TAMIL CHARACTERS

A. R. Venkatachalapathy (b. 1967) is a professor at the Madras Institute of Development Studies, Chennai. He studied in Chennai before doing a PhD in history at Jawaharlal Nehru University, New Delhi. Chalapathy has taught at Manonmaniam Sundaranar University, Tirunelveli; the University of Madras; and the University of Chicago. He has held research assignments in Paris, Cambridge, London, and Harvard. He was the Indian Council for Cultural Relations Chair in Indian studies at the National University of Singapore (2011–12). He has published widely on the social, cultural, and intellectual history of colonial Tamilnadu. Apart from his writings in English he has written and published extensively in Tamil. His more than thirty books include non-fiction, compilations, scholarly editions and translations. Over the last few years he has been writing in the popular media. He was awarded the VKRV Rao Prize for History in 2007. Presently he is working on a biography of Periyar.

D1255246

Also by A. R. Venkatachalapathy

AUTHORED

Who Owns That Song? The Battle for Subramania Bharati's Copyright

The Province of the Book: Scholars, Scribes, and Scribblers in Colonial Tamilnadu

In Those Days There Was No Coffee: Writings in Cultural History

EDITED

In the Tracks of the Mahatma: The Making of a Documentary (written by A. K. Chettiar)

Chennai, Not Madras: Perspectives on the City

Love Stands Alone: Selections from Tamil Sangam Poetry (translated by M. L. Thangappa)

Red Lilies and Frightened Birds: Muttollayiram (translated by M. L. Thangappa)

Beyond Tranquebar: Grappling Across Cultural Borders in South India (with Esther Fihl)

TRANSLATED

JJ: Some Jottings (written by Sundara Ramaswamy)

TAMIL CHARACTERS
Personalities, Politics, Culture

A. R. Venkatachalapathy

PAN

First published 2018 by Pan
an imprint of Pan Macmillan Publishing India
Pan Macmillan India, 707, Kailash Building
26 K. G. Marg, New Delhi – 110 001
www.panmacmillan.co.in

Pan Macmillan, 20 New Wharf Road, London N1 9RR
Basingstoke and Oxford
Associated companies throughout the world
www.panmacmillan.com

ISBN 978-93-86215-60-4

Copyright © A. R. Venkatachalapathy 2018

Illustrated by Mohamed Rashmy Ahamed

Typeset by Manmohan Kumar
Printed and bound in India by Gopsons Papers Ltd.

for
RAM GUHA

CONTENTS

CONTENTS

III   CULTURAL QUESTIONS

PREFACE

TAMILNADU POSES A CHALLENGE to common sense. The contours and complexities of its politics and culture often befuddle observers. Media persons from outside Tamilnadu are puzzled when they chase stories from the region. This despite the prodigious volume of international literature that focuses – much to the chagrin of adjacent regions such as Kerala, Andhra, and Karnataka – on matters Tamil.

On the one hand is the long history of claims to Tamil distinctness and exceptionalism. The 'South', especially Tamilnadu, has posed problems to the Indian nation as well as to historians. Thomas Trautmann, the distinguished American historian-anthropologist, once observed that, 'The idea of an Indian South that differs in kinship and language is a very old one'. The south of India therefore has always demanded a separate history.

Tamilnadu has been part of the Indian mainstream, yet maintains its distinctiveness. A party which has ruled the state a good part of the last fifty years had, until not so long ago, a secessionist demand built into its founding constitution. Fringe Tamil nationalist elements always function and attract attention. The Tamil ethnic question in the adjoining sovereign state of Sri Lanka question continues to resonate here.

The caste system, marked by the absence of the intermediary Kshatriya and Vaisya varnas, has its own Tamil iteration. With probably the smallest proportion of Brahmins in its population, Tamilnadu is the progenitor of a non-Brahmin movement – over a century old, this movement is still alive. While an organised Dalit movement is of recent origin, two generations before

Dr B. R. Ambedkar, the Tamil region produced an intellectual who argued that the 'Untouchables' were the original Buddhists, and that their conviction resulted in discrimination. Systematic caste-based reservations in employment and education were introduced in Tamilnadu nearly a century ago, while most of India is still struggling to reconcile itself to such positive discrimination and affirmative action.

Dravidian kinship remains one of the world's distinct kinship systems. If couples from the same *gotra* can be hounded in the cow belt, marriages between cross cousins, and between maternal uncles and nieces are still preferred in many parts of Tamilnadu.

Language occupies a central place in the eponymous tract. Linguistically, Tamil is part of a family of languages, Dravidian, which is distinct from the Sanskrit-derived Indo-Aryan family. Tamil has asserted independence from Sanskrit over the centuries; possibly Tamil is the only language where a purist movement has succeeded to a great extent. Since the turn of the twentieth century a demand to recognise Tamil as a classical language has been articulated; and this recognition was won through governmental fiat for the first time anywhere in the world. The region has witnessed two major anti-Hindi agitations – against the compulsory study of Hindi in schools (1937–9) and against the constitutional recognition of Hindi as the sole official language of the Indian Union (1964–5) – and the underlying sentiment shows little signs of diminishing. Devoted to language, scores of youths have given up their lives in the cause of language, tragically burning themselves to death.

Across the towns of Tamilnadu one can see statues of a bearded old man with the words 'There is no God' inscribed on the pedestal. Yet the Bhakti movement, which originated here more than a millennium ago and transformed the Hindu religion across the subcontinent, continues to thrive. There may not be a single neighbourhood in Chennai which does not have a Pillaiyar (or Gangai or some other Amman) Koil

Street – much to the confusion of postal delivery staff and courier boys. Tamil temple architecture, or Dravidian as it is called, is arguably Tamil's greatest contribution to world culture, its influence permeating South East Asia. Embedded in the social structure, the massive edifices of stone are the site of struggle, as once-marginalised communities stake claim to cultural rights. For nearly a hundred years now, Hindu temples have been administered by a secular state.

Cultural issues obtain great purchase in Tamilnadu. At the time of Independence, through great public pressure, the state acquired the copyright of the poet Subramania Bharati – a first in the history of global copyright. Barely two years ago hundreds of thousands mobilized on the streets of Tamilnadu to fight for the right to conduct the indigenous bullfight, *jallikattu*.

The hold of cinema is a dominant feature of Tamil culture. The Tamil cinema industry is vibrant, and gives Hollywood and Bollywood a run for their money. If a Bollywood star were to walk on the streets of Tamilnadu it is unlikely that the star will receive a second glance. It has been four decades since the composer Ilaiyaraaja practically wiped out Hindi film songs from Tamil popular culture. The intertwining of film and politics is most apparent in the fact that the state has been ruled for nearly fifty years by four chief ministers whose popularity was derived in large measure from their film career. As this book goes for printing, at least three – or is it four? – film stars are eyeing the chief minister's chair.

It is over half a century since the Dravidian movement dethroned the Congress, and no 'national' party has any reasonable hope of coming to power in the near future. Tamilnadu continues to be the bulwark against the Hindutva juggernaut. For years now the state has been synonymous with populism – free nutritious noon meal scheme in schools, free distribution of rice, TV sets, electric fans, laptops, etc. – and corruption.

One chief minister was the subject of an early commission of enquiry. Another chief minister's crime abated because the court apparently waited for the accused to die to deliver the verdict. The 2G scam implicating Tamilnadu politicians was once seen as the 'mother of all scams'.

Logically speaking, such a state should be a laggard, low down on the development scale. Yet, it is exactly during the time of Dravidian politics that the state has made great strides in development. Jean Drèze and Amartya Sen, in *An Uncertain Glory* (2013), summarise these achievements in the clearest terms. Describing the 'rapid progress in a relatively short period', they talk of how Tamilnadu, very poor until even the 1960s, now has one of the highest per capita incomes and lowest poverty rates in India. In all human development indicators – education, health, communication, roads and public transport, and civic amenities – Tamilnadu ranks high. All these resulted, they demonstrate, not from political largesse, but through pressure from the bottom, 'an outcome of democratic politics'.

～

This book addresses the political issues of these times refracted through the prism of personalities – both political and cultural – and specific cultural issues. This was not planned as a book, but, in a manner of speaking, I absentmindedly ended up writing it. In my intellectual career I have worn two hats: that of a professional historian writing in English, and a Tamil writer producing essays and monographs on cultural history for the general reading public.

Though annoyed by the banality of much comment on matters Tamil in the English media I have hesitated to write for a general audience in English. Rarely have I written opinion pieces – what is the opinion of a historian worth, in any case?

Historians, by definition, don't write in the heat of the moment. They are more like Mao: on being asked about the impact of the French Revolution on the course of world history, he supposedly said, 'It's too early to say!' One wonders if even Mao could have got away in these days of the explosion in the electronic media.

Tamilnadu has kept the media busy over the last decade. Willy-nilly I have succumbed to its pressure to offer sound bites and write on contemporary issues. The time between Jayalalithaa's incarceration in September 2014 and her death in December 2016 was particularly eventful, calling for periodic columnal interventions. For a slow writer, who takes months and years to formulate an essay, a tight deadline with a strict word limit and a defined subject was a challenge – the equivalent of the proverbial gun to the head (the Tamil equivalent is – literally – more pressing: 'a knife to the throat'). I have seen myself as a middle-distance runner (long academic essays) who occasionally ran the marathon (full-length monograph and book). Writing for the popular press is more like a 100-metre sprint. But the exhilaration at the end, akin to a runner's high, makes it all worthwhile. It is for readers to judge if I have crossed the finish line in good time.

Thanks are due to the many editors who reposed confidence in me. Special mention needs to be made of the *Hindu*. Who would have thought that 'the Mahavishnu of Mount Road' would be the primary forum for my opinions? The *Mirror*, at the time of Jayalalithaa's death, asked me to profile her. In these days of short attention span, a limit of 3,000-plus words can only be termed god's bounty. This invitation led me to attempt a full-fledged profile written furiously over five hours even as the official pronouncement was awaited. The critical response it received emboldened me to attempt the profiles of Karunanidhi and MGR.

Further thanks are due to *Economic and Political Weekly*, *India Today*, *Outlook*, *Week*, *Economic Times*, *Hindustan Times*,

Seminar, Biblio, Wire, Scroll, Sahapedia, Orient BlackSwan, Penguin Random House, and Oxford University Press for opportunities to write.

Late last year Prasun Chatterjee proposed the idea of putting between covers my essays on contemporary Tamilnadu. I liked the idea, but was not sure if there was enough for a book. The result surprised me more than anyone else. Though the book originated as individual essays and columns in the popular press, and as afterwords and forewords to books, I have revised and expanded them substantially. The profiles of Karunanidhi and MGR were written specially for this book.

The book falls into three sections. The first section profiles key political personalities of the past century. Missing is K. Kamaraj. Tamilnadu has produced some of the finest cultural talents in modern India, but sadly little is known about them beyond Tamil boundaries. I hope the second section will kindle interest in their life and work. The last section comments on important cultural questions – anti-Hindi agitations, the classical language issue, prohibition, jallikattu – by marshalling historical data. Together I hope these essays both inform and provide an insider's perspective on modern Tamilnadu.

Historians of contemporary India are deprived access to recent archival resources ('the thirty-year rule', as it is called). The chapters on contemporary political figures and events therefore rely on lived experience, readings in contemporary published material, memory, and hearsay. It is strange for me to pen a book completely bereft of footnotes and references. I had friends read chapters to confirm information and insights. I sought prior comments on a few tricky essays. Special mention needs to be made of Kannan Sundaram who read the political pieces at short notice just before I shot them off to the press. The endorsement of Sukumaran, poet and journalist, was particularly gratifying. The final manuscript has benefitted enormously from the careful reading it was subjected to by Gopalkrishna Gandhi. My wisdom lies in accepting most of his corrections and suggestions for revision. All blame for remaining errors is mine.

The chapter on Dalits and cultural rights was written jointly with J. Balasubramaniam. It is included here with permission.

I am delighted that Rashmy's vivid sketches embellish the book.

Thanks are due to S. Thillainayagam for help with the final proofs.

Ramachandra Guha, apart from single-handedly creating the space for popular history in India, has been a personal inspiration. Over the years Ram has prodded me to write more in English, though it has taken me a while to submit to it. I have drawn on his sagacity and wisdom often, including in the writing of some of these essays. The playful yet perceptive title capturing the nub of this book is his. The dedication acknowledges my debt to his scholarship and friendship.

ABBREVIATIONS

AIADMK	All India Anna Dravida Munnetra Kazhagam
Anna	C. N. Annadurai
BJP	Bharatiya Janata Party
CBI	Central Bureau of Investigation
CICT	Central Institute of Classical Tamil
CPI	Communist Party of India
CPI (M)	Communist Party of India (Marxist)
CSP	Congress Socialist Party
DK	Dravidar Kazhagam
DMDK	Desiya Murpokku Dravida Kazhagam
DMK	Dravida Munnetra Kazhagam
ECR	East Coast Road
EPRLF	Eelam People's Revolutionary Liberation Front
IAS	Indian Administrative Service
ICS	Indian Civil Services
INC	Indian National Congress
IPKF	Indian Peace Keeping Force
LTTE	Liberation Tigers of Tamil Eelam
MGR	M. G. Ramachandran
MHRD	Ministry of Human Resources Development
MLA	Member of Legislative Assembly
MP	Member of Parliament
NCBH	New Century Book House
NDA	National Democratic Alliance
NNR	Native Newspaper Reports
OMR	Old Mahabalipuram Road
PUCL	People's Union for Civil Liberties

Rajaji	C. Rajagopalachari
RSS	Rashtriya Swayamsevak Sangh
RTI	Right to Information
TADA	Terrorist and Disruptive Activities (Prevention) Act
TELO	Tamil Eelam Liberation Organization
TMC	Tamil Maanila Congress
TNA	Tamilnadu Archives
TULF	Tamil United Liberation Front
UPA	United Progressive Alliance

I
POLITICAL
PERSONALITIES

PERIYAR
Prophet from the South

> The prophet was known as 'Periyar'. It was a Tamil word,
> meaning a sage or a wise man. I knew the name Periyar, but only
> just; I knew nothing about the man. I began to learn now, and
> I was astounded as much by what I learned as by the fact that,
> with all my reading about the independence movement in India,
> I had read or registered so little about this prophet of the South.
> – V. S. Naipaul, *India: A Million Mutinies Now*

THINGS HAVEN'T CHANGED TOO much since V. S. Naipaul wrote
this in 1991. The political and cultural changes following the
Mandal agitation (1990) – against the state policy of reservation
for backward castes in government institutions – and the rise of
an aggressive Hindu fundamentalism gave a new visibility to his
name beyond the borders of south India.

A curious paradox however marks Periyar's name and fame. In
Tamilnadu, he is an icon for most political parties even if they have
sold out on his radical ideology. His statues dot the landscape,
with a rather combative slogan engraved on the pedestal:

> There is no god, there is no god at all.
> He who invented god is a fool.
> He who propagates god is a scoundrel.
> He who worships god is a savage.

Many government artefacts – bus stations, buildings,
projects – are named after Periyar. His ideas are extensively

debated in the Tamil public sphere. In the last less than a decade three different editions of his collected writings, running into a cumulative hundred volumes, have appeared – a bonanza that was preceded by a sustained campaign to free Periyar's writings from a copyright regime and put them in the public domain for unrestricted use.

Barely four decades ago, when I was first introduced to Periyar as a schoolboy, his name was scarcely mentioned in polite (and academic) company, though a sneaking admiration among non-Brahmins could be discerned. Sometime in early 1981, I was drawn to a literary meeting which had advertised a quiz competition for school students. The literary circle which organised the competition was run by a fifty-year-old man who conducted literary meetings every month, and this was only its fifth meeting. Little did I know then that this would be a life-changing moment. My encounter with the short, soft-spoken Mamani transformed this middle-class boy eventually into a man of letters and a historian. But this was nothing compared to the transformation Mamani had undergone himself. The son of a poor widowed woman in the working-class neighbourhood of north Chennai, he never had the opportunity to go to a regular school. On the eve of Indian Independence, as celebrations rent the air, Mamani, then sixteen years old, listened to the speech of an old man with a Socratic beard, Periyar, who spoke in a colloquial tongue: Indian Independence was a sham; what was political freedom worth if it did not usher in social emancipation? The articulation of what was a most unpopular view set this young man thinking. He began to attend meetings of the political party to which the old man belonged. Impelled by a desire to read his radical views he went to night school even as he toiled during the day in sweatshops. Soon he found himself as a printer's devil in Periyar's own printing press. Not long thereafter he found a clerical job and rose to be part of the middle class. He fashioned his life on the ideas of Periyar: he became an atheist, and spurned religious rituals. This most modest-looking man became, for me, a hero. For some years, every Sunday, in the afternoon at 2 p.m., I would meet him. Over two to three hours he would share his knowledge of not only Tamil history and culture, but of everything under the sun. As I parted after a cup of hot tea he would lend me his books, many of them bought with money saved paisa by paisa when he was a wage labourer.

This was how I was introduced to not only Periyar, but much of Tamil history and culture. Until then Periyar was little more than an old man, who held contrarian views about god and religion. But the writings of Periyar that I began to read were breathtaking despite their evident period quality. Characteristically enough, Periyar's writings in those days were available only as booklets and pamphlets printed on cheap newsprint in a far from fetching manner; the three-volume V. Anaimuthu edition of his collected writings was a rarity which could be consulted only in a library.

The book that shook me the most was Periyar's *Penn Aen Adimaiyanal* (Why the Woman Is Enslaved) consisting of essays written mostly in the late 1920s – a year before *Marriage and Morals* was published, the book that cost Bertrand Russell his job at the City University of New York. Periyar's questioning of patriarchal norms regarding marriage, chastity, and motherhood was breathtaking, and his rationalistic analysis of caste, religion, and god exhilarating. Not only was he advocating contraception, he was advocating it on the grounds of pleasure and weakening patriarchy. Reading Richard Dawkins in the early 2000s left me with a sense of déjà vu. The ideas that burst forth in Periyar's writings were at variance with what was taught in school and in college. The intellectual mainstream was averse to his stark rationalism. In the larger world of letters and ideas, dominated by a certain variety of Marxism that privileged economic processes and class analysis, Periyar was loathed whenever he was given attention, which was not often. This was also inflected by the fact that Indian intellectuals were largely Brahmins, whom Periyar reviled. If at all he was known at an all-India level it was more-often-than-not as an anti-national, a secessionist who demanded an independent Tamilnadu/Dravida Nadu, a stooge of the British, a Brahmin-baiter, an atheist, a caste-ist, and an ethnic chauvinist. Paradoxically though, the Dravidian movement commanded considerable academic attention from universities in the West. From as early as the late 1950s a steady stream of Western academics studied one or the other aspect of Periyar and his movement, though his complex politics and ideology have eluded their full grasp.

~

For all his importance as a radical thinker Periyar was no philosopher or even a systematic thinker. He had a rebellious childhood and barely went to school. A rakish youth, he bloomed late as a political personality. Periyar left behind no systematic treatise on any philosophical, social, or political subject, but rather reacted to issues as they cropped up.

E. V. Ramasamy Naicker (1879–1973) lived a long life and was active in the public sphere for some sixty years. Starting his life as a prosperous merchant in the small town of Erode in the Kongu region of western Tamilnadu, far from the bustle of provincial, not to speak of national, politics he was pushing forty when he made his entry into politics. In a manner of speaking one could say that he was an old man all his life! From the stepping stone of municipal politics he took the plunge into nationalist politics through an immersion in the Indian National Congress (INC), the premier nationalist organisation in the nation's struggle to win political freedom from British colonialism.

Periyar cut his political teeth in the Congress's first mass-political phase (1919–22) when it launched the Non-Cooperation Movement against draconian laws imposed by the colonial government. In the half a decade or so that he spent in the Congress he emerged as one of the two most popular leaders who could mobilise the masses for a political programme. The high watermark in this phase was his leadership in 1924 of the satyagraha in the temple town of Vaikom in the adjoining native princely state of Travancore, in present-day Kerala. Taking over the leadership of a sagging movement he galvanised it into a successful struggle for the right of lower-caste Ezhavas to walk the streets surrounding the temple in the face of resistance by both the state and the upper castes.

Periyar was involved in another game-changing issue during this time. Political nationalism brings in its wake cultural nationalism. One of the issues that confronted Indian nationalists was the de-nationalising effect of a Western form of education that created willing collaborators of colonialism: 'a class of persons Indian in blood and colour, but English in tastes, in opinions, in morals and in intellect'. Following Gandhi's call to boycott English schools, schools based on the traditional Indian model, *gurukulam*, were established, one of them in Cheranmadevi in the deep south of Tamilnadu by V. V. S. Aiyar, scholar and early nationalist, and friend of V. D. Savarkar. From clothing to pedagogy Western methods were eschewed in this school and an 'Indian' model was sought to be recreated. In 1923 a controversy flared up in the school. It turned out that students in the school were segregated on caste lines, and Brahmin students were served separately in keeping with traditional conceptions of caste-based commensality. This controversy split the nationalists in Tamilnadu, and forever changed the social character of its politics, anticipating similar changes at the all-India level by half a century. Periyar was at the heart of this controversy and, as a result, his ideas about politics and society underwent a radical transformation.

Periyar began to entertain serious doubts about political independence and to reflect on the nature of real social emancipation. Convinced that political independence would only reinforce existing caste-based hierarchies, especially the supremacy of Brahmins, he advocated, as a first step, constitutionally mandated proportionate representation for various castes in elected political bodies. It was on this proximate issue that, in 1925, he broke away from the Congress (in the high noon of nationalism, when even cigarettes used Gandhi as a brand name).

As Periyar increasingly contended with caste in relation to the goal of national independence he began to develop a sharper understanding of the ideological power of caste. He developed the radically new conception that caste underpinned every social and ideological institution. Consequently, his social programme was to attack all such institutions to demolish the system of caste. By this time he was subscribing to an eclectic mix of Enlightenment ideals and freethinking, that positioned 'Reason' above received knowledge. By the mid-1920s he had turned his rationalistic attention to a radical critique of religious texts: scriptures, epics, and devotional literature. In what has been described as a 'hyper literal' reading of texts (the reverse of fundamentalism), he demonstrated how these texts legitimised and perpetuated hierarchical differences based on birth. Periyar also called for the public burning of such texts, and a campaign to do so in the 1940s and 1950s greatly extended the reach of his movement. His writings in this vein became controversial, and to this day, in popular memory, Periyar is chiefly remembered as an atheist and as an iconoclast.

The route from religious texts to the institution of religion was not long, and soon Periyar was attacking all religions, but especially 'Hinduism' (which he argued was not a 'real' religion, but only a fabrication). He also published, in translation, texts such as Lenin's *On Religion* and Russell's *Why I Am Not a Christian*, and the American freethinker Robert Ingersoll's essays. However, he made tactical use of Islam. While being an admirer of Kemal Ataturk, he advocated conversion to Islam (for Dalits), despite its many inequities, especially in terms of gender relations, as a means to overcome the oppression of untouchability.

Soon Periyar extended the net to include politics and state. In his view the nationalist Congress sought to recreate a Brahmin Raj, and in Gandhi he saw the prime architect of this dystopic vision. Periyar offered one of the most radical critiques of Gandhi that continues to have relevance to this day. While he supported colonialism for introducing piecemeal, and largely inadequate, social reforms he was often critical of the colonial state for its weak-kneed response posed by Indian nationalism.

Periyar tried to build strategic relationships with other lower-caste movements and minorities. He won the lifelong respect of Ezhavas following his role in the Vaikom Satyagraha (1924–5). At a time when Dr B. R. Ambedkar, the great 'Untouchable' leader, was sought to be marginalised by all dominant political formations, Periyar was one of the earliest leaders to recognise him as the sole spokesman and genuine representative of the Dalits of India. His advocacy of separate electorates for Dalits provided crucial support to Ambedkar at the time of the Poona Pact (1932). He was the earliest to produce translations of Ambedkar's important writings such as *The Annihilation of Caste*. Arguing that the Shudra status of non-Brahmins would not be wiped out until the varna category (of Dalits) was annihilated, he asserted that Dalits had unconditional claim over every advance that the Non-Brahmin Movement made. Periyar's interventions in the Dalit question therefore have a wider import. Ironically enough, Periyar is often blamed for the delayed emergence of the

Dalit movement in Tamilnadu by some fringe Dalit intellectuals. Periyar's ideas therefore continue to occupy a central position in contemporary debates on caste, Dalits, and untouchability.

Similarly, in M. A. Jinnah and the Muslim League he saw a real challenge to the upper-caste Hindu-dominated Congress, and was an ardent supporter of his demands vis-à-vis the Congress. In 1941 he spoke at the Muslim League's all-India conference in Chennai sharing the dais with Jinnah.

During the late 1920s and the early 1930s Periyar dallied with socialism and communism. The first (albeit incomplete) translation of *The Communist Manifesto* in any Indian language was the one published by Periyar in Tamil in 1929. In 1932 he toured the Soviet Union and Europe, and was fascinated by Soviet society. During this time he also engaged with contemporary nudists and freethinkers, especially in Germany, and with the League Against Imperialism. In England, in association with Shapurji Saklatvala, he attended many working-class meetings. The Soviet trip left a deep impress on Periyar. On his return to India he combined self-respect and socialism and campaigned across the region mobilising considerable support for the programme. In the face of imminent repression by the colonial state he gave up socialist propaganda. His relationship with communists in India was deeply fraught with rivalry and distrust. The cream of Indian communists were Brahmins who shied away from confronting the caste question.

Periyar's critique of the Congress continued after Indian Independence. His massive mobilisation against the Supreme Court's decision declaring caste-based reservation in the *Champakam Dorairajan vs Government of India* case was instrumental in forcing the passing of the first amendment to the Constitution of India. In fact, Periyar was deeply critical of the Indian Constitution and launched agitations to burn it.

In 1949 his party suffered a split. The occasion was his marriage to Maniammal, his thirty-year-old secretary. Periyar had a deeply ambivalent attitude to electoral politics. Believing – like the vanguard of Leninist strategy – in being ahead of the masses, in terms of ideas, he put much faith in the state as an agent of change. For him electoral politics inevitably entailed the dilution of ideology, compromise on ideals, and corruption of processes. Periyar therefore eschewed electoral politics, and a majority of his party, led by the charismatic C. N. Annadurai, using the marriage as a pretext, split the party and launched the Dravida Munnetra Kazhagam (DMK). Periyar was left with only a rump, but, at the age of seventy he took it upon himself to lead and conduct the movement single-handedly. During the 1950s he launched various agitations to burn and break images of the Hindu gods Ram and Pillaiyar (Ganesh), burnt the national flag and the constitution, defied the courts, and repeatedly courted arrest. He also volunteered support to the Congress ministry led by K. Kamaraj, ensuring in the process that the Tamilnadu unit of the party was de-Brahminised.

~

Periyar's primary mode of expression was public speaking. According to one count he travelled for 8,200 days, traversed over 800,000 miles, attended 10,700 public events, and spent about 21,400 hours addressing the public. From 1925, when he launched a weekly (*Kudi Arasu*) and a decade later a daily (*Viduthalai*), he was never short of forums to record and publicise his writings. His published writings thus have the impress of his speaking.

Periyar was no systematic thinker. He responded to contemporary issues as they emerged, and his ideas evolved as he grappled with reality. The published articles were not finished pieces, and evolved as issues changed shape. Repetitions were therefore inevitable.

Periyar never gave a thought to whether the words that he employed were formal words. Subject–object–verb order would frequently be mixed up. And he cared a fig for singular or plural nouns and verb endings. As one contemporary said, 'Grammar, conjugation, commas, semi-colons and periods should tremble at Periyar for he never gave them a damn'. Tamil, in linguistic terms, is diglossic, with a sharp divide between the written and the spoken registers. While it was the norm for public speaking to be conducted in the formal register – the divide accentuated by Dravidian orators employing a highly stylised form of speaking – Periyar always used the spoken register.

Periyar's speeches, and therefore his writings, bristle with tales, similes, illustrative stories, proverbs, and popular sayings. Every chronicler of Periyar has wondered where this school dropout drew them from. Proverbs are often untranslatable, but it would be unfair not to give a sampling. 'Like a well taking up half a garden'; 'Like fixing a silver ferrule to a cucumber'; 'How to string pearls the size of pumpkins?' Some of the best proverbs have stories underpinning them, and Periyar employed them to telling effect. One could easily compile a nice volume of Tamil folklore from his speeches and writings alone.

Situational humour, never easily captured in cold print, is also evident even in the published versions of his speeches. His analogies and tales could more than occasionally sound illogical when reduced to print, but at the time of utterance made the audience crack up.

Periyar is credited with coining Tamil neologisms for 'Enlightenment' and radical terms and concepts such as 'democracy', 'reason', and 'socialism'. Periyar's engagement with democracy and elections has considerable contemporary relevance as India continues to grapple with its democracy even as it is challenged by emerging identities and problems of governance. Periyar and his ideas remain a contentious force – as the new generation engage with his ideas as well as see him as a symbol.

~

Despite his advancing age, illness, and lack of organisational structure, Periyar very much set the political and social agenda of the state, until his death in 1973. The arch iconoclast was buried with full state honours.

2

C. N. ANNADURAI
Gentle Persuader

WHEN CONJEEVARAM NATARAJAN ANNADURAI (1909–1969) died, his funeral was one of the largest the world had seen – it is even a Guinness record. Anna, as he was fondly called, was born of rather undistinguished parentage for which he was often ridiculed by petty-minded political rivals. In the rise of this barely five-and-a-quarter-feet man with a balding pate, tobacco-stained teeth, stubble chin, but a captivating husky voice, lies the story of modern Tamilnadu.

Anna, whose name also means 'elder brother', was the first leader of post-Independence India to have not come from the freedom struggle. Education – BA (Honours) in Economics from Pachaiyappa's College, Chennai, and an 'MA' proudly tagged to his name – was his only claim to respect until he cut his political teeth in the non-Brahmin Justice Party, translating into Tamil the high-flown public speeches of its leaders. It was a fitting honour therefore when A. Ramaswamy Mudaliar, the doyen of the first phase of the Non-Brahmin Movement and known for his English oratorical skills, whose speech he translated early in his political career, unveiled Anna's statue at the northern end of Mount Road, Chennai, later named Anna Salai.

The turning point in Anna's life came when he met Periyar in a conference at Tiruppur in May 1934. Periyar was always taken in by educated non-Brahmin youth and, when the twenty-six-year-old young man confidently asserted that he had no wish to take up government employment, but wanted to enter public life, Periyar probably saw in him the makings of a lieutenant.

The ill-advised move of C. Rajagopalachari's (Rajaji) first Congress ministry to introduce compulsory Hindi in schools triggered a great movement and Anna rose to prominence through this struggle. It can be said that Anna's political career spanned the period between two anti-Hindi agitations – of 1938 and 1965.

The first anti-Hindi agitation of 1937–9 established his skills in both 'word and deed' – with language and in organisation. Even though the modern form of public oratory had emerged with the nationalist political movement early in the twentieth century, Anna created his own style of eloquence which came to be patented as Dravidian rhetoric with its own aesthetic. And his style was never short of emulators and imitators. Anna drew from his wide and voracious reading, and breaking conventional forms of Tamil grammatical sentence structures (by inverting the standard subject–object–verb order), he created a forceful though not a stentorian form of delivery. It was this oratorical skill that won for him a huge following of idealistic youth. He was in great demand in various colleges as politically minded students invited him to speak despite great conservative opposition from authorities. His speeches, in the 1940s, in Pachaiyappa's College, Madras Christian College, and Annamalai University were immediately published, and have continued to remain in print for over more than half a century. When Deivasikamani Achari published his primer of Tamil platform-speaking, *Medai Tamil*, it was punctuated with illustrations from Anna.

Anna adapted his distinctive style of delivery to the written mode as well. His earliest story was published in 1934 in *Ananda Vikatan*. He maintained a steady stream of writings – stories, sketches, essays, and polemics. *Dravida Nadu*, the weekly he launched in 1942, was virtually filled in by his own pen. His regular epistolary essays, written as *Thambikku Anna-vin Kadithangal* (Letters to the Younger Brother), on a variety of contemporary themes laced with his political perspective, won him innumerable readers.

The Justice Party that Anna had joined in 1934 had within a few years undergone a dramatic change when Periyar took over its leadership. Periyar gave it a radical new orientation which antagonised the rump of the old Justice Party wedded to conservative legislative politics. Anna was Periyar's able lieutenant as he took control of the party and made it a viable, if non-electoral, opposition to the Congress which was sensing power with the imminence of Indian Independence.

Within a decade, with freedom only a matter of time, Anna gave the crucial reorientation to the Non-Brahmin Movement which would rid it of the stigma of loyalism. Anna represented a new breed of political activists with grass-roots support at variance with the earlier Justice Party leadership steeped in an elite and upper-class culture. At the Salem Conference (1944) he proposed the party's rechristening as the Dravidar Kazhagam (DK), called for the renunciation of all titles given by the British government, and prepared it for the challenges of a newly independent nation state.

Anna's alliterative rhetoric, radically new to the Tamil language, changed Tamil public speaking forever. He used the new technology of the public address system to telling effect, conserving energy for long orations, modulating the voice, and punctuating it with pregnant pauses. Combined with his insatiable reading in Western rationalism his linguistic skills enthralled the Tamil youths from upwardly mobile non-Brahmin castes. His defeat of senior scholars such as Somasundara Bharati and R. P. Sethu Pillai in public debate, when still in his early thirties, greatly enhanced his rising reputation. By the mid-1940s Anna had added script-writing for films to his political quiver. In the context of the history of Tamil talkies the move from playwriting to film scripting was only logical. Films such as *Velaikkari*, *Nallathambi*, and *Or Iravu* catapulted him to fame winning acceptability across the ideological spectrum.

Anna's successes with the pen, on platform, on stage, and on the silver screen did not come easily. Many of his books such as *Ariya Mayai* and *Ilatchiya Varalaru* were proscribed and forfeited. He was also convicted for 'creating enmity between various classes' and served prison sentences. The record of the Congress government in banning political books would have shamed the British. DMK films, which articulated social reform ideas in catchy and alliterative dialogue, had often to escape the eagle eyes of ever-vigilant censor officers who tried to snip any attempt to propagate what was considered party propaganda.

Anna's meteoric rise presaged differences in the party. Despite being a trusted lieutenant of Periyar and sharing his ideology he had a different political vision. In the politics of collecting a purse for the poet of the Dravidian movement, Bharatidasan, and organising a grand function in 1946 the fault lines became clearly visible. The first open sign of break however came when Periyar declared 15 August 1947 as a day of mourning. In perceptively judging the public mood jubilant at the prospect of shaking off the colonial yoke, a trait he was to display many times in his political career, Anna declared that of the two enemies – the Brahmin and the British – there was now one less.

Anna soon began to sense that he was being sidelined in the party and slighted by its leader. Never one for openly expressing bitterness he responded with suggestive short stories – 'Rajapart Rangadurai', a story of the rift between a theatre producer and its lead player, is a brilliant allegory. Periyar's controversial marriage in 1949 provided the opportune moment for Anna to break free and launch a new party, the Dravida Munnetra Kazhagam (DMK). It is to Anna's great credit that, despite many tempting suggestions, he refused to confront Periyar and claim the party for himself, which, given the overwhelming grass-roots support that he commanded, he might well have been successful in doing. His inaugural speech at Robinson's Park, Chennai, on 16 September 1949 was full of emotion – an unexpected thundershower metaphorically standing for the tears caused by the sadness of the split. Periyar for a long time derisively referred to the DMK as *kanneer thulikal* (tears). Anna however swore that Periyar was his leader, and the president's chair would remain empty; the new party would never have a president, but only a general secretary. Over the next two decades while Periyar was ruthlessly critical of Anna and the DMK, Anna himself was very civil in his response.

What contributed to Anna's ultimate success was his ability to harness and tame the ideas and energies let loose by Periyar – diehard Periyarists would say Anna watered down his views. Be that as it may, given his controversial and radical ideas on nation (anti-'national'), caste (strongly anti-Brahminical), religion (atheistic and iconoclastic), women (he declared that motherhood was a shackle), and language (advocated an unsentimental approach to it), understandably Periyar eschewed electoral politics, a commitment he maintained until his death twenty-five years after Independence. While Periyar's movement was enormously empowering in the public sphere and civil society, what about politics?

In Anna the emergent backward castes saw a leader who could take them to political power. He skilfully repackaged Periyar's iconoclastic ideas to make them palatable in the public domain. Much of Anna's writings and speeches can be seen as aesthetic adaptations of Periyar's ideas. Anna was also a man for memorable phrases and catchy slogans. Periyar's rustic and brutal atheism became '*Onre Kulam, Oruvane Devan*' (One God, One Community) in a skilful appropriation of a poem

by the venerated medieval Tamil saint-poet Tirumular. When
Periyar went about breaking the idols of Pillaiyar, Anna famously
observed that he would neither break the idol nor the coconut (in
worship)! Phrases such as '*Ippadai thorkin eppadai jeyikkum?*' (If
this army was to lose, which is the one that would triumph?, from
P. Sundaram Pillai's *Manonmaniam*) and '*Ethaiyum thangum
idhayam vendum*' (A heart for every fate!, from Tennyson) will
remain etched in Tamil political vocabulary.

The DMK did not contest the first general elections (1952),
instead offering support to anyone who pledged a commitment
to the DMK's political demands. If the Congress in the very
first elections after Independence failed to get a majority in the
Madras legislature it was in some measure due to the DMK's
undermining of Congress's legitimacy.

With a heady, if ambiguous, mixture of romantic nationalism
and socialism the DMK pretty much set the terms of the debate
in early post-1947 Tamilnadu. Over the 1950s Anna built a party
which expressed the dissatisfaction of the Tamils with the Indian
state. He coined the slogan of '*Vadakku Vazhkirathu Therku
Theikirathu*' (The North Flourishes; the South Withers). The
party conducted major agitations against Nehru for calling the
DMK's demands 'nonsense', protesting the naming of Kallakudi
as Dalmiapuram (after a cement factory owned by the Marwari
house of Dalmias).

Anna was a true democrat. He built a network of reading
rooms across the state not only as an aid to political education
(local barbers' saloons and cycle repair shops as the locus of
local leadership was a hallmark of the DMK's rise), but also to
build a democratic party structure. Anna was always on his feet,
constantly touring the length and breadth of the state. But he was
a careful strategist and it is said that – to avoid overexposure – he
would come back to give a talk at a town only after a substantial
time gap; he would invariably give the slip if he had to commit to

a talk against his wish. Even though he was notorious for coming late to meetings Anna never failed his audience. It is said that he would be the last to eat in a communal feasting, after mega meetings and conferences, as organisers were wont to neglect the rank and file if the leaders ate first and left.

Anna sensed the rank-and-file's desire to contest in the elections. He conducted a poll in the DMK's state conference at Trichy in 1956 to gauge the party's mood. In the same party conference, in 1956, V. R. Nedunchezhiyan was elected general secretary of the party. As he passed the baton to him, Anna famously said, 'Thambi vaa, Thalamai erka vaa' (Come brother, don the mantle of leadership). Rarely has it happened in Indian politics that a leader gave way to new leadership. In the 1957 elections the DMK won fifteen seats in the state assembly.

Anna's DMK was studded with a galaxy of stars – from the erudite Nedunchezhiyan and Chezhiyan and a natural poet Kannadasan to the star speaker E. V. K. Sampath and the gifted M. Karunanidhi. Every personality in the party ran a journal of his own. The DMK historian K. Thirunavukkarasu has counted over 300 Dravidian movement journals during this period – practically every one of them perished as Karunanidhi asserted his hold over the party. Anna never felt threatened by the rise of peers and younger leaders. When in 1960 he became general secretary again it was only to stem a rift in the party. Anna's magnanimous handling of the split in the party next year, following Sampath's mutiny, is noteworthy. Accusing the party of swerving from its ideological path and questioning the disproportionate importance given to film stars – criticisms not without substance – Sampath went on a sudden hunger strike precipitating a crisis. Despite Anna's best efforts the party suffered a split and Sampath formed the Tamil Desiya Katchi which however soon merged with the Congress.

A contemporary American political analyst, Selig Harrison, in his *India: The Most Dangerous Decade*, had observed, as early as in 1960, of Anna that 'there is no doubt that this powerful orator is the single most popular mass figure in the region' – a point missed by his contemporary political rivals.

The DMK grew from strength to strength, and in the 1962 elections won an impressive fifty seats in the legislature. However, the Congress plotted the defeat of Anna in his home turf, Kanchipuram, shamelessly using the communal card and playing on religious sentiment. A positive spin-off of the debacle was that Anna went to the Rajya Sabha where he held his own among stalwart parliamentarians, gaining national prestige.

If Anna left an indelible mark on the Tamil language and irreversibly changed the way Tamil was spoken on the platform, his English was no pushover either. As indicated earlier he had begun his political career by translating the English speeches of Justice Party stalwarts who modelled their orations on Burke and others. Anna also briefly worked on the editorial staff of the party's English organ, *Justice*. In 1959 he had launched and edited the DMK's English weekly, *Homeland*.

Anna's move to the House of Elders gave him the opportunity to articulate a distinctive Tamil/Dravidian/south Indian perspective. He made his mark among stalwart parliamentarians, with quick repartees to interventions. As always Anna tried to convince rather than assert views and positions. He pointed out the dangers of a homogenising state with power accumulated at the centre. His denunciation of Hindi imposition, the state's attempt to impose one language as the official language of the union, bears reading even now.

Anna's most challenging moment during his term as a member of parliament (MP) came in the wake of the Chinese aggression. Anna demonstrated his shrewd political acumen by abdicating the nominal secessionist demand in the DMK's programme. Even here he had the last laugh when he stated on the floor of the house that:

I am perfectly aware of the constitution ... of the National Integration Committee under the able leadership of Dr C. P. Ramaswami Aiyar, a sturdy champion of India's sovereignty and integrity, so sturdy indeed that as Dewan of Travancore he announced the independence of Travancore and proclaimed a pact with Pakistan.

But what propelled Anna and the DMK to power were the years leading up to 26 January 1965 when, through the union government's review of the constitutional provision, Hindi was to be enshrined as the sole official language dislodging English's status as associate official language. The DMK was to spearhead the decisive anti-Hindi agitation of the 1960s. The 1950s were marked by minor agitations such as the tarring of Hindi letters on signboards at railway stations. In the various party conferences organised by Anna the imposition of Hindi was a recurrent theme. Paradoxically, nobody strengthened the case against Hindi more than the Hindi fanatics themselves. As the pitch of the pro-Hindi camp became more and more shrill every argument of that side was effectively nailed. Countering the argument of Hindi being the language of a majority Anna quipped that, in that case, the common crow and not the peacock would have to be India's national bird. Nehru's legally-not-binding assurance that English would remain as long as the south wanted did little to solve the problem. With the DMK declaring Republic Day 1965 as a day of mourning the stage was set for unprecedented turmoil in independent India. The DMK called for the burning of the constitution in protest. Thousands were arrested and top DMK leaders incarcerated, lending them an aura which was to be converted into electoral power in a few years. The near-spontaneous uprising of students – many of whom were first-generation literates – marked the changing social base of politics in

Tamilnadu. Self-immolation as a form of protest, an expression of subaltern commitment and despair, was a favourite stick to beat Dravidian politics with until upper-caste protestors took to it in the wake of Mandal. The repression let loose by the state effectively ensured that the Congress would be defeated in the 1967 elections.

And when the DMK swept the polls in 1967 – in a pre-election alliance with Rajaji's Swatantra Party, the Communists, and the Muslim League, thereby gaining political acceptability across the board – it surprised no one except the Congress.

But the electoral success disturbed no one more than Anna himself for he feared that success had come a little too early – the DMK's first cabinet was the youngest in India then. He was pained by the defeat of K. Kamaraj (whom Periyar had backed) at the hands of a greenhorn, a student activist named P. Srinivasan. In a magnanimous gesture Anna drove to Trichy and met Periyar after a hiatus of twenty years – a gesture that moved the venerated old man – and dedicated his government to him. And again in one of his memorable slogans he called the DK and DMK a double-barrelled gun.

The new DMK government legalised the non-ritualistic self-respect marriages championed by Periyar, renamed Madras state as Tamilnadu, scrapped the three-language policy for a two-language one, and initiated many welfare schemes. The spectacular World Tamil Conference organised in early 1968 was the high watermark of the new government. Anna was also to win many other honours. Notable was the award of the Chubb Fellowship by Yale University and an official visit to the USA in 1968.

The dazzling rise of Anna was however cut short by throat cancer. A compulsive chewer of tobacco and user of snuff, Anna's erratic lifestyle with reading late into the night and constant tours took its toll. He was not yet sixty. He left behind no property and it is said that he never even had a bank account.

What the future course of Tamil politics would have been had Anna lived longer is a moot question. But the Indian nation state owes to him the accommodation of Tamil nationalism within it – not as a concession, but as an enriching.

3

M. KARUNANIDHI
Political Artist

THE YEAR 2018 MARKS the birth centenary of T. Balasaraswati, the great Bharatanatyam dancer. Two years earlier the birth centenary of M. S. Subbulakshmi was celebrated. Both came from a devadasi community, now going by the name of Isai Vellalar. A once-respected community of singers, dancers, and musicians it came to be stigmatised from the late nineteenth century. The colonial state, and the modernising intelligentsia it spawned, looked down upon it. Despite this the women of this community excelled in the arts – as dancers, as singers, and as actresses on the stage and on the silver screen. Traditionally, in this community, the birth of a girl was celebrated, and the arrival of a son, bemoaned. Following a matrilineal descent women controlled property, and men were relegated to the sidelines.

From such a community came the longest serving chief minister and legislator of Tamilnadu. His political successes apart, he won the support and undying veneration of hundreds of thousands of followers who admired his linguistic flair, literary skills, and eloquence on the platform. The political history of the last half a century and more, not only of Tamilnadu, but also perhaps the whole of India, can scarcely be written without more than a mention of Thirukkuvalai Muthuvel Karunanidhi (1924–2018), whose abbreviation in Tamil is DMK – completely appropriate, as he was synonymous with the party.

For over seventy years Karunanidhi was an inescapable presence in Tamil politics. For at least five decades no major political event in Tamilnadu occurred without Karunanidhi's imprint – positive or negative – on it. Following his mentor C. N. Annadurai, he smoothly integrated the state into the national mainstream, made the strongest case for state autonomy in a federal set-up, empowered the backward classes, and reinforced language as a key component of identity. In much of these areas his contribution was symbolic – and all the more powerful for that.

First elected to the legislative assembly in 1957, Karunanidhi was a sitting member until his death. Only two other Indian politicians – Pawan Chamling of Sikkim and Jyoti Basu of West Bengal (with Biju Patnaik of Odisha snapping at the heels) – occupied the chief minister's seat for a longer duration. Ascending to the chair of the chief minister in 1969, on Anna's death, he won the elections in 1971 and regained power only to see his government dismissed in January 1976 during the National Emergency (1975–7). After thirteen years without power he bounced back as chief minister in January 1989, in the wake of M. G. Ramachandran's (MGR) death. Two years later he was to be 'out' again, being the victim of Article 356 when his government was dismissed by the centre for allegedly supporting Tamil militants in neighbouring Sri Lanka. In 1996 he returned with a sweeping majority, completed a full term, lost the elections in 2001, but was back in the driver's seat again from 2006 to 2011. In between Karunanidhi played a key role in the formation of V. P. Singh's government (1989–90), the United Front government (1996–8), the National Democratic Alliance or NDA (1998–2004), and United Progressive Alliance or UPA I and II (2004–9; 2009–14).

Besides his contributions to politics Karunanidhi was a major cultural figure in Tamil cinema and letters, commanding the love, admiration, and respect of a multitude of supporters.

Born in 1924 in Thirukkuvalai, a village near Thiruvarur (under UPA I, Karunanidhi managed to locate a new central university of Tamilnadu here) in the fertile Kaveri delta, Karunanidhi had modest beginnings. In school he was taught by S. Dandapani Desigar – a Tamil-Saiva scholar who deserved more than a Padma Shri, which was bestowed upon him for having been the teacher of one particular pupil. But the likes of Karunanidhi are not produced in schools. From a young age he displayed precocious writing talents. Drawn to the Dravidian movement he joined the anti-Hindi agitation of 1937–9 as a fourteen-year-old student and was rusticated. Even in his youth he scripted plays and acted in them. Organising party events he once invited the star poet Bharatidasan to Thiruvarur. By 1943 he had started *Murasoli*, as a handwritten journal which, in the years to come would become the DMK's official organ despite being owned by his family.

For details of his early life one has to rely on Karunanidhi's own testimony, especially as chronicled in his multivolume biography *Nenjukku Needhi*. Unique among Dravidian party leaders he had a keen sense of history, and at every possible moment exercised his grip over its writing. Perhaps that explains why the official history of the DMK or the collected editorials of C. N. Annadurai remain unpublished despite the DMK having been in power for over a quarter of a century. Such volumes would perforce have to give space to others, an idea one can hardly expect Karunanidhi to favour. At six volumes running to about 4,000 pages, his autobiography stands in for the official history of the party. A permanent exhibition depicting the chronicle of the party on display at Anna Arivalayam, Chennai, the party headquarters, has little place for any one except him.

The autobiography draws its title from a poem by Subramania Bharati. 'Needhi' means justice and fairness. However,

Karunanidhi's rivals can hardly expect its dispensation in the text. It is rather animated by self-justification.

The autobiographies of Indian politicians, often ghostwritten, are usually published when they are out of power and seek to relive their past fame. This is one criticism that cannot be directed at Karunanidhi. Unlike the Western autobiography, which narrativises the realisation of the self, Tamil autobiographies have invariably focused on the transformations taking place around them. Karunanidhi's work falls squarely within this tradition and parallels can be drawn to the autobiography by his 'country-cousin' Thiruvarur Vi. Kalyanasundara Mudaliar (1883–1953), the scholar and labour leader of an earlier age. There are few references to the personal and *Nenjukku Needhi* is but a narrative of political events refracted by Karunanidhi's personality.

It is easy to understand why practising politicians never attempt the autobiography. Apart from the problem of having to explain and justify the occurrences of volte-face there is also the need to keep future political options open. Karunanidhi deftly manages this through certain strategies. Whenever he should be at a loss to explain such about-turns he resorted to quotations from the media – journals as varied as *Dinamani, Ananda Vikatan, Economic Times, Eenadu, Illustrated Weekly, Sunday, India Today,* and *Hindustan Times.* Another strategy was to use literary allusion and alliteration to rationalise his shifting political stances. Scathing criticism bordering on libel against political opponents often took the form of quotations from their present-day allies. Quick to an associate's fault Karunanidhi never failed to settle scores by quoting their past words.

Karunanidhi had a facile pen and was never known to be at a loss for words. But the easy style in which he wrote, resonating to the rhythm of Tamil public speaking, did not leave much scope for nuance. Yet the usefulness of his multivolume autobiography for understanding contemporary Tamil politics as well as getting an insight into the mind of one of Tamilnadu's foremost politicians can scarcely be contested. The other option is to turn to equally skewed – to the opposite side – tirades by his political adversaries such as Kannadasan, Jayakanthan, and Pazha. Karuppiah.

THE SUN RISES

Karunanidhi's rise began with the popularity of talkies. With the introduction of playback singing in the mid-1940s the scales were tilted against singing stars who could barely emote or deliver dialogues with conviction. At this moment Dravidian movement ideologues entered the film world and began to write scripts. Anna himself led the charge. His *Nallathambi* (1948) and *Velaikkari* (1949), with their social reform content and crisp, provocative dialogues, crafted the template for what came to be known as the DMK film. These films rendered Periyar's subversive ideology in a palatable form to a popular audience. But it was Karunanidhi who did this to greatest effect. Though Karunanidhi was not credited for his first script within years he had become a star writer: *Manthiri Kumari* (1950) had a separate title card for the dialogue writer even as the names of actors (not excepting MGR) were all bunched in one card. But the film that succeeded beyond all expectations was *Parasakthi* (1952).

Sivaji Ganesan's spectacular debut in *Parasakthi* changed Tamil film history. The climatic courtroom scene where he delivers a long defence, imitated and mimed extensively, is possibly the single most memorable dialogue in Tamil film history. Karunanidhi skilfully slipped in subversive ideas past vigilant censors. That sometimes censoring drew pointed attention to the censored ideas was another matter. For instance, in the famous line, 'When did she [the Goddess] ever speak? She is just a *kal* [stone]!', 'kal' was muted by the censor board. But in

Sivaji's exaggerated lip-synch, the muted word thundered over the voiced ones.

Through the 1950s, *Manohara*, *Malaikallan*, *Thirumbi Paar* followed one after another, and Karunanidhi's dialogues could almost single-handedly ensure the success of a film. Coupled with Sivaji Ganesan's histrionics his dialogues proved to be crowd-pullers. Laced with politics, the screenplays and the dialogues were keenly consumed. Soon Karunanidhi was also producing films.

Karunanidhi not only scripted dialogues for actors to mouth. He was also a superb orator. Even among other talented public speakers that the DMK spawned – Anna, Nedunchezhiyan, Anbazhagan, Sittrarasu, E. V. K. Sampath, K. A. Mathialagan – Karunanidhi stood out. In his early years he used to thunder on the podium and later collapse tired into his seat. But soon he exploited the power of the public address system. With pregnant pauses, alliterative sound patterns, suggestive phrases, and modulated voice he was a star speaker. Suffused with literary and puranic allusion his speeches had enough for both the uneducated and the cognoscenti. Caught in the most delicate of situations Karunanidhi could weasel out with a cheeky line or a playful phrase. Never one to shy away from the press – unlike, say, Jayalalithaa or Narendra Modi – he countered the most tricky questions with quick repartees and quips, and was thus the media's delight.

When considering Karunanidhi's output the word 'prolific' readily comes to mind. Apart from film scripts he wrote short stories, novels, epistles, sketches, political commentary, and so on – and none of them were ghost written. (One should add that he never employed a speech writer.) In poetry, even though he eschewed prosodic forms, his lines mimicked traditional cadences. Rephrasing classical literature into contemporary language was his forte. His retellings of Thirukural, Tholkappiyam (the earliest Tamil grammar), and Sangam classics won him a huge readership, and helped the popularisation of these classics. Some of these retellings found expression in films as well: for instance, *Poompuhar*, the film version of Silappadhikaram, the great epic with a woman protagonist, Kannagi.

Karunanidhi took his literary reputation seriously. He had fellow litterateurs endorse his achievements. Scholars were roped in to fix their imprimatur on scholarship. When in power Karunanidhi expected and won literary accolades. He received the Rajarajan Prize of the Tamil University, and the inaugural Kural Peedam Prize – need one say, instituted by him – went to him. During his last term in office the Madras University commissioned and subsidised English translations of his many works. Also said to have eyed the Sahitya Akademi Award, he missed it.

Karunanidhi's writings are innocent of modernist elements. Yet he sought appreciation from modern writers. His 1992 interview to the middle magazine *Subamangala* is revealing of how distant he was from the richness of contemporary Tamil writing. Never one to take criticism in his stride, he could be abrasive when his literary standing was questioned – as the Tamil writer Jeyamohan found out once. Karunanidhi's literary minions worked overtime on his carping critic Jayakanthan in his last years to win his endorsement. Not known to forget or forgive, he bore a grudge towards Kannadasan for the portrayal of his ambitions in his autobiography *Vanavasam*.

Despite his tremendous will to political power Karunanidhi prided himself as a man of letters. 'Kalaignar' (the artist), was the most favourite of sobriquets – Doctor (DLitt), Muthamizh Arignar (the scholar of literature, music, and drama), Tamil-ina Thalaivar (the leader of the Tamil community) – that he eagerly adorned himself with. Writing was not only the runway from which his political career took off, but also the fuel station where he refuelled himself.

FIRST STINT IN POWER

From the early 1950s the DMK was inching close to electoral politics. Those were busy times for Karunanidhi, active as he was in films, journalism, politics, and public speaking. Karunanidhi revelled in all these activities. He rode to political stardom when during the DMK's 1953 *mummunai porattam* (three-pronged agitation) he suddenly and dramatically put his head on the railway track at Kallakudi station – against the government decision to rename it as Dalmiapuram, after the north Indian industrialist Ramakrishna Dalmia – as the train was about to be flagged off. This event was given epic treatment in *Kallakudi Makaviyam* (The Saga of Kallakudi) by the same Kannadasan who wrote stinging exposes of Karunanidhi in later years.

Another event that put Karunanidhi in the limelight was the celebration of the DMK's victory in the 1959 Madras municipal corporation elections. Towards the end of the felicitation speech, in which he heaped praise on Karunanidhi for his campaigning, Anna pulled out a gold ring and slipped it on his fingers. When an agitated Kannadasan, who had played no less a part in the electioneering, confronted Anna on this he is said to have replied calmly, 'Buy me a ring and I shall do the same for you at the next conference!'

At the 1956 Trichy conference, after a secret ballot, the DMK formally committed itself to contesting elections. In the elections shortly afterwards the DMK was off to a good start winning fifteen assembly and two parliamentary seats. Karunanidhi was returned from the Kulithalai assembly constituency. For the next sixty years Karunanidhi would maintain an uninterrupted electoral winning record, his last victory being in 2016 (the only assembly election he did not contest was in 1984).

One of the first two DMK MPs was E. V. K. Sampath. A nephew of Periyar, Sampath was a superb platform speaker.

Unlike other DMK speakers he relied less on alliteration and more on substance, and won his own band of followers. With a good command over English he also had a keen understanding of national and world politics. In 1949, Sampath had rebelled against Periyar and followed Anna to join the DMK, thus abdicating claim to Periyar's legacy and wealth.

When the DMK split in 1949, Anna walked away with virtually every significant personality. Though the undisputed leader he constituted an informal committee of five leaders – the so-called *aimperum thalaivar* – to direct the party. In 1956 he even stepped down from the secretary-ship of the party boldly making way for Nedunchezhiyan. Karunanidhi's uncanny political acumen was evident in the fact that he felt least threatened by the galaxy of leaders at the higher echelons of the party. The leaders, for their part, saw little threat in Karunanidhi – only to rue their attitude a decade later. Always many steps ahead of his rivals Karunanidhi saw Sampath, of more or less his age with considerable skills and following, as his competitor. Karunanidhi provoked him and carried on a barely invisible campaign against Sampath. Sampath grossly underestimated his rival, and adopted the strategy of campaigning against the prominence given to film personalities, arguing for reorienting the party's policies to keep pace with the changing times in a post-Independence scenario. However, he was consistently outwitted and out-manoeuvred. After a dramatic fast in 1961, Sampath left the DMK, formed a party of his own, which ultimately merged with the Congress, his promising political career coming to a sad end.

In 1967 the DMK came to power. Karunanidhi was made the PWD minister, and was third in rank in the new cabinet. But Anna fell ill, and died in early February 1969. Karunanidhi composed a tearful elegy – a recording of its recital is still broadcast at party events. At one point, as he cites one of Anna's famous lines about facing adversity, Karunanidhi chokes. The cynic may be excused for reading a rehearsed performance, but it easily captivated the emotionally charged cadre.

Karunanidhi moved quickly and garnered the support of a majority of legislators even as senior leaders seemed baffled by the ambition of, from their perspective, an upstart. Only one leader, Nedunchezhiyan, backed by his younger brother, Era. Chezhiyan, actually threw his hat in the ring, but was stunned by the utter lack of support for his candidature. History was soon made. A member of a stigmatised caste became Tamilnadu's chief minister at the age of forty-four.

Unsurprisingly, Karunanidhi was high on power and exulted in it. In a brilliant move ahead of the 1971 general elections he forged an alliance with Indira Gandhi who was desperate to defeat the 'syndicate' – contesting elections as Congress (O) under Kamaraj. Indira Gandhi conceded all the assembly seats to the DMK, contesting only ten parliamentary seats. Despite the controversy over the 'insulting' of Hindu gods in a DK conference in Salem, an unholy alliance between Rajaji and Kamaraj, and a desperate campaign by conservative elements – epitomised by Cho Ramaswamy and his political journal *Thuglak* – Karunanidhi returned with an overwhelming majority. He also established his hold over the party. By the mid-1970s most of the senior leaders had joined his rival MGR's party. The few who did not accepted Karunanidhi's leadership unquestioningly. He also manoeuvred to make himself its president in violation of Anna's solemn pledge that the seat would be forever Periyar's. The decimation of the original DMK's leadership is indexed by how the many journals run by its leaders all folded up leaving *Murasoli* alone, tall.

During his tenure Karunanidhi introduced some highly visible welfare measures such as instituting a slum clearance board for relocating urban ghettos and the abolition of hand-pulled rickshaws. Apart from constituting a backward classes commission, he made a law to ensure that any trained person, irrespective of caste, could become a temple priest. This progressive act was challenged in court, and over forty years passed before the Supreme Court endorsed it. An attempt to abolish horse racing was however completely struck down. Prohibition was withdrawn after a quarter of a century, and in a desperate move to shore up finances lottery tickets were introduced. Though perceived as corrupt Karunanidhi won the reputation of being an excellent administrator who could deliver, thereby commanding the respect of civil servants. On the floor of the legislative assembly, he was brilliant in rebutting the opposition's charges.

The Thiruvarur chariot festival was revived after a long hiatus cementing his credentials among believers. Symbolic edifices were established. In Poompuhar he planned and executed a cultural complex to commemorate Silappadhikaram. In Chennai, Valluvar Kottam, a massive celebration in stone, mimicking a fortress, of Thirukural was commissioned. A statue of Karunanidhi was installed in the arterial road of Anna Salai.

The years preceding the Emergency were turbulent. In the context of high inflation and rising prices, labour was restive. The police did not cover itself with glory in tackling labour unrest. The suppression of the Simpson's strike was particularly brutal. In this context Annamalai University's decision to confer a doctorate honoris causa on Karunanidhi did not go down well. (Following his example, MGR and Jayalalithaa had a similar degree conferred on them from the University of Madras.) The resulting protest of students was quelled with police firing, producing a martyr.

In his ascendance to chief ministership in 1967 Karunanidhi had been backed by MGR. But soon MGR emerged as a threat. At this moment a lifelong weakness of Karunanidhi became more prominent – the love for his family. Earlier, in 1967, when Anna had vacated his South Madras parliamentary seat, Karunanidhi got the party's nomination for his nephew Murasoli Maran. In a bid to undermine MGR, Karunanidhi promoted the entry into films of his son Mu. Ka. Muthu, born of his late first wife, Padma. Muthu brazenly imitated MGR. The same talents were hired to make his films. The party machinery was employed for publicity. Muthu had a great singing voice – inherited from his maternal uncle, Chidambaram S. Jayaraman – but lacked in every other department, his leaden feet in sharp contrast to MGR's sprightly steps. At best Muthu's films were pathetic copies of out-of-date exemplars. (Wasting himself on drink and drugs Muthu was to cause much grief to his father, compounded by the serious embarrassment of his joining the All India Anna Dravida Munnetra Kazhagam [AIADMK] and accepting a purse from arch-rival Jayalalithaa. Seriously ill, this firstborn could not even take part in his father's funeral.)

A split was inevitable. In 1972, MGR launched his own party, the AIADMK. All attempts were made to wreck MGR's big-budget *Ulagam Suttrum Valiban* released the next year, but its box office success was unstoppable.

IN POLITICAL WILDERNESS

In June 1975 a beleaguered Indira Gandhi invoked a state of internal emergency. Amidst the horrors of Emergency, Tamilnadu was the one refuge for fugitives such as George Fernandez and E. M. S. Namboodiripad until the DMK ministry was dismissed at the end of January 1976. Many of DMK's leaders and cadre, with the sole exception of Karunanidhi, were arrested. His son M. K. Stalin was imprisoned. In attempting to save Stalin from police beatings Chitti Babu, a DMK MP, died. In an attempt to pile on the pressure the Sarkaria Commission was instituted to inquire into corruption charges against Karunanidhi. Many second-line leaders ditched him fearing persecution. But he stuck resolutely to his anti-Emergency position. As *Murasoli* faced strict censorship he used ingenious methods to get his message through. For instance, stopped from releasing a list of arrested DMK cadres, he printed it under the rubric of those who failed to turn up at Anna Samadhi, an annual party ritual on the occasion of Anna's death anniversary. Karunanidhi's Emergency-period boldness somewhat salvaged a reputation sullied by acts of omission and commission during his first stint in power.

The years between 1976 and 1988 were difficult for Karunanidhi. For ten years MGR stood between him and political power. Karunanidhi's political skills were put to the severest test during this decade. His heroic stand during the Emergency produced no electoral fruits. In the March 1977 general elections, despite being in an alliance with the Janata Party that won power at the centre, the DMK fared badly. Three months later it fought the assembly elections alone, but came a cropper. When MGR took oath as Tamilnadu chief minister, Karunanidhi would have scarce imagined that he would be in political wilderness for ten years – or that he would outlive his rival by over three decades, serve two full terms in office, and become a major player in national politics.

To his credit Karunanidhi kept MGR on his toes. He was the chief minister in waiting, ever alert to a misstep by his rival. In the legislature he often had the ruling government on the mat. To be fair to MGR, despite limited speaking skills, he stood his ground. Karunanidhi raked up scandals such as the Bulgarian shipping scandal, went on a long march from Tirunelveli to Tiruchendur when a trustee of the Tiruchendur temple was murdered – a minister's hand was suspected – and severely embarrassed MGR by leaking an enquiry commission report on the issue.

Karunanidhi also kept himself busy, scripting a series of films with political overtones. Times had changed, and his political barbs were blunt. Yet these films helped to keep the party flock together.

In late 1979, Karunanidhi smelt his first chance. The Janata government had collapsed. In the January 1980 general elections Karunanidhi, swallowing his pride, forgave Indira Gandhi for her Emergency crimes, and forged an alliance with the Congress. As was his wont Karunanidhi deployed linguistic dexterity to justify political opportunism, coining the alliterative phrase '*Nehruvin magale varugu, Nilaiyana atchi tharuga*' (Come Nehru's daughter to bestow a stable government). And in another opportunist move – a move that would backfire and return to haunt him – he forced Indira's hands to dismiss MGR's government when the DMK–Congress alliance won the parliament elections.

The consequent 1980 assembly election results were to coincide with his 56th birthday on 3 June. Karunanidhi had planned to take office at Valluvar Kottam – Emergency had earlier thwarted his plans to inaugurate it. But Karunanidhi had not factored in MGR's resistance – he fought an inspired rear-guard battle – and the fractious nature of his ally. The DMK and the Congress had divided the seats equally, with the understanding that the largest partner would claim chief ministership. The DMK and the Congress worked at cross purposes and the poll results left Karunanidhi shell-shocked. The prematurely ordered victory banners and posters remained unclaimed in the printing presses.

A wiser MGR now built bridges with Indira Gandhi in his second innings, thus keeping Karunanidhi at bay. In early October 1984, MGR fell gravely ill. Karunanidhi saw another chance. But his hopes were dashed when, within weeks of MGR's hospitalisation, Indira Gandhi was assassinated. Wanting to capitalise on sympathy, Rajiv Gandhi announced snap polls. It was a double whammy – the sympathy wave created by a martyred prime minister and an ailing chief minister was impossible to counter. In an effort to stem the tide, after attempts to suggest that MGR was no more failed, a desperate Karunanidhi invoked his old friendship with MGR, promising the electorate that he would abdicate when his friend returned. It was another instance when Karunanidhi's image as a man of cunning and intelligence worked against him. His emotional appeal did not cut ice with the electorate.

The Congress–AIADMK swept the elections. As the AIADMK was wracked by intra-party wrangling under a visibly unwell MGR, Karunanidhi kept up the pressure. The years were eventful especially in relation to the ethnic conflict in Sri Lanka. Given its investment in identity politics the DMK had always shown a keen interest in the island's politics and the travails of the Tamils under Sinhala majoritarianism. The state-sponsored July 1983 anti-Tamil riots in Sri Lanka gave a new urgency to Tamils in India. Following the failure of decades of non-violent resistance Tamil youths took to arms, and various militant groups, aided by the Indian state, flourished in the atmosphere. Further, many of these groups found their own backers in Tamilnadu political parties.

While MGR was perceived to be close to the Liberation Tigers of Tamil Eelam (LTTE) and its supremo V. Prabhakaran, Karunanidhi was identified with the Tamil Eelam Liberation Organization (TELO). In 1986, in the first of its coordinated fratricidal attacks, the LTTE targeted TELO slaughtering all its members, including its chief Sri Sabaratnam. In mid-1987 the Indo–Sri Lanka Peace Accord was signed between Rajiv Gandhi and J. R. Jayawardene, and the so-called Indian Peace Keeping Force (IPKF) was despatched to the island to battle the separatists. Despite the unanimous rejection of the accord by all Tamilnadu political parties, the Indian government went ahead. MGR however acquiesced to the arrangement – he endorsed the accord in a massive meeting on Marina Beach when he appeared with Rajiv Gandhi. Karunanidhi was in the vanguard of those criticising the accord.

In December 1987, MGR died. Karunanidhi rushed to his Ramavaram residence to pay his last respects, and made a dignified tribute befitting the occasion. But AIADMK cadres went on a rampage, attacking the DMK's party offices. Karunanidhi's statue, on Anna Salai, was vandalised. Said to have brought him ill-luck, the statue was never replaced. It was not the first time that Karunanidhi's rationalism would come under a cloud.

If Karunanidhi had thought the chief minister's chair was his now, Rajiv Gandhi had other plans. In a bid to reinstate the Congress the AIADMK government was dismissed, the assembly dissolved, and the state placed under President's Rule for a year. Rajiv Gandhi made a dozen visits to the state, but the IPKF debacle was too serious to be whitewashed.

BRIEF INTERLUDE IN POWER

In elections held in January 1989, with the AIADMK split into rival factions between MGR's widow Janaki Ramachandran and Jayalalithaa, Karunanidhi saw his chance. Sure of a victory in a four-cornered contest he astutely dropped his former alliance partners such as the Communist Party of India (CPI) who had stood by him through tough times. Despite being out of power for thirteen long years Karunanidhi had kept the party intact, well-oiled with periodical, keenly fought intra-party elections. The DMK was always prepared, a government in waiting. The humongous numbers that it won – 179 out of 234 – however belied real weaknesses.

Power had a therapeutic effect on Karunanidhi's health. But his second stint in power was not a happy one. Family was his Achilles heel. First, inner party feuds were simmering. For a start he sensed a threat to his son M. K. Stalin's position as heir apparent in the ambitious Vaiko (then going by the name of V. Gopalsamy). Rajathi Ammal – famously described by Karunanidhi on the floor of the legislature as 'my daughter Kanimozhi's mother' – began to be seen in the public presaging their daughter Kanimozhi's entry into public life in the next decade. The second threat was the mercurial Jayalalithaa. At least initially she did not seem to be in politics for the long haul and showed little will to fight. But backed by ambitious hangers-on she soon posed a challenge. Karunanidhi handled it badly. Pushed to a corner she fought viciously and troubled Karunanidhi more than MGR ever did.

But the biggest trouble came in the form of the LTTE. Over the years Karunanidhi had carefully fabricated the image of being 'Tamil-ina Thalaivar'. Karunanidhi was caught in a cleft. The Indian state was fighting the LTTE in Sri Lanka, without either clear political objectives or ground plans. In Tamilnadu itself public opinion was against the IPKF. Support, material and moral, flowed towards the LTTE from Tamilnadu. Central and state agencies worked at cross purposes. Karunanidhi went soft on the LTTE. But never attentive to niceties, the LTTE seriously, and repeatedly, embarrassed him. In June 1990, in broad daylight, in the heart of Chennai, the LTTE gunned down twelve members of the Eelam People's Revolutionary Liberation Front (EPRLF – then in power in the Northern Province of Sri Lanka) – including its leader K. Padmanabha. Public opinion turned, and Jayalalithaa whipped up a campaign that law and order had broken down.

The consequences were immediately visible. In the historic November 1989 general elections, though V. P. Singh formed the government defeating a beleaguered Congress, the DMK, a member of his National Front, could not win a single seat. Yet Murasoli Maran, as a Rajya Sabha member, was given a cabinet berth. Karunanidhi had struck a fine personal rapport with V. P. Singh, and the adoption of the Mandal Commission recommendations by the National Front government was touted as a victory for the Dravidian movement ideals.

44

Meanwhile, the Jayalalithaa–Rajiv Gandhi combine proved a formidable force, relentlessly attacking Karunanidhi. Each passing day was an ordeal. It must have taken great courage, in this situation, for Karunanidhi, as chief minister, to refuse to welcome the returning IPKF forces for its violence against the Sri Lankan Tamils.

In November 1990 the central government fell. V. P. Singh was replaced by Chandra Shehkar of the Samajwadi Janata Party, whose government depended on the support of Rajiv Gandhi's Congress. Jayalalithaa, who had developed a cosy relationship with the Congress, put persistent pressure on Chandra Shekhar to undermine the DMK. The central government, flouting every constitutional norm, dismissed the DMK government in January 1991. Even the fig leaf of a governor's report was absent. (For the good turn of not sending the report Surjit Singh Barnala would be rewarded with a second term of governorship when Karunanidhi returned to power in 1996.) Karunanidhi thus had the dubious distinction of being dismissed from power under Article 356 of the Constitution twice. Criticism about the DMK's slack handling of Tamil militancy gained strength when Rajiv Gandhi was brutally assassinated in May 1991 in the midst of general election campaigning. In the state elections held simultaneously Jayalalithaa crushed the DMK, which won only two of 234 seats. Only Karunanidhi could retain his seat and that too by a wafer-thin margin – he resigned promptly. After such a wipeout few would have dreamt of a comeback. But Karunanidhi was not one to be written off easily.

THE SECOND COMEBACK

Even as Jayalalithaa scaled new heights of authoritarianism in her first term in office, in 1993, Karunanidhi faced the biggest intra-party challenge of his political career. Over the years

Karunanidhi's leadership in the DMK was a settled question, with seniors like K. Anbazhagan content to be a permanent standby. Challengers were not brooked. If his son Mu. Ka. Muthu was the red flag that enraged MGR leading to his mutiny, twenty years later it was M. K. Stalin's turn. As Stalin was unobtrusively groomed, his image getting a makeover in the 1990s – Karunanidhi's repeated assertion that the DMK was no Sankara Mutt to anoint successors notwithstanding – there was considerable resentment among those second-line hopefuls. One of them, Vaiko, known for his thundering speeches and creditable interventions as a three-time DMK member of the Rajya Sabha, launched a challenge. In 1989, in a disparate act of brinkmanship, the sitting MP took a boat illegally to the LTTE-controlled jungles of northern Sri Lanka even as the IPKF was fighting the guerrillas. Dressed in camouflage fatigues, his pictures with Prabhakaran and other LTTE leaders were designed to prop up his image and win brownie points among the cadres. The DMK government was deeply embarrassed.

Matters came to a head in late 1993. In a dramatic move Karunanidhi declared that the LTTE planned to eliminate him to ease Vaiko's path to DMK's leadership. It was a pre-emptive strike that forced Vaiko on the back foot. But Karunanidhi had misjudged the resentment against the family within the party – both among its leaders and the cadres. To his shock, one-third of the district secretaries – the pillars of the party – and nearly a half of the general council members went with Vaiko. In hindsight one can scarcely believe that Karunanidhi saw a challenge in a vacuous and impetuous Vaiko. Perhaps it was more an index of his assessment of Stalin's abilities. Over the next few years, though, Vaiko was comprehensively outsmarted by Karunanidhi who had humbled bigger challengers.

Jayalalithaa's first term in power during 1991–6 was marked by hubris and high-handedness, which made her enormously unpopular. Karunanidhi was back to form positioning himself as the saviour of the state. As the Congress went on – it is said blackmailed – to form an alliance with the AIADMK for the 1996 elections it split under the leadership of G. K. Moopanar as the Tamil Maanila Congress (TMC). The tide of 1991 was reversed, and it was the AIADMK's turn to be trounced at the hustings.

At the national level that year the DMK also decided to join the United Front, which meant a share in the parliamentary cake. Prime ministership was within Karunanidhi's striking distance. Three decades earlier Kamaraj had spurned it in his broken English: 'No Hindi. No English. How?' When queried on his prime-ministerial ambitions Karunanidhi retorted with a Tamil phrase, '*En uyaram enakku theriyum*' (I know my height!). His ally Moopanar, shall we say, did not know his height, and resented the fact that Karunanidhi did not propose him to prime ministership. (It went to H. D. Deve Gowda.) Moopanar nursed this disappointment, and this ultimately led to a falling out with the DMK, pushing him into Jayalalithaa's hands in the 2001 elections. Ironically, the DMK which played a key role in the formation of the central government also caused its downfall with the Jain Commission report's leaks about the DMK's alleged connivance in Rajiv Gandhi's assassination leading the Congress under Sitaram Kesri to withdraw its support.

Mid-term elections followed in February 1998. Shortly before L. K. Advani arrived in Coimbatore to campaign serial blasts rocked the textile city – the handiwork of Muslim fundamentalists. Tamil Muslims formed the traditional voter base of the DMK, but the radicalised Muslim youth of the post–Babri Masjid demolition had little patience for accommodative politics. The DMK lost. To make matters worse for Karunanidhi the Bharatiya Janata Party-(BJP) led NDA government was at the complete mercy of Jayalalithaa for its very survival. For the next thirteen months it is difficult to say who had a worse time:

Karunanidhi or Prime Minister A. B. Vajpayee. Jayalalithaa relentlessly hounded Vajpayee to dismiss the Karunanidhi government. A historic third dismissal from power hung over Karunanidhi's head. But Vajpayee did not yield – either out of conviction or because his hands were tied by the Supreme Court verdict in the S. R. Bommai case. In the event, in a dramatic vote of confidence motion in the parliament in April 1999, Karunanidhi did the unthinkable: the secular DMK, with a history of anti-Brahminism and a strong anti-Hindu communal ideology, voted with the BJP. But the government fell for want of one vote. Nonetheless, the DMK went on to form an alliance with the BJP and join the union government after its victory in elections later that year.

The DMK's alliance with the BJP was a blot on Karunanidhi's secular record. But the lure of power was too strong to resist. Murasoli Maran's hand is discernible in Karunanidhi's ideological slip. Not incidentally it was during the NDA regime that the media empire of the Maran family's *Sun TV* became a Frankenstein and ultimately threatened Karunanidhi himself. As the NDA government was on its last legs a dying Maran further dented Karunanidhi's reputation. Long after the break with the NDA was a foregone conclusion, the DMK continued in government just so that Maran, fighting for his life in hospital, would die in harness. At the time of the Gujarat riots in 2002 the DMK kept a deafening silence (Kanimozhi's condemnation was exceptional) even as there were rumblings from the other members of the NDA government. In Tamilnadu itself, Rashtriya Swayamsevak Sangh (RSS) front organisations made inroads into Tamil civil society with the active acquiescence of the DMK.

But we are getting a little ahead of the story.

Victory in the 1999 general elections had won Karunanidhi a temporary reprieve from Jayalalithaa. For all the troubles in the centre the 1996–2001 DMK government was arguably the best government in living memory. Apart from bringing Jayalalithaa to book, it kept corruption largely under check and launched many development initiatives. Concrete roads were laid in the rural areas and farmers' markets were set up to enhance peasant earnings. Caste conflicts that had flared up at the end of Jayalalithaa's tenure however continued if on a lower key. In a major reversal of policy, to contain violence triggered by the naming of a state-owned transport corporation after a Scheduled Caste hero, Sundaralingam, Karunanidhi had to drop all names. This turnabout hit the nadir with the death of seventeen Dalit plantation workers in what came to be known as the Tamiraparani massacre. Karunanidhi's attempt to start Periyar Samattuvapurams – government colonies of mixed castes – despite being well-intentioned failed.

But once again, contradictions in the family were brewing which revolved around who would inherit the party. Every term in office had seen the rise of one offspring or the other of Karunanidhi. In 2001 it was his errant son, M. K. Alagiri's turn to act up. Decades earlier Karunanidhi had banished him to Madurai in an effort to keep him in check. The local DMK leader, P. T. R. Palanivel Rajan, had acted as a counterweight to Alagiri. At the time of the 2001 state assembly elections things went out of hand and Alagiri was expelled. Apart from the electoral alliance that Jayalalithaa had stitched together, Alagiri's rebellion was a factor in DMK's defeat. Two years later Tha. Kiruttinan, the DMK leader and former minister, was murdered brutally when out for his morning walk – an incident dramatised in the Tamil film *Subramaniapuram*. The rivalry between Alagiri and Stalin was said to be the reason for the murder. Alagiri was the prime accused. Despite the AIADMK being in power, and the case being transferred to the neighbouring Andhra Pradesh to ensure a fair trial, the acquittal was a foregone conclusion.

Jayalalithaa astutely stitched together an alliance in the 2001 elections. She found an unlikely partner in G. K. Moopanar's TMC, formed in 1996 in protest against the Congress aligning with the AIADMK. But the alliance arithmetic worked and Jayalalithaa became chief minister for a second time. The DMK's defeat was followed by a grave threat to Karunanidhi's life. On the midnight of 30 June, Karunanidhi was arrested. No protocols were followed. Speculations were rife about plans that might have been had on his person. Luckily they went haywire. In a brilliant move Karunanidhi delayed the arrest for a crucial while by which time Union Minister Murasoli Maran and others arrived at his home. As he was ushered out of his house by a posse of policemen Karunanidhi staged a resistance. A scuffle ensued. All of which was caught on a spy camera, then a newfangled device. Before the police realised they had bungled, the dramatic footage was aired on *Sun TV*. Karunanidhi's pathetic cries of '*Ennai kolraangale, ennai kolraangale*' (They are killing me) inflamed the populace, triggering a groundswell of sympathy. Karunanidhi had survived another ordeal. As a bonus he enjoyed Z+ security until his death.

Within a few years Jayalalithaa had once again managed to become universally unpopular. In the 2004 parliamentary elections Karunanidhi negotiated a grand alliance of all opposition parties, and won all thirty-nine parliamentary seats. The Congress-led UPA scored an unexpected win over the BJP-led NDA. The DMK wielded the winning cards and wrested plum portfolios. Murasoli Maran's younger son Dayanidhi Maran became cabinet minister.

ANOTHER COMEBACK

But Karunanidhi's eyes were set on the chief-ministerial chair. A long-term critic of populist measures, he now promised many freebies. Karunanidhi became chief minister for a fifth time in 2006. But this term was even more fraught, overshadowing even the travails of the Emergency. For a start with only 96 of the 234 seats, the DMK government was dependent on the Congress – a check on the DMK's bargaining power at the centre. Jayalalithaa rubbed it in by repeatedly calling it a minority government.

Power at the centre as well as the state fed already-untrammelled ambitions both in the party and in the family. Though Stalin's hopes of becoming chief minister were belied, he became deputy chief minister. Karunanidhi had once again forgiven Alagiri, and he was back in the party. Within a year the first crisis erupted. The Sun TV empire had enlarged itself by the acquisition of the Tamil newspaper *Dinakaran*. The daily published an opinion poll – the agency that conducted the poll or the methodology it adopted remains unknown – that listed the most popular leaders in the state. Stalin topped it with a huge percentage while Alagiri was given 2 per cent. In broad daylight the *Dinakaran* office was ransacked and three of its employees murdered. It was common knowledge who was behind it.

The Maran brothers were expelled from the party, and the DMK now had to fend for itself in the media. A media channel, Kalaignar TV was started and a state-owned cable TV operation was promoted to take down Sun TV's near-monopoly on satellite telecast distribution. (A longstanding demand of the media world, it was given a decent burial once the family quarrel was settled.) In 2009, the notorious Thirumangalam Formula for winning elections through money power was forged. Karunanidhi decorated his son Alagiri with a new position – South Zone Organizing Secretary – for which the party constitution had no provision.

By this time his health was failing. Karunanidhi had had a colourful youth. But as he aged he brought discipline to his life – in stark contrast to the diabetic Jayalalithaa who was gorging herself on ice cream and milkshakes in her hospital bed. He stopped eating meat and practiced yoga regularly. But age and time are not so easily defeated. Added to these was the punishing schedule he maintained. An early riser (journalists dreaded his early morning calls, as he challenged them on their comments and analysis), he worked long hours – running the administration, controlling party affairs, writing for *Murasoli*, entertaining unending streams of daily visitors and admirers, scripting films and TV serials. To these must be added the almost weekly felicitation functions that he graced, his tired face aglow as he heard cloying praise heaped on him. Karunanidhi took to a custom-made wheelchair. Despite his love for his son, however, he turned a deaf ear to suggestions that he abdicate in favour of Stalin.

But the biggest challenge loomed from the south. In Sri Lanka the embattled LTTE had painted itself into a corner, and 9/11 had undermined all support for armed struggle. The LTTE was weakened by the mutiny of its eastern commander, Karuna. To make matters worse the Sinhala majoritarian state was now headed by a determined leader in Mahinda Rajapaksa. The LTTE's vacuous politics was accentuated by its aging military leadership. To add to all these India was now led by a party whose leader had been assassinated by the LTTE. The security establishment disgraced by the IPKF debacle was back in saddle. Under this constellation nothing could have saved the LTTE. As it suffered reverse after reverse, sentiments in Tamil swelled. The onus was on Tamil-ina Thailaivar to save the Eelam Tamils. Karunanidhi's skills were severely tested. As he desperately tried to save his chair, family, party, and government, the Eelam insurgency was being wiped out. The police suppressed protests brutally. Even a proper funeral for Muthukumar, who had immolated himself in protest, was not permitted. As the Sri Lankan army closed in on Mullaithivu, Karunanidhi staged a farcical fast on Marina Beach for all of four hours.

If a government which did not have the reputation of being pro-Tamil had not been in power in Tamilnadu how the law and order situation might have panned out is a moot question. Karunanidhi's reputation as Tamil-ina Thalaivar was a casualty. His desperate attempts to salvage his reputation by organising an international Tamil conference only added to the effect.

The 2009 parliamentary elections coincided with this debacle. Though the polls were won by the UPA of which the DMK was a part, the Congress was no more dependent on the DMK for a majority in the parliament. When a wheelchair-bound Karunanidhi flew to Delhi to bargain for cabinet seats, the bonhomie of 2004 was conspicuously missing. He still managed a cabinet berth for Alagiri only to have Alagiri's refusal to attend parliament and take questions severely denting the party's national image.

His favourite daughter Kanimozhi's political ambitions added to the troubles. Shattered by her disastrous first marriage her literary turn in the late 1990s gave some happiness to her artistically oriented father. Her feminist sensibilities gave the DMK an edge that it had lacked all along, and the party gained a certain acceptability among intellectuals. In 2006 she was nominated to the Rajya Sabha. But her political hopes, a manifestation of her mother's ambitions, it is said, triggered animosity in the first family. The Maran brothers, still nursing their wounds, broke the 2G scam story – related to the out-of-turn 2G spectrum allocation for telecommunications companies – putting DMK minister A. Raja and Kanimozhi in the dock.

In this context, in the 2011 assembly elections the Congress arm-twisted the DMK into giving it sixty-three seats – even as the negotiations were going on in the ground floor, the Central Bureau of Investigation was raiding Kalaignar TV's offices on the first floor. In the face of a spirited campaign by Jayalalithaa the Tamil electorate dumped the DMK, its term in office bringing back memories of Jayalalithaa's first term. The DMK even lost the opposition party status to the new film star on the political block, Vijayakanth. The biggest blow came when Kanimozhi was arrested and imprisoned for many months. As his health continued to falter the reins quietly passed into Stalin's hands, a fact deeply resented by Alagiri. It reached its nadir when Alagiri stormed into Karunanidhi's Gopalapuram residence – and as a tearful Karunanidhi recorded on camera – spewed the most unspeakable words at his father.

The 2011 election defeat was followed by an even cleaner sweep-out in the 2014 parliament elections. The DMK lost all thirty-nine seats. Despite Jayalalithaa suffering a series of setbacks – legal, judicial, health – resulting in a complete failure of governance, an ailing Karunanidhi could not exploit the situation. As his health collapsed forcing him to turn away from the electoral battlefield, the 2016 assembly elections were completely managed by Stalin. And the result: it was an election in which the DMK snatched defeat from the jaws of victory.

Coincidentally, when Jayalalithaa was hospitalised in the months preceding her death in December 2016 Karunanidhi was also in a hospital barely a few kilometres away. It is not clear how he reacted to the passing away of his bitterest rival.

The last two years of his life were tragic. Karunanidhi was occasionally wheeled in before the camera, dressed in his trademark yellow shawl – a concession, it is said, to his superstitious family – and gave a barely recognisable smile. In and out of hospital he was evidently not in control. A great scriptwriter, left to himself, Karunanidhi would have scripted a more fitting ending.

~

The historian is not only tasked with marshalling data and writing a narrative. He is also called to judge. But how does one judge a man who lived such a long and eventful life, teeming with twists and turns, highs and lows, principled stances and volte faces. It is a task that is rendered more difficult when the historian is part of the very processes heavily inflected by this man. More than anyone else Karunanidhi was aware of this predicament, and he played it to his advantage. He was substance, but also symbol, and what a symbol. Pushed to a corner he always fought back with symbolic force.

As Karunanidhi lay in state on 6–7 August 2018 it was precisely this war of symbols that was fought in the courts. Should he be interred beside his beloved mentor, Anna, on the hallowed grounds of the Marina in Chennai, or should he be given a decent but not fitting burial in out-of-the-away Guindy Park? As such wars go the loser is the winner, irrespective of jurisprudential wisdom. The Government of Tamilnadu's refusal to grant him space on Marina Beach smacked of vendetta at best or meanness at worst. If the court ruled against the government, it would be befitting Karunanidhi's stature. If not, it would be one more instance of denying a great leader from an underprivileged community his due. In life and in death Karunanidhi is not defeated in symbolic wars. In the event he was buried on the Marina Beach.

Despite his many populist welfare measures and able administration Karunanidhi's reputation rested largely on symbolic action. Backward caste reservation is a case in point. No one epitomises the backward caste assertion better than Karunanidhi. But what does the record say? In 1970 he appointed the backward classes commission with A. N. Sattanathan as chairperson. While Karunanidhi marginally enhanced backward caste reservation from 25 to 31 per cent, who raised it to a substantial 50? MGR. Who ensured that the overall quota of 69 per cent was not pared down to 49 per cent? The reviled Jayalalithaa. Karunanidhi was *the* advocate of state autonomy. But who exploited the admittedly limited powers of the state provided by the Constitution? Jayalalithaa. Who authored India's greatest welfare measure, the nutritious noon-meal scheme for schoolchildren? MGR. One can easily produce a longer list of such instances.

But then Karunanidhi was the master of symbols. Whether getting the chariot of the Thiruvarur temple rolling after years, or introducing an invocation to Mother Tamil as the state's anthem, or getting Tamil recognised as a classical language, he understood the emotional quotient of cultural gestures. As we know symbolic wars are more than symbolic. When Karunanidhi, in 1970, legislated that any trained person, irrespective of caste, could be a temple priest, the move had the power to undermine deeply entrenched structures. It may not have come to fruition until a few weeks before his death, after nearly a half a century of legal battles, but the principle had been established.

Karunanidhi revelled in another set of symbols – erecting structural edifices symbolising Tamil pride: the fortress-like Valluvar Kottam in Chennai and the 133-metre statue to celebrate the sagely author of Thirukkural; the seaside memorial for Anna; the Poompuhar complex to celebrate the Tamil epic, Silappadhikaram.

In this process of forging symbols Karunanidhi himself became one. In this he will remain unrivalled.

Over seventy years Karunanidhi was an inescapable presence in Tamil politics. Just to get a temporal span over which he cast his shadow, it is nearly half a century since Anna died and more than three decades have passed since MGR's death. It is already long since MGR's name got any political purchase. Jayalalithaa, soon to be forgotten, will be one more memorial on Marina Beach. But there is little mistaking Karunanidhi's mark on Tamil political life. MGR is said to have had three lives. Karunanidhi's one life achieved as much, and more. Anna, MGR, and Jayalalithaa left no heirs, and history will judge them on their own terms. It is unlikely that Karunanidhi will have that privilege. The post-Anna phase of Tamil politics will have Karunanidhi's name indelibly etched on it. But Karunanidhi's name will have those of his heirs, immediate and distant, scribbled all over it.

4

M. G. RAMACHANDRAN
Star Politician

ON THE MARINA BEACH, where MGR lies buried, a steady stream of visitors, the numbers now overtaken by those visiting the grave of his protégé, Jayalalithaa, circumambulates his tomb. As they reverentially walk around, many press their ears to the granite slabs, expecting to listen to the ticking of his watch. In one of the biggest funerals ever seen MGR was interred dressed in his trademark off-white synthetic *vetti*, full-sleeved shirt, impenetrable sunglasses, and fur cap. On his right hand, over the cuff, as ever, was his watch. Thirty years after the interment his admirers still fancy that they can hear his watch ticking. MGR, the man, was as much the image and the myth.

The lame duck Edappadi K. Palaniswami government, serving time at the mercy of the BJP government, in a bid to bolster its image celebrated MGR's centenary in all districts of Tamilnadu during 2018 – after the centenary year was over. It is believed that MGR was born on 17 January 1917 in the hill town of Kandy in Sri Lanka. His parents were Nairs from Kerala, and his Malayali origins were held against him by his great rival M. Karunanidhi. In an effort to rid him of this stigma, in a state where Tamil identity is of paramount importance, one of his ministers recruited a genealogist to invent a new pedigree for him. The scholar 'demonstrated' using epigraphs, genealogies, and other historical narratives to establish that MGR was a Kongu Vellalar, no less.

But the people who voted for MGR in droves cared little about his antecedents. The fervour with which he was adulated in his lifetime and after defies logic and belief. His success was rooted in 'the image trap' (in the arresting phrase of a social theorist) that he created on the screen.

For someone whose charisma was built through the screen MGR's career graph was far from smooth. Unlike his great film rival, Sivaji Ganesan, who appeared with a bang, fully formed, MGR's take off was long and painful, extending to over a decade and a half. Like all other early Tamil film personalities MGR's career began on the theatre stage.

In the early decades of the twentieth century mythological and pseudo-historical themes formed the staple of the stage. In MGR's days women, with the exception of devadasis – a community of women dancers dedicated to the temple – were wary of appearing on stage. To tide over the difficulty of finding women for the stage only boys were employed, and they would play both male and female roles. Thus was born 'Boys' Companies', an institution that dominated Tamil theatre in the early part of the twentieth century. MGR was primarily associated with the renowned Madurai Boy's Original Company. The proprietors of such companies were often tough, whimsical, even tyrannical. Abuse was not uncommon. Talented boys were in demand, and rival troupes often poached on young talent. When the boys approached puberty and their voice broke, their careers often ended disastrously. For an indigent family with little resources, MGR and his brother Chakrapani had to suffer in order to keep the family going. MGR revered his mother Sathyabama, and in all his films he played the unquestioning and obedient son to the noble mother. His respect for his mother was such that he not only named his film studio after her, but, as chief minister, also a state-owned transport corporation.

The 1920s were the time of the influx of silent films from Hollywood which had universal fascination. Rudolph Valentino and Douglas Fairbanks were great heroes, and MGR's choice of swashbuckling roles can be easily traced to the influence of the latter. In many MGR films a regulation fencing sequence was eagerly anticipated by fans.

The appearance of the Tamil talkie in 1931 dramatically transformed the film world. Almost overnight Hollywood motion pictures gave way to films with local colour, content, and conversation. MGR's film debut came five years later: *Sathi Leelavathi*. He made a brief appearance as a police constable. But the film itself hasn't survived. Some footage was retrieved and included in an autobiographical docu-film made by its director, Ellis R. Dungan. MGR had good looks: a photogenic face and fantastic physique said to be the result of consuming *thanga basmam* (a medicinal concoction in which gold was a key component). His fair complexion was a big draw, admired and envied by many. But before the invention of playback singing such physical attributes counted for little. In the first few decades of Indian films actors occasionally spouted some dialogue in between seemingly never-ending songs. No wonder the singing stars M. K. Thyagaraja Bhagavathar and P. U. Chinnappa dominated Tamil films despite their distinct lack of acting skills.

Two changes in the Tamil film world occurred in the mid-1940s: the introduction of playback singing and the advent of Dravidian movement ideologues. While the former obviated the need for actors to be singers, the Dravidian movement ideologues brought in sensational and radical social content that militated against the mythologicals. They espoused a new discourse and articulated rebellious ideas in catchy, alliterative dialogues.

After a series of non-descript small roles in many films spread over a decade, MGR began to get noticed. During the mid-1940s he found a life partner in his co-star, V. N. Janaki – forty years later she would be chief minister of Tamilnadu for a few weeks. MGR made his name with *Marmayogi* and *Manthiri Kumari*, both of which appeared in 1950. With some fine trick shots by its maker K. Ramnoth MGR's swashbuckling role in *Marmayogi* attracted attention.

With Indian nationalist inclinations in his early life he was soon swayed by the Dravidian movement, it is said, at the instance of Karunanidhi. Unlike Karunanidhi, MGR was not known to have an intellectual bent of mind. But in fact he read a lot. At his Arcot Street home in Theagaraya Nagar, Chennai – now an MGR memorial – his library is on display. A prized part of the collection is the volumes of Periyar's weekly, *Kudi Arasu*.

In contrast, his fellow actor Sivaji Ganesan moved away from the Dravidian movement (following a controversial visit to the Tirupati temple) to join the Congress under Kamaraj. MGR's understated acting – in contrast to Sivaji Ganesan who visibly strained every nerve to emote – and screen presence would very soon make him the heartthrob of millions. With his contrasting acting style Sivaji was his arch rival, and at a time when the two of them made at least four or five films every year, the clashing dates of their release caused much commotion. While Sivaji was considered the actors' actor, MGR's fan following was immense, as reflected in the consistent box office collections.

In the 1950s hits followed one another: *Malaikallan*, *Alibabavum 40 Thirudargalum*, and *Genova*. *Madurai Veeran*, based on the life of a medieval Dalit folk hero, with its fantastic script by Kannadasan was a spectacular hit. By 1957 MGR had made his own film *Nadodi Mannan* demonstrating his consummate understanding of the craft of Tamil film-making. Very soon he left no one in doubt that he was in full control of all his films.

As Tamil films transitioned to colour MGR gave more spectacular hits. *Aayirathil Oruvan* continues to be a classic with its appealing shots of seafaring, cutlass-wielding pirates, catchy songs, and engaging fight sequences. More films followed, sealing his near-complete domination of the film industry. He had crafted a perfect formula for making trademark MGR films. The noble and incorruptible hero, who is a devoted son, impervious to the pleasures of the flesh, fighting the bad guys defined the storyline.

MGR chose a string of heroines who exuded sexuality which ensured repeat audiences. The fanatical adulation of B. Saroja Devi, the actress who starred opposite him until she was overtaken by Jayalalithaa, is difficult to imagine now. Camera angles were strategically chosen to focus on tightfitting clothes that exaggerated bodily parts. As if this was not enough, in later films a second heroine was enlisted to add to the oomph quotient. MGR never let down his past heroines, giving them bit roles in his films. Stories abound about how he took control over not only the professional, but also the personal lives of his heroines.

Apart from a comic sidekick, his films were known for their songs. A key genre of the song was what came to be called *kolgai padal* (a programmatic song). With strong political overtones these songs articulated a glorious vision of a just and fair life. Decades later one can still hear the songs blaring out of conical speakers, mobilising voters for his party.

Given his power over the film industry MGR could make or break careers. It is known that he wielded this power not infrequently. While he rewarded loyalty by retaining a trusted set of junior artistes over many films and over many years he often kept film producers on tenterhooks. An expensive set would have to be dismantled if he so fancied. When he fell out with the lyricist Kannadasan, he was replaced by Vaali, and later by Pulamaipithan, Naa. Kamarasan and Muthulingam. He introduced S. P. Balasubrahmanyam to Tamil films, and in the 1970s he chose K. J. Yesudas as his playback singer, replacing T. M. Soundarrajan, a most unlikely choice, but pulled it off. In a surprising move, he chose C. V. Sridhar, reputed to be an auteur, to direct his films.

The adulation that MGR won remains incredible. The urban and rural poor saw in him their messiah. Instances of women tearing his posters to sleep on them have been recorded. How MGR's films played havoc in the lives of lower-class fans is portrayed in Jayakanthan's novelette, *Cinemavukku Pona Chitthalu*. Children loved his fight sequences. In short, MGR films had everything for everyone. This adulation was capitalised for political purposes.

~

Through the 1960s MGR's film success was paralleled by his interest in politics. He did not hesitate to invoke DMK symbols and ideas in his films. Many of them had inputs from Dravidian and Tamil nationalist elements.

MGR shared a special bond with Anna. In him Anna saw a crowd-puller and a reliable funder and fundraiser. MGR first became a Member of the Legislative Council – the upper house of the state legislature – and held party positions. MGR's role in the rising popularity of the DMK and its electoral successes cannot be underestimated.

On 12 January 1967 a dramatic incident – incredible even by film standards – occurred. MGR was shot by fellow actor, the maverick and exceptionally talented M. R. Radha. Radha shot himself immediately after. Radha usually essayed the role of the villain in many of MGR's films, until it became the monopoly of the evil-looking M. N. Nambiar. But what caused the shoot-out in the first place remains unknown, even after a sensational case that ended in a seven-year sentence for Radha. But one thing was clear – unlike in MGR films, in real life there were no untainted heroes and villains personifying evil.

A bleeding MGR was rushed to the Royapettah Government Hospital. Pictures of MGR, his throat and neck in bandages, surfaced. Polling dates followed soon after. MGR was a contestant in the St Thomas Mount constituency adjoining Chennai city. Need one say he won hands down? MGR's survival was near miraculous. That a bullet lodged in his throat was never removed is probably urban legend. A resultant slur rendered his enunciation of some tricky Tamil words comic, and inspired both friendly spoofs and vicious caricatures.

MGR did not aspire to a political position, but continued acting in his films. If anything he gave bigger hits. When Anna died in early 1969 he backed Karunanidhi's bid for chief ministership. But things began to sour between the two. As Karunanidhi once remarked in one of his pregnant phrases there could not be two swords in one scabbard. Meanwhile MGR's films were exhibiting stronger political overtones. His *Nam Naadu* was a searing attack on corruption and black marketing. The friction was exacerbated when Karunanidhi started promoting Mu. Ka. Muthu. Though a cardboard cut-out like Muthu was no match for him, MGR was not amused.

Matters came to a head in 1972. A split was imminent. Indira Gandhi was looking to cut the DMK with its demands of state autonomy to size. The role of central agencies, especially the threat of opening income tax files, cannot be discounted in giving the push to MGR. Karunanidhi had antagonised many political rivals. Communists looking for a way to undercut DMK were behind-the-door Chanakyas. MGR launched an attack by calling for party accounts. Karunanidhi responded by expelling him from the party. Communist leaders, M. Kalyanasundaram and P. Ramamurti, counselled MGR on the formation of the party and devised political strategies in the initial years – that they lived to rue the AIADMK's rise soon is a different story. The party was initially named Anna Dravida Munnetra Kazhagam. ('All India' was prefixed during the Emergency making the name somewhat of an oxymoron.

But it was a political statement. MGR was loath to be identified with separatism of any sort.)

Over the years MGR had built a strong network of *rasigar mandram* (fan clubs), which mobilised energetic youth across the state. The clubs became the kernel for party units. MGR's mega budget *Ulagam Sutrum Valiban* – shot in Japan during the international Expo '70 – with four heroines was in the making. The government in power went all out to sabotage the film. Attempts to hijack the film cans were reported. But in vain. The film was a huge success running for over 200 days. Further bad news awaited the DMK. In the first by-elections that the AIADMK contested, MGR's candidate, Maya Thevar, won. The ruling DMK came third. MGR's political fortunes were on the upswing.

During the years leading up to the Emergency and the dismissal of the DMK government MGR continued with his film-making. A visibly aging MGR with sagging face muscles appeared in colourful costumes prancing with younger heroines. MGR acted in more than a dozen films until his last *Maduraiyai Meetta Sundarapandiyan* was released just after he became chief minister. By definition MGR's films cannot be a financial failure. Seen critically they were duds, but served his political needs. By this time younger heroes (Rajinikanth and Kamal Haasan) and newer film-makers (Mahendran, Bharathiraja, and Balu Mahendra) had entered the scene marking a brief Indian summer in the Tamil film world – but that is another story.

MGR was politically silent during the Emergency years. In the 1977 parliamentary elections he allied with Indira's Congress, but fought the subsequent state elections independently. The results gave him a clear mandate. The AIADMK won 144 seats out of 234. With the AIADMK's victory the state would be set on the path of a virtual two-party system – the DMK and the AIADMK – with crumbs being left behind to be picked up by national parties.

MGR had created a history of sorts. A film star had successfully entered politics and won political power. In 1983, N. T. Rama Rao would repeat this performance in Andhra Pradesh. Chiranjeevi tried to repeat it in 2008, but met with varying success. If the dream of power gleams in the eye of every film star now – Kamal, Rajini, and possibly Vijay – its seeds were sown by MGR.

For the next ten years MGR ruled with scarce a challenge on the political front. Karunanidhi was the ideal opposition leader keeping him constantly on his toes.

The contrasting images of MGR and Karunanidhi explain much about their career and success. Karunanidhi, with his linguistic skills, rhetorical flourishes, and unarguably sharp mind, had an image of being a shrewd man which paradoxically contributed to a distrust among the common people, while MGR's non-intellectual image was disarming and won him public confidence.

For two years, from 1970, MGR had serialised his autobiography in the popular weekly, *Ananda Vikatan*. It is a surprising document. Shorn of rhetoric, a transparent honesty animates the rambling *Naan En Piranthen*. The contrast with Karunanidhi's autobiography, *Nenjukku Needhi* is hard to be missed. Using an unassuming language, MGR's narrative nevertheless engages the reader, and sounds convincing and never comes across as being self-serving.

Within two and a half years of power MGR's government met with a crisis. He had supported the Janata Party government under Morarji Desai and later the short-lived Charan Singh government. In the January 1980 parliamentary elections the DMK–Congress combine swept the polls, with the AIADMK losing all but two seats. Karunanidhi opportunistically egged Indira Gandhi to dismiss the MGR government. To Karunanidhi's great surprise MGR staged a brilliant countercampaign. He toured the length and breadth of the state, demanding justice. The electorate rewarded MGR with an even bigger mandate in June 1980.

On his return to power MGR put to use the lesson he had learnt: he never rubbed the central government on the wrong side again. Soon he cosied up to the Congress and the seat-sharing arrangement with his alliance partner was perfected. In subsequent elections, while the AIADMK retained two-thirds of the seats in the assembly, he conceded the same proportion to the Congress in the parliament. This so-called MGR Formula paid rich dividends and dashed Karunanidhi's hopes of defeating the AIADMK in MGR's lifetime.

~

MGR's was a repressive regime. Learning from the success of DMK campaigns that were fuelled by students, he banned college elections and suspended student bodies. It was a body blow to the DMK whose leadership was forged in colleges. Prohibitory orders – in terms of restrictions on public congregations – became the norm rather than being occasional. The provisions of the Dramatic Performance Act mandating the prior approval of play scripts by the police was strictly enforced. The Naxalite movement was crushed through the extrajudicial route. While he cared little for the print media – secure in the belief that his core rural supporters did not follow them and the urban reading public would never vote for him – MGR once had *Ananda Vikatan*'s editor imprisoned for publishing a cartoon. The police were empowered to carry on his political agenda. The intelligence wing was used to keep a tab on political opponents – it was perfected by Karunanidhi later. The police officer K. Mohandas was legendary for being MGR's trusted hatchet man.

Soon after his return to power MGR introduced what was called the nutritious noon meal scheme. The scheme envisaged the provision of a free meal to all schoolgoing children at lunch time. It was to cost the public exchequer what was then an astronomical sum of hundred crore rupees per year. Provisioning for this involved considerable fiscal jugglery and tough negotiations with the central government for subsidised rice. Among the elite and in political circles the scheme was universally derided. Economists said it wouldn't work. Politicians, led by Karunanidhi, argued that people were being reduced to beggars. But MGR stood his ground.

The results were dramatic. The number of school dropouts and irregular attendance saw a significant drop. Malnutrition levels plummeted. The sight of children with brown hair, a visible sign of melanin deficiency, became a thing of the past. Overall health indicators improved, outstripping other states in India. Altruism – intended or unintended – apart, it was a political master stroke. It inaugurated the moment of welfare populism in Tamilnadu that has progressed phenomenally over the next decades. Carping political critics soon followed suit. On his return to power Karunanidhi added eggs to the menu. This was a system amenable to corruption from the top to the bottom, but this hardly took away from what had been gained.

Another significant contribution of MGR was the expansion of lower-level technical education. Scores of industrial training institutes and polytechnic colleges were set up all over the state, laying the foundation for a successful automobile industry. In the early 1980s he also enabled the establishing of self-financed engineering and medical colleges. That it profited liquor barons and his own hangers-on is a different matter.

MGR is often blamed for giving a pro-Hindu slant to Dravidian politics. As chief minister he once visited the Kollur Moogambikai temple. His tenure was marked by two landmark events in the history of communal relations in Tamilnadu: the Meenakshipuram conversion (1981) and the Mandaikadu riots

(1982). In a distant village near Tenkasi in southern Tamilnadu there was a mass conversion of Scheduled Castes to Islam. Hindu communalist organisations saw this as a threat, and planned long-term strategies to counter such conversions. It had all-India implications. The aggressive Hindu Munnani was founded in the wake of the conversions. The Mandaikadu riots between Hindu Nadars and Christian fishermen of Kanniyakumari district had a significant impact on state policy towards religious minorities and on how communal violence should be encountered.

~

The climax of MGR's career was a long-drawn affair with many twists and turns. In October 1984 MGR fell gravely ill, suffering from kidney failure, and was flown to New York for treatment.

As he lay ailing in Brooklyn Hospital, New York, prayers were conducted across temples, churches, and other places of worship. A tearful Sowcar Janaki lip-synching *'Andavane un pathangalai naan kanneeril neerattuvaen ...'* (O Lord, let me bathe your feet with tears) from the MGR-starrer *Oli Vilakku* prefaced film screenings across cinema halls in the state. Despite the mocking by an avowedly rationalistic opposition party – the DMK – the spontaneity and fervour marking these prayers cannot be discounted.

In the wake of Indira Gandhi's assassination on 31 October 1984, Rajiv Gandhi went in for snap polls a few months ahead of schedule. The AIADMK was in alliance with the Congress. Those were pre-satellite channel days, and the print media carried great prestige, but could easily be thwarted by the government. During the long months of treatment there was little real news of MGR's condition but for the periodical press releases that H. V. Hande – now a member of the BJP, a physician himself and a minister in his cabinet – issued. The press releases carried little credibility, and in one of his famous wordplays Karunanidhi called it '*Hande pulugu, anda pulugu, aakasa pulugu*' (untranslatable; but the rhyming reference is to 'blatant lies of universal proportions').

Access to MGR and his wife, Janaki Ramachandran, was controlled by a major faction of the party led by R. M. Veerappan, film producer and a minister in the cabinet. In this the Congress was a willing ally. MGR filed his nomination papers to the Andipatti constituency from his hospital bed in the presence of India's Ambassador to the United States. Those were pre-RTI (Right to Information) days and no one has seen the signed nomination papers to date. Indira's assassination and MGR's ill-health formed an unbeatable combination. Until MGR's miraculous recovery and return to India some months later, the state did not have an acting chief minister. And when MGR was sworn in, Doordarshan and Films Division, the only media allowed inside the Raj Bhavan, decided to mute the cameras!

MGR ruled for three years until his death on Christmas Eve of 1987. His recovery was certainly miraculous, but his health was not good enough to hold the reins of power. His memory failed often and he could at best mumble a few words. Who really controlled him during those years is still a mystery. The suspicion was on R. M. Veerappan, but he himself was once dismissed from his ministership. The DMK platform speakers constantly ridiculed his disability, but to no avail. Finally, on a cold night in late December 1987, MGR appeared on stage with Rajiv Gandhi to unveil Nehru's statue at Kathipara junction at the gateway to Chennai on the way to the airport. MGR caught a chill and died a few days later on 24 December, which also happened to be the fourteenth death anniversary of Periyar.

The last years of MGR remain one of the many dark spots in Tamilnadu's post-Independence governance.

5

JAYALALITHAA
From Actress to Amma

IN 1981 A TAMIL film titled *Aaniver* was released. A lower-caste girl from a village clears the civil services examinations and becomes a district collector. But her childhood sweetheart and husband is illiterate, creating considerable difficulties as she tries to perform her social and official roles. Unable to resolve this tension, in melodramatic fashion, she resigns from the IAS to play the dutiful role of a homebound wife. A nondescript film by any standards, I remember it for a review published in the now-defunct Tamil weekly, *Idhayam Pesugirathu*. Feminism was an unknown term in those days, certainly in the Tamil popular media, and it was therefore surprising to see a critique of the heroine's decision. That the reviewer was a former actress, not known for doing exactly intelligent roles, added to the surprise. The reviewer was Jayalalithaa.

Jayalalithaa's film career had effectively ended in the mid-1970s. She had given a series of spectacular hits with MGR. Starting from the blockbuster *Aayirathil Oruvan* she had played MGR's love interest in many of his subsequent films. She had replaced B. Saroja Devi, who had dominated in the preceding decade. It was now Jayalalithaa's turn to be shown the way out by younger and more voluptuous actresses such as Manjula, Latha, and Radha Saluja. Tamil cinema can be unforgiving towards actresses.

~

Like all spectacular success stories the antecedents of Jayalalithaa are shrouded, not in mystery, but in contradictory details. Jayalalithaa was born in a Mandya Iyengar family in Mysore in 1948 – or according to another version, she hailed from the temple town of Srirangam. Her father, Jayaram, died when she was two and it was left to her mother, Vedavalli, to raise her. Following her sister's foray into film acting her mother too donned the make-up. Shedding her given name (her daughter would name her Poes Garden home as Veda Nilayam), she came to be known as Sandhya.

Following Sandhya's entry into films the family moved to Chennai, then the capital of the south Indian film industry. Her indifferent run in films notwithstanding, Sandhya sent her daughter to the elite Church Park convent, perhaps in a conscious decision to shield her from the murky world of films. Though Jayalalithaa only matriculated, her excellent spoken English was a convent legacy. Her sophisticated accent once willy-nilly fooled a prestigious English daily to term her as the most educated of Tamilnadu's chief ministers. (In her notorious dilatory tactics Jayalalithaa persuaded the special court trying corruption charges against her to translate the voluminous court documents into Tamil as she claimed not to know English.) The convent of the Presentation Sisters, apart from giving her good English, also managed to instil an anti-Christian sentiment in her. She would enact an anti-conversion bill, warming the heart of many a Hindu zealot, during her second term in power.

Jayalalithaa was taught Bharatanatyam and her *arangettram* (the formal debut) was presided over by Sivaji Ganesan. Evidently Sandhya had plans for her daughter. With her fair skin, charming looks, and attractive figure the mother might have fancied that her daughter would succeed where she had failed. Jayalalithaa had a lonely childhood with no protective father figure around. The life of a single mother struggling to earn a living as a B-grade actress can well be imagined. The intentions and bearing of the many men swarming around are not likely to have been honourable. The young girl, not surprisingly, detested the tinsel world and the men who peopled it, a feeling that would be reinforced by her romantic relations in later life. By all accounts Jayalalithaa did not want to follow in her mother's footsteps. But, as it often happens, the most reluctant are the ones who thrive when thrust unwillingly.

When it became clear that the affluence that she experienced was a facade, Jayalalithaa took the plunge into the film world, immediately after matriculating. She was lucky to be spotted by the film-maker B. R. Panthulu who gave her a few minor roles in Kannada films, before casting her opposite MGR in the big budget *Aayirathil Oruvan*. But her Tamil debut itself was in C. V. Sridhar's *Vennira Adai*. Both films, released in 1965, were shot spectacularly in Eastmancolor, adding to her glamour. Coincidentally, *Vennira Adai* also saw the debut of Nirmala, who also caught MGR's eye. MGR patronised Nirmala with small roles in all his films, and two decades later nominated her to the Legislative Council. When it transpired that Nirmala was an insolvent and the nomination illegal, MGR abolished the council of elders in the bicameral legislature. The Nirmala affair gives us a window into how MGR's mind worked. Jayalalithaa probably drew many lessons from MGR's handling of controversies.

Apparently, MGR was obsessed with Jayalalithaa. And she in her turn developed a strong bonding with a man old enough to be her father. On screen the duo was a spectacular success, delivering hit after hit. MGR's screen presence and Jayalalithaa's overt sexuality proved to be a great draw. Off screen, however, it was a rollercoaster ride. MGR was a married man with many interests and a busy film and political career. Jayalalithaa felt the emotional stress acutely.

By the standards of the Tamil film world Jayalalithaa had a long career. As MGR chose younger actresses Jayalalithaa acted opposite other actors, it was rumoured, to MGR's great resentment. It was at this time that she developed an intimacy with Sobhan Babu. The Telugu actor, older to her by about ten years, was a married man and the relationship was bound to fail. A strong personality such as Jayalalithaa could hardly be content with playing second fiddle. These relationships evidently left her deeply scarred, reinforcing her distrust of men. To add to this injury political opponents – men with suspect morals themselves – did not hesitate to slander her all through her life. Perhaps this was at the root of her desire to see men fall at her feet publicly in abject surrender.

The souring of the relationship with Sobhan Babu and the drying up of film opportunities should have ended her public life. But it was not to be. Jayalalithaa was still young and ambitious. It was at this time that she projected her image as a thinking woman and drew the attention of one of the factions surrounding MGR. The review mentioned at the beginning of this essay dates to this period, when she also wrote columns in *Thuglaq* and *Thai*, apart from a short novel, *Nee Indri Naan Illai*, in *Malaimathi*.

THE POLITICAL ROLLERCOASTER

Jayalalithaa's political graph compared to her film career was even more erratic – she scaled phenomenal heights and plumbed even greater depths. In less than a decade she was elected chief minister, a Brahmin leader of India's most successful Non-Brahmin Movement, with an unprecedented majority. The beginning was made in the coastal town of Cuddalore in a party conference. MGR anointed her in a newly created post of propaganda secretary – what ideology the AIADMK possessed worthy of propagation was a moot question. A few years later in a public function, suffused with Freudian symbolism, Jayalalithaa handed over a six-foot ornamented sceptre to MGR – an image she later used to claim her mentor's mantle as she set about charting her political career. The anointment was noted with alarm on both sides – within the party, the faction led by R. M. Veerappan, MGR's most successful film producer and party organiser, on the one hand, and M. Karunanidhi, MGR's political rival, on the other.

Even as party rivals feared her meteoric rise MGR nominated her to the Rajya Sabha. Shortly after Jayalalithaa's nomination to the house of elders Indira Gandhi was assassinated in October 1984 and the Congress came under a new generation of leaders as Rajiv Gandhi stepped in. Jayalalithaa charmed leaders of various political parties with her suave manners and fine communication skills, and won Rajiv's respect. The networks established during this time helped her command Tamilnadu's polity in the following decades.

As often happened in her career, right when the going was good Jayalalithaa suffered a setback. MGR fell seriously ill in October 1984. During this time Jayalalithaa was sidelined, with little or no access to her mentor, and fought a rearguard battle with the help of some dissidents. Matters reached a head when MGR died in December 1987. Jayalalithaa was not permitted to see his body in his Ramavaram home and she had to rush to Rajaji Hall where he lay in state. In a symbolic move she stood at his head – in Tamil culture, a wife's rightful place – for over a day until she was abused and pushed down violently from the military hearse.

ENTER SASIKALA

During the difficult times following this Jayalalithaa found solace in a friendship with V. K. Sasikala.

Sasikala hails from the Kallar caste, one of the three endogamous communities which have come together under the category of Mukkulathor to garner political and social power. Though originally from Thiruthuraippoondi in the Thanjavur delta, the family soon moved to nearby Mannargudi. Known for its great Vaishnava temple, soon its fame was eclipsed by its association with her family, with the alliterative name 'Mannargudi Mafia'. Apart from the fact that she was some years younger than Jayalalithaa, little else is known of her early life and education.

Sometime in the 1970s Sasikala was married to M. Natarajan in a function presided over by Karunanidhi. During 1964–5 thousands of college students had joined the agitation against making Hindi the sole official language of the Indian union. In the wake of brutal state repression the agitation threw up many activists who later joined the DMK and propelled it to power in 1967. The DMK rewarded many of these activists with a newly created government position called 'public relations officer'. Natarajan was one of them.

In the 1980s Jayalalithaa had settled into her Veda Nilayam home in the posh Poes Garden locality. Jayalalithaa was a loner with a complex psychological disposition. Sasikala had started a video rental shop in a nearby neighbourhood, and in renting video cassettes to a bored yesteryear actress soon came to develop a friendship with her. The years leading up to Jayalalithaa's electoral victory in 1991 were turbulent. Sasikala became her trusted aide, displacing the few relatives and other domestic helpers that the Poes Garden household employed. It was a relationship that lasted till the end, but not without its ups and downs. Speculation was rife about the nature of their relationship. Jayalalithaa herself described her once as 'a not-blood sister' (*udan piravaa sahodari*). But the real answer came perhaps when they appeared together with garlands on Jayalalithaa's sixtieth birthday at the Thirukadaiyur temple where couples exchange garlands ritually on the man turning sixty.

MGR'S SUCCESSOR

When MGR died, in a smart move that backfired, R. M. Veerappan got MGR's wife Janaki Ramachandran elected as the chief minister. The assembly session following it, in January 1988, witnessed chaotic scenes as members of legislative assembly (MLAs) backing Jayalalithaa were outnumbered and manhandled. Fishing in troubled waters, the Congress government at the centre dissolved the assembly. The fishing was serious. With P. C. Alexander playing the pliant governor, the Congress desperately tried to shore up its fortunes. In the January 1989 elections the Congress contested on its own. The results not only exposed Congress's limitations, but also confirmed Jayalalithaa's claim to MGR's mantle.

The two factions – the Janaki group with a pair of doves as its election symbol and the Jayalalithaa group, appropriately it was said, with a fighter cock symbol – contested the elections. The DMK romped home. But the biggest takeaway was the rout of the Janaki faction – Janaki herself was defeated and lost her deposit in her husband's pocket borough. Though Jayalalithaa won only twenty-seven seats (she became the official leader of the opposition), there was little doubt who MGR's political heir was. The two rivals for MGR's affections came to a pragmatic understanding, considering his will about the inheritance of his property in case of a dispute. Janaki gave up the party and the invaluable asset of the twin-leaves election symbol for an undisputed bequest of more material assets.

Jayalalithaa had worsted one rival. But managing the rival DMK and its leader Karunanidhi was no easy task. The bitterness between the two was visceral and defies rational explanation. The two rarely faced each other on the floor of the legislative assembly.

Matters came to a head within weeks of the DMK's return to power. The budget session ended in utter pandemonium, the decorum of the house a regular casualty in the following decades. The elements of what transpired at that time are clear – Jayalalithaa was taunted with offensive words, she snatched the budget papers from the chief minister's hands, and an honourable member of the house tugged at her sari – but not the sequence. The video footage of the events has never seen the light of day. Not so, pictures of a Jayalalithaa with hair tousled in a dishevelled sari. Her words that she would step into the legislature again only as chief minister rang like Draupadi's vow.

The vow came to fruition two years later. Karunanidhi's strategic mistakes were capped by the assassination of Rajiv Gandhi in May 1991. The DMK was routed. Dressed in a trademark green cape, said to conceal a bullet-proof vest, Jayalalithaa was now chief minister at the age of forty-three. The LTTE threat translated into Z+ security cover. With it her isolation from the people was ensured.

In less than a year the process of squandering popular goodwill began its inexorable roll. At the once-in-twelve-years Mahamaham festival at Kumbakonam, in February 1992 Jayalalithaa's ritual dip along with Sasikala resulted in a stampede and the death of some fifty pilgrims. During these years all dissent was curbed, political opponents humiliated, and the media hounded. Jayalalithaa's megalomania and hubris apparently knew no limits. One state-owned bus company was named for her, and another for her mother. Tamilnadu came to be identified with sky-high cut-outs of Jayalalithaa. The apogee was reached when the mother of all marriages, the marriage of Sasikala's nephew, V. N. Sudhakaran (one of those convicted along with Sasikala in February 2017), was celebrated with an obscene display of wealth. Sasikala's control over Jayalalithaa was evident from the fact that Sudhakaran was declared the foster son of Jayalalithaa.

The last straw came when the Congress was arm-twisted into forging an alliance for the 1996 elections with an unpopular AIADMK. Even the supine Congress leadership could take it no more, resulting in a split under the leadership of G. K. Moopanar. Within five weeks of the formation of the TMC, the party, in alliance with DMK, routed the AIADMK with Jayalalithaa herself losing her Bargur seat to a greenhorn.

Winning on the promise to bring the corrupt to book, Karunanidhi launched a series of legal moves to punish her. Jayalalithaa went to prison briefly, but soon gathered the best legal minds to defeat the Indian legal system. She succeeded in dragging the disproportionate assets case for eighteen years. But when it suited her she managed to get her appeal heard in three months. One case turned on whether the signature was hers!

As the legal process went ahead the political tide had begun to turn. Caught on the wrong foot in the wake of the Jain Commission's findings suggesting DMK's complicity in the Rajiv Gandhi assassination, in 1998 the Congress withdrew support to the United Front government. To add to the DMK's misery serial blasts rocked Coimbatore just ahead of L. K. Advani's election campaign in February 1998. Victory for the BJP–AIADMK alliance was a foregone conclusion. But the BJP's happiness was short-lived. Dependant on a whimsical Jayalalithaa for support the A. B. Vajpayee government bent and crawled, but fell short of dismissing the DMK government.

Jayalalithaa's bluff was called when Vajpayee decided he could take no more. In an unexpected move the DMK allied with the BJP and joined the NDA government in 1999. A checkmated Jayalalithaa bounced back by winning the 2001 state elections relying on electoral arithmetic and capitalising on bickering within the DMK. She fashioned a new persona in her second term. Evidently to overcome her image of a yesteryear actress, she was now addressed as Amma. In keeping with numerological fancy her name was now spelt with an extra 'a' at the end – as Jayalalithaa.

But she herself had changed little. Within weeks of her victory Karunanidhi was arrested at midnight. It was a botched arrest – the dramatic images of a septuagenarian leader roughed up by policemen foiled whatever sinister designs Jayalalithaa might have had. Her ire now turned to other targets. Citing a grave financial situation more than 200,000 striking government employees were sacked overnight. A controversial anti-conversion bill was passed. The age-old practice of sacrificing goats and fowl in popular shrines was banned. By 2004 she had antagonised every political force, and in the parliamentary elections she was alone while all other parties joined together winning all thirty-nine seats, leading to the DMK grabbing plum posts in the UPA I government. This alliance continued in the 2006 state assembly elections. While the DMK alliance won 163 seats, on its own it could garner only 96 seats (118 being a simple majority). Jayalalithaa had to remain content by dubbing it 'a minority government'.

Paradoxically, being in power at both the state and the centre proved to be the DMK's undoing. Cabinet positions in the central government are often cash cows, and various members of Karunanidhi's family vied for it. This scuffle for the fishes and loaves of office accelerated in the UPA II government. The family rivalry was expanded with the addition of Karunanidhi's grandnephews, Kalanithi and Dayanidhi Maran, and daughter, Kanimozhi. In short the 2006–11 DMK minority government brought back memories of Jayalalithaa's first ministry of 1991–6. In a two-horse race the Tamil people had to inescapably look to the other force. And to Jayalalithaa's credit she single-handedly led the charge. In a brave move she launched campaigns in Madurai, considered to be Alagiri's impregnable fort, and other cities. In the 2011 election campaign she could easily connect with the electorate. In alliance with Vijayakanth's Desiya Murpokku Dravida Kazhagam (DMDK) she bounced back to power. But within months she showed the DMDK its place, snubbing Vijayakanth and engineering a split in the party.

Soon after Jayalalithaa became chief minister Sasikala, with her family, was again expelled from the party and sent out of her home. She was reinstated some months later only after signing a letter of abject apology and disowning her entire family. But in public perception, if not in reality, the Sasikala family continued to rule. With Jayalalithaa's failing health, if anything, the grip tightened. The route to power in the AIADMK was through Sasikala, and she had a big hand in political negotiations, the forging of alliances, and the distribution of tickets. O. Panneerselvam was her choice to be a makeweight chief minister when Jayalalithaa was forced to step down from power on two occasions, first in 2001–2 and then in 2014.

Due to this control the AIADMK came to be seen as a party of the Mukkulathor, and whenever the party was in power tension between them and Dalits in southern Tamilnadu got accentuated. As Jayalalithaa completely distanced herself from public Sasikala was seen to be the real power.

JUSTICE DELAYED AND ILL-HEALTH

In the early years of this decade Jayalalithaa, despite rumours of serious ill-health, was cruising along. And then came two setbacks. The AIADMK won thirty-seven of the thirty-nine parliamentary seats on its own, cornering 44 per cent votes in the 2014 parliamentary elections. But it turned out to be a meaningless victory. Jayalalithaa's plans for a larger role – not excepting the role of even the prime minister – were dashed as the BJP under Narendra Modi won an absolute majority. Then came the legal setback.

The wheels of justice turned slowly but decisively, or so it seemed. Eighteen years is a long time, long enough to produce one whole new generation of voters. But the events of the distant past between 1991 and 1996 caught up with Jayalalithaa. Call it irony or poetic justice, it was perhaps the delay that cost Jayalalithaa dearly. She might have paid a smaller political price if she had let the case be decided earlier. As corruption occupied the centre stage of Indian politics and courts began to take a less and less acquiescing stance vis-à-vis corruption the Prevention of Corruption Act began to give nightmares to politicians.

On 27 September 2014 J. M. da Cunha, the judge of the special court at Parapana Agrahara, found her guilty in the disproportionate assets case – the last of the many cases filed in 1996, and considered to be an open and shut case; she had somehow wriggled out of all other cases. While an academic reading of the guilty verdict would suggest that justice had ultimately prevailed, it had an unintended popular response. Over the years inflation and competitive corruption had made the figures paltry and Jayalalithaa became even more popular after her conviction.

The conviction of Jayalalithaa did little to undermine her support base. The orchestrated protests and sham tears shed by the new cabinet as it was being sworn in could not detract from the genuine, if misplaced, sympathy Amma evoked among her supporters. Hadn't she been electorally punished more than once? Isn't sixty-six crores of rupees a pittance? This logic befuddles the moralist, but political commentators can ignore it only at their own peril.

'MY LEADER, RIGHT OR WRONG'

The months following the special court's verdict were marked by unprecedented public displays of prayer and devotion. Ardent AIADMK party men sought divine intervention in favour of Amma. Sceptics termed these as sycophancy orchestrated by motivated party leaders. But the wide popular support and sympathy among the plebeian classes, especially among the women, were hard to miss. 'My leader, right or wrong' seemed to be the guiding principle. Corruption, disproportionate assets, the mother of all weddings – all seemed to count for little in the popular mind.

Prayers for Jayalalithaa's acquittal dominated many state-administered temples. Various 'great tradition' rituals including *annadhanam* (free feeding of the poor), *vilakku pujai* (lamp ritual), and *yagna*s were organised with great gusto by local party leaders. There was also a ritual involving temple elephants. Scale apart, there might be little to comment on these demonstrations of piety and prayer. What was striking was the parallel performance of popular religious rituals. *Mulaippari* (the fertility rite of offering of germinated seeds), *paal kudam* (offering milk in pots), the full range of *kavadi*, *man choru* (the votive ritual of eating food straight out of an earthen floor), the self-mortification rites of *alagukuthuthal* (piercing the body with hooks) and *chedal* (hook-swinging), and walking on fire and carrying the fire pot were performed extensively. Many years ago a former AIADMK woman minister had donned the ritually prescribed neem-leaf skirt.

Great or little, the prayers apparently paid off, and Jayalalithaa was released on bail. But she was a broken woman, and she was scarcely seen in public. Twenty-eight days in the Parapana Agrahara jail evidently broke her health and spirits. The acquittal by the Karnataka High Court in May 2015 did little to uplift her.

If anything, the governance of the state went down in a tailspin and it was capped by the criminal failure of the mishandling of the Chennai floods at the end of the year. Jayalalithaa sported a jaded look in the last few years of her life. Her last election campaign, in the 2016 Assembly elections, was lacklustre. Public appearances were stage-managed to give a modicum of normalcy. If heavy make-up disguised possible signs of ill-health, special arrangements were made not to expose her limited mobility. It is said that her government's PR department released photoshopped pictures regularly giving an impression that she was meeting visitors. And the sojourns in her Kodanadu estate, if anything, got only more frequent and longer.

Yet, in the 2016 elections, the AIADMK registered a historic win; for the first time since 1984 a government had stemmed anti-incumbency to make a comeback. That it was achieved without an alliance can be read as the DMK snatching defeat from the jaws of victory.

In September 2016 Jayalalithaa was admitted to Apollo Hospitals, ostensibly with fever and dehydration. That was the last the public saw of her until her body was laid in state at the Rajaji Hall. Her seventy-five days in the hospital demonstrated, if ever proof was needed, that Sasikala was in full control of not only the Jayalalithaa household, but also of the entire party. Despite the phenomenal media glut information was in short supply in 2016. Apollo Hospitals' medical bulletins could not have convinced a primary school student. That even ministers of the central cabinet and the governor of the state could not meet her only confirmed the hold of Sasikala and her extended family. A one-man commission appointed by the Government of Tamilnadu is now conducting an enquiry into her death. Few believe that anything will come of it.

The government remained paralysed, and none dared even hint that an acting chief minister should hold the baby. At that moment the BJP was as soft as the Congress was during MGR's times, desisting from calling the state government to account.

As Jayalalithaa battled for life the Supreme Court's verdict continued to be reserved. It was on 14 February 2017, two months after her death, that the Supreme Court overturned the Karnataka High Court's acquittal and restored the trial court's conviction. While technically the case against Jayalalithaa abated with her death, there is little doubt that the judgement holds her culpable of the crime of corruption. Aware of the imminent judgement, perhaps she had lost the will to live.

AFTER AMMA

Jayalalithaa's was a truly remarkable career. A woman with no social base to speak of rose to the pinnacles of power in a patriarchal society. Despite being a Brahmin she won the support of an avowedly Non-Brahmin Movement. The taunts and abuse and slander that she received would have deterred the most robust of personalities. MGR's inheritance was not her birth right, but won through hard struggle. And, most spectacularly, she expanded her support base to even eclipse that of her mentor. Winning 44 per cent of the popular vote in the 2014 elections on her own without an alliance partner is yet to be explained by any psephologist. A personality with great strengths, it was also marred by many blotches. Her greatest achievement was holding MGR's party together and even expanding it.

Ryszard Kapuściński, the great Polish journalist, begins his classic *Travels with Herodotus* with a story. In a suggestive lesson that he imparts to a fellow Greek dictator, Thrasybulus of Miletus walks him through a field of crops. Without uttering a direct word, every time he sees an ear of grain standing higher than the rest he lops it off. The best of the crop is thus destroyed leaving behind the mediocre and average. Jayalalithaa was known to be an avid reader. One is not sure if she read Herodotus. But there is little doubt that she practised Thrasybulus's lesson perfectly. In contrast to her mentor MGR, who attracted a bevy of talent disillusioned with the DMK under Karunanidhi, Jayalalithaa shuffled party hierarchy with the quickness of a child bored with her toys.

In party propaganda Jayalalithaa was referred to as *niranthara pothu cheyalalar* (the permanent general secretary) – the AIADMK never had a party president in keeping with C. N. Annadurai's declaration that Periyar alone qualified to be thalaivar (president). Unlike in the DMK which until not too long ago conducted bitterly fought inner-party elections, the AIADMK went through the motions only to keep to the letter of the Representation of People's Act. Over the years the DMK's district secretaries became hereditary regional satraps, but in the AIADMK they held power only at the will and pleasure of the general secretary.

The first pretender to her throne is now in prison.

Fairy tales exist about a royal elephant throwing a garland to anoint a queen. But Lady Luck was never expected to choose the queen's confidante. V. K. Sasikala's jackpot came in the form of an unexpected friendship. Her claim to fame or infamy rested solely on her bonds with Jayalalithaa. For three decades, until her death in December 2016, Jayalalithaa had dominated Tamilnadu's politics, and all through these years Sasikala hovered behind her. Sasikala was the Chinnamma, the small Amma, to Jayalalithaa, the Amma. Ironically the exercise of this control proved to be her undoing. Everyone had underestimated the affection that the masses had for Jayalalithaa. That they could not catch even a glimpse of their revered Amma rankled in the minds of her admirers, and added grist to the rumour mills about the cause of Amma's death and the hands responsible for it.

The unseemly haste with which Sasikala became the general secretary of the party, and later the manner in which she humiliated the sitting chief minister, Panneerselvam, confirmed the people's perception. Her attempt to do an Amma by wearing a green sari, a streak of vermillion on her forehead, and aping Amma's sartorial style and coiffure ended up only infuriating Amma's devoted folk. In a matter of weeks Sasikala transformed into a universally reviled figure. In this atmosphere even a worm would turn. Panneerselvam sensed the popular mood, and in an inspired moment launched an offensive against her by first symbolically meditating at the Jayalalithaa memorial. It turned out to be his fifteen minutes of fame.

But in the barely concealed machinations of the BJP hoping to gain a toehold in the state by weakening the two Dravidian parties, a rapprochement was effected between Panneerselvam and Edappadi K. Palaniswami anointed by Sasikala as the chief minister before she was jailed. But it was Edappadi who turned. Since assuming power in February 2017 he has entrenched himself. Sasikala's new choice, her own nephew T. T. V. Dinakaran, is touring the length and breadth of the state, hoping to inherit Jayalalithaa's mantle. In its turn this has created further rifts in the Mannargudi family. These uncertainties are set to continue until general elections are called, an idea that does not seem to find favour with the BJP which seems to have lost all hope in the state.

That the AIADMK did not implode is primarily due to the timing of Jayalalithaa's death. It's barely six months since the AIADMK was returned to power. The victory margins were low, and the ruling party and the opposition were separated by a thin majority.

~

Jayalalithaa's unchallenged control over the party underpinned her not infrequent ideological pendulum swings. From her original abhorrence of the LTTE and its separatist demands to when she promised the Tamil electorate, in May 2009, an independent Eelam there was scarcely a murmur in the party. While her political opponents fumbled to rationalise their decisions Jayalalithaa could switch positions without batting an eyelid. Alliance partners loved this as it ensured near-complete vote transfer. No party functionary dared defy her decisions. Another fallout was the avenues for upward mobility for cadres lower down the line. Who really remembers the names of district secretaries or even ministers from the AIADMK?

That Jayalalithaa belonged to a caste with a numerical minority gave her a liminal position; she could win support across castes and communities – this despite the disproportionate share of political power she delivered to dominant castes such as the Mukkulathor and the Kongu Vellalars. Yet she could break many of the pieties of received wisdom. When she divested the respected Ayyaru Vandayar of his ministership within weeks nobody even noticed. She could also field a Dalit candidate ('Dalit' Ezhilmalai) in a general constituency and ensure his victory.

Jayalalithaa revelled in playing a high-stakes game where she never blinked. In a game of chicken she was unbeatable. Who would have the audacity to allege that the governor of the state, no less, had misbehaved with her? She once even recorded her conversation with the union home minister and leaked it.

If MGR made history by winning three successive elections Jayalalithaa had similar, and other dubious, records to her credit. And her stint in power had not only been longer, but also spread over a quarter of a century.

Indian democracy has seen extraordinary stories and fascinating personalities. Jayalalithaa's story will remain on top of the list for some time to come. The telling of that story demands the flair of a novelist, the insight of a psychoanalyst, and the analytical skills of a political scientist. A historian can only throw up his hands.

6

'CHO' RAMASWAMY
The Old Guard

'CHO' RAMASWAMY PASSED AWAY in Chennai in the early hours of 7 December 2016. That the end came barely a day after J. Jayalalithaa's death is coincidental – he had been in and out of hospital for a year – but apposite. The great Hindi writer Premchand died a day after Maxim Gorky; S. A. Dange, who represented a strand that believed in the progressive character of the Indian national bourgeoisie, passed away a day after Rajiv Gandhi's assassination; and the protagonist of Sundara Ramaswamy's *J.J.: Sila Kurippugal*, the fictional Malayalam writer, JJ, Joseph James, breathes his last immediately after Albert Camus's fatal car accident. Cho was Jayalalithaa's great admirer, and some would say, even apologist. A trenchant critic of V. K. Sasikala and the Mannargudi family's influence on Jayalalithaa, it must have broken his heart to see the prominence accorded to them in the funeral.

Cho was gifted with a brilliant and incisive mind. Born in 1934 in a family of lawyers in Mylapore, Chennai, he followed the family tradition and acted as a legal adviser to Brahmin industrial houses and firms. Cho came into his own when he took to the drama stage, an involvement that continued late into his life. He also had a successful run in the tinsel world donning the role of the hero's funny sidekick.

Until he took to journalism, in 1970, Cho's claim to fame was as playwright, stage artist, and film actor. At a time when theatre was the domain of professional troupes Cho belonged to the emerging amateur theatre. While professional troupes toured across the Tamil hinterland, staging plays in makeshift halls, amateur theatre groups drew their audiences from the Brahmin middle class and were confined to Chennai and the bigger cities. This was the heyday of the sabha, voluntary cultural associations, based largely in urban Brahmin neighbourhoods, sustained by subscriptions and business sponsorship by Brahmin-managed firms, both in private and public sectors. The sabhas provided, in the pre-TV days, entertainment in the form of plays and music concerts. The artistes and the audience were not known for their social diversity.

This was the time when the DMK was on the ascendant, undermining not only Brahmin political power, already on the wane, but also its cultural power. The propagandist plays staged by the Dravidian movement's cultural vanguard such as M. R. Radha offer a study in contrast. The sabhas were a non-confrontationist cultural response.

While ridiculing the alliterative and highfalutin dialogues of the Dravidian movement plays, Cho's scripts often used the colloquial Brahmin dialect. He was the pioneer in employing the Chennai street dialect, derisively referred to as *Madras bashai*, the demotic language of the lower classes, but he had little empathy for it, using it only for comic effect. While a major theme of the serious arts and literature in immediate post-Independence India was disenchantment and the souring of idealism, Cho articulated the elite distrust of democratic politics, especially the rise of the Dravidian movement.

Cho fancied himself to be a Shaw – his *Manam Oru Kurangu* was an adaptation of *Pygmalion* – and his plays were full of words. Enacted on the proscenium stage, players walked from one wing, mouthed their lines, and exited from the other. Despite his biting satire and humorous asides that regaled audiences, his plays lacked seriousness, and were singularly bereft of a wider social vision. Despite his unacknowledged borrowing of the name *Thuglak* for his political journal from Girish Karnad, Cho never demonstrated any awareness of the modern theatre in Kannada, Marathi, Bengali, and Hindi, and he is not known to have mentioned names such as Badal Sircar, Vijay Tendulkar, and G. P. Deshpande. Nor is he known to have welcomed Tamil new theatre efforts by groups such as Pareeksha, Nija Nataka Iyakkam, Koothu Pattarai, and so on.

As a comedian, and often writing the comedy track himself – he scarcely demonstrated originality of talent like a Chandrababu or a Nagesh – Cho expressed similar views in his films as well. While he maintained a lifelong aversion to Periyar and Anna his most trenchant criticism was reserved for Karunanidhi.

In 1970, Cho became a figure of note, with the launch of a new political journal, *Thuglak*. It had been three years since the DMK had been swept to power, and two years after Karunanidhi had become chief minister. *Thuglak* articulated the anxieties and insecurity of a section of middle-class Brahmins. The new political culture, of grand spectacle and welfare populism, threatened this section of conservative Brahmin intellectuals and turned them into reactionaries.

Periyar was still active at that time. In January 1971 he organised a conference in Salem against superstition where tableaus depicted scenes from the Hindu puranas. This was compounded by alleged desecration of divine images. *Thuglak* published a special issue, and whipped up a frenzy. The confiscation of copies of the journal fuelled its popularity. The controversy soon subsided and, contrary to expectations, the DMK returned to power, drubbing the alliance between K. Kamaraj and Rajaji which Cho had banked on.

Emergency saw Cho play a crusading role in defence of democracy. The cover of one issue of *Thuglak* was printed solid black, and included the review of a film titled *Sarvadhikari* (Dictator)! At this time he headed the People's Union for Civil

Liberties (PUCL). But soon he left it as he refused to make a distinction between the violence of the state and non-state actors. His anti-civil liberties position would take him to extraordinary length in later times, as he defended and legitimised even encounter deaths.

While Karunanidhi remained a target Cho relished attacking MGR and his politics. Pouring scorn and ridicule on his politics, he portrayed him as a clown. In his view the AIADMK was a populist party with no ideology to speak of. However, when Jayalalithaa took over the party, and followed in his footsteps, the same lack of ideology ceased to matter for him.

A summary of Cho's political positions would cause any liberal to squirm. Cho's nationalism was often a garb for Hindu supremacy. When democracy delivered undesirable results he questioned democracy itself. Caste-based reservation undermined merit. Human rights questioned the state. Feminism challenged the traditional role of women. The Hindu caste order ensured harmony. In Sri Lanka, Tamils were advised to put up with Sinhala majoritarianism. In economics he was critical of licence-quota raj and the public sector. Despite his aversion for Indira Gandhi, Cho believed in a benevolent despotism. His preference for Narendra Modi, forgetting his earlier support for L. K. Advani and A. B. Vajpayee, is therefore of a piece.

This vision, Cho articulated through jokes, witty comments, and wisecracks. By turning everything into a joke he undermined the seriousness of public debate. Rather than make his readers introspect he confirmed their fears and apprehension, and turned them into disgruntled cynics. In the late 1980s, with the rise of a new generation of 'investigative journalism' – especially *Junior Vikatan* and *Nakkeeran* – *Thuglak* lost out. The fortnightly turned into a weekly, but remained a one-man show.

In later life Cho turned into a commentator on the Hindu view of life. He retold the Mahabharata and Valmiki's Ramayana, and wrote a wholesale polemical defence of Brahminism – but he was no Rajaji, lacking his moral vision.

What then explains Cho's stature and all-India visibility? Before the media revolution he was someone who delighted with quick, sharp, and convenient quotes in English, endearing himself to Delhi journalists already biased against the for-them-inscrutable politics of the Dravidian south. Despite his apparently anti-establishment views he was in close touch with people of power. Not surprisingly he was nominated by the BJP to the Rajya Sabha (1999–2005) during the NDA government.

Cho dabbled directly in politics and facilitated alliances. In 1996 he smoothened the alliance between the DMK and the breakaway Congress under G. K. Moopanar. A man critical of an ideologically vacuous MGR, he did not hesitate to consistently advocate Rajinikanth's entry into politics. Every year, at the time of Pongal in mid-January, he organised a massive hall meeting that tested the political waters and directed the parties of his choice towards course.

In tributes Cho has been termed as a right-wing public intellectual. But he was no Arun Shourie or Swapan Dasgupta. Despite being an extraordinarily intelligent man Cho never indulged in sustained argument, and could therefore never convince anyone.

Thinking of Cho one image comes to mind. In days past, in the *thinnai*s (patios) of the Brahmin *agraharam*s (streets of exclusive Brahmin residence) old women would sit and grumble over the coming of the Kali age when everything had turned topsy-turvy.

From Subramania Bharati and A. Madhaviah to Sundara Ramaswamy and Gnani Sankaran (and T. M. Krishna) Tamil Brahmins have produced a host of self-critical intellectuals who enriched public life and intellectual discourse. It is tragic that a man of Cho's abilities did not belong to that line.

7

C. S. SUBRAMANYAM
Communist Chronicler

FOR SOME INSCRUTABLE REASON, death either takes away communist leaders prematurely or gives them extraordinarily long lives. Comrade C. S. Subramanyam (1910–2011), or CS, one of the founding leaders of the CPI in south India and the chronicler of its history, passed away a year after he turned a hundred.

No decent account of his life and work exists. Organs and front-magazines of the CPI and Communist Party of India (Marxist) (CPI [M]) published notices and tributes at the time of his death in September 2011. If they are woefully inadequate little blame will attach to them. For CS was extraordinarily self-effacing and reticent about discussing what was an undoubtedly eventful life, at least in its early phases. Individuals did not count in the impersonal march of history, or so he resolutely believed. Even when conversation ineluctably turned to his life he would quickly skirt discussion. In the 1980s, when the JNU histoiran Bipan Chandra tried to conduct a full-fledged interview with him as part of a massive project to record the oral histories of the nationalist movement, CS refused to be interviewed. Several attempts on my part to conduct formal interviews too failed. It now turns out that I was able to tease out far more information about him than others, and the following account is based on such tantalising information that I could recollect from conversations with him, occasional correspondence (hence the numerous I, me, myself), some archival data (of the colonial Government of Madras), and a reading of his publications.

In mid-1984, I stepped into the portals of the Tamilnadu Archives (TNA), Chennai. Not yet seventeen, I had just entered college. Fascinated by the tragic-hero of the early nationalist movement in Tamilnadu V. O. Chidambaram Pillai (VOC, 1872–1936), I had entered the musty corridors of TNA to track him. The research hall of TNA used to teem with scholars, and heated discussions would overflow into the makeshift canteen outside. Every day, at about 11 in the forenoon, a thin figure with a shock of silver hair, dressed in khadi dhoti, shirt, and towel would walk into the research hall. I never saw him in laundered and pressed clothes. A lump on his forehead was prominent – how he managed to escape the police when look-out notices were issued to apprehend him was a surprise. Recognised as a freedom fighter, the archives staff would treat him with deference. This was Comrade CS.

The name immediately brought to my mind the two-volume *Bharati Darisanam*, the primary resource for the history of the Swadeshi movement in Tamilnadu. In the early 1970s a young communist cultural activist, Ilasai Manian of Ettayapuram, had managed to acquire microfilm copies of the only extant copy of the first volume (1906–7) of Subramania Bharati's weekly, *India*, from the National Library, Kolkata. Demonstrating further resourcefulness he had improvised a microfilm reader and transcribed large parts of the journal. When they were eventually published, in 1976–7, it was CS who served as the editor, classifying the articles and providing annotations. *Bharati Darisanam* remains a milestone in the bibliography of Bharati. At this time CS also published a booklet on Bharati's essay on Tolstoy and the Russian Revolution: his framing introduction was my first lesson in the Marxist method of situating texts in their historical context.

From my mentor T. Kovendhan, a Soviet Land Nehru awardee, who worked for some time in CPI's New Century Book House (NCBH) – CS's primary publisher – I learnt a great deal about CS's early life and achievements. A stickler for rules CS would scarce speak in the research hall; even for a short conversation he had to step out. In the early 1980s he had established the Institute of South Indian Studies (ISIS) under the aegis of the CPI and NCBH. ISIS was located on 6, Nallathambi Street at the confluence of Anna, Wallajah, and Ellis roads. The ISIS was an institute only in name. The doors would open on the evenings when CS came. It was a set of rooms: the main hall had long tables and chairs where CS worked and met visitors; an adjoining room had a small but impressive collection of books on the nationalist and left movements.

CS was seventy-four at that time, and I was a good half-a-century-and-more younger. I was naive, enthusiastic, curious, and particularly ignorant of etiquette – a combination that must have amused the old man and somewhat loosened his tongue. I had also recently edited and published a collection of VOC's letters, and CS was evidently impressed.

One evening, in late April 1985, I was waiting for CS to arrive at the institute, but he failed to turn up. When I saw him the next day he explained that it was his wife's sixth death anniversary. It was a rare occasion when a glint of emotion could be detected in his calm eyes.

CS's marriage to Dr Sugunabai was the turning point in his life. His father, Sundaram Iyer, was an officer in the colonial education department. The family hailed from Comal, a village near Mayiladuthurai, in the undivided Thanjavur district. As his father was transferred from one town to another, CS studied at Voorhees College, Vellore, and Presidency College, Chennai – at the latter institution the communist leader P. Ramamurti was a fellow student. His family was affluent enough, and sometime in 1930 he embarked for England to sit the Indian Civil Services (ICS) examination. CS studied at Balliol College, Oxford, which trained so many British Indian officers. The interwar years were the time when left ideas and ideals captured the imagination of the youth. CS became a member of the October Club at Oxford and did voluntary work for the *Daily Worker* at the time of the Second Round Table Conference (1931). He interacted with Rajani Palme Dutt (a founder of the Communist Party of Great Britain, and the Comintern's in-charge for India), among others, and returned to India, without taking the ICS examination, as a communist. (His younger brother, C. S. Ramachandran went on to become a well-known ICS officer.) I remember him mentioning that Christopher Caudwell was his junior in college.

When CS returned to India, circa 1933, the Communist Party barely existed. According to a confidential report of the Government of Madras, when the Government of India was contemplating a legislation to ban the Communist Party, the only organisation actively engaged in Bolshevik propaganda in south India was Periyar's Self-Respect Movement. During 1931–2, Amir Hyder Khan, deputed to establish the party in Tamilnadu, organised the Young Workers' League in Chennai. He was arrested in 1932 and spent a year and a half in jail, and the organisation of a formal party had to await the arrival of CPI's first general secretary S. V. Ghate from Bombay in early 1936. CS met Khan clandestinely in July 1934. Meanwhile, the Congress Socialist Party (CSP) acted as a front for communists, and CS played a part in its organisation. By the time the CPI was banned in 1934, he was among its top leaders. When the *Janasakti* was launched in 1937, CS was entrusted with the responsibility of running the party's weekly apart from managing the press and the party office. CS used to work in the office dressed in shorts – like most communist leaders of the day – and undervest. He was more a backstage man rather than a street fighter. His early life thus epitomises the early history of the CPI in Tamilnadu.

In 1940 the Government of Madras instituted the Madras Communist Conspiracy case under the Defence of India Act against P. Ramamurti, Mohan Kumaramangalam, and CS. They went underground, and a lookout notice was issued with a reward of a hundred rupees. Eventually CS was arrested and sentenced to eighteen months of rigorous imprisonment.

With the Soviet Union joining the Allies in the War the ban on the party was lifted. CS was released from prison in July 1942 along with other leaders. A party in the forefront of an anti-imperialist struggle was now in the uncomfortable position of having to oppose the Quit India movement and mobilise the masses for what they had only recently described as an imperialist war. When the issue was debated in the party CS was one among the small minority that voiced reservations on the party's stance.

At the Calcutta Congress, in early 1948 the party called for the armed overthrow of the Indian state and was consequently banned. Many leaders went underground. During this phase of the party CS developed a romantic relationship leading to marriage with Sugunabai who had long endured domestic violence at the hands of her husband, a party man. The party, known for its moralistic position on such issues, promptly expelled CS. But CS never left the party!

In the late 1980s, in the context of the Gorbachevian glasnost, following some openness in the party structure, CS was asked to give a letter requesting rehabilitation. Rather than give such a letter, CS asked if it might not be simpler for the party to revoke the resolution expelling him!

Following his expulsion, in 1952, CS moved to Gobichettipalayam, where his wife established practice as gynaecologist and obstetrician. It is not clear what occupied CS during the 1950s and 1960s. The year of Khrushchev's denunciation of Stalin and the brutal suppression of the Hungarian uprising by Soviet troops that cleaved communist parties across the world in 1956, barely caused a ripple in the Tamilnadu party. Not surprisingly the 1964 split saw CS firmly with the CPI.

In the late 1960s, G. Adhikari embarked on the major project of compiling the documents of the history of the CPI. Presumably, CS had had a close association with Adhikari from the early days, and it was at his instance that CS took upon himself the task of chronicling the communist movement in Tamilnadu. Evidently – pace the copious details on M. Singaravelu Chettiar (1860–1946), an early communist and thinker, in the volumes – CS provided considerable support to Adhikari. CS may not have realised at the outset that the chronicling of the communist movement would come to occupy his life, and give it meaning and substance making up for not being able to work for the party directly.

Notwithstanding CPI's original foundation in 1920 at Tashkent, the party celebrated its golden jubilee in 1975. In the years leading up to it, once again at the instance of Adhikari, CS embarked on a biographical study of M. Singaravelu. An early Buddhist, Singaravelu had been introduced to communist ideas even at the time of World War I, had played a stellar role in the rash of strikes following the War, had celebrated the first May Day ever in India (in 1923), and had maintained extensive (not to say, intercepted) correspondence with M. N. Roy in the early 1920s. Based on an impressive exploration of sources *Singaravelu: First Communist in South India* was published by People's Publishing House. This book, and its vastly expanded Tamil version published in 1990, remains the standard work not only on Singaravelu, but also on the early history of the communist movement in Tamilnadu.

The biographical study of Singaravelu was followed by two short books in Tamil on Shapurji Saklatvala, the first Indian communist member of the British parliament, and S. V. Ghate, an early communist leader and an accused in the celebrated Meerut Conspiracy Case (1929–33). The focus of the Saklatvala book was on his Indian tour of 1927, and includes a rare picture of him with Singaravelu. In 1998, to mark the 17th party congress of the CPI held in Chennai, CS wrote *Our Party's Growth in Tamil Nadu: A Brief Sketch*. Re-reading this short book one is left with a sense of how grievously incomplete remains the task of writing a history of the communist party in Tamilnadu.

CS reclaimed Singaravelu for the communist movement in Tamilnadu. But for his work Singaravelu would have been confined to a brief chapter in the history of the Dravidian movement when Periyar's Non-Brahmin Movement spectacularly adopted socialist ideas. CS continued with his work on Singaravelu. In a booklet he demolished the calumny that Singaravelu had apologised to the government to escape the Kanpur Communist Conspiracy Case (1924). CS also edited a series of publications of the uncollected and unpublished writings of Singaravelu. One of them was a manuscript on the fundamentals of communism written in Tamil. Other volumes put together essays published in *Pudu Ulagam* (New World), a monthly that Singaravelu was associated with at the time of his break with the Self-Respect Movement.

No account of CS would be complete without reference to his comrade, K. Murugesan. A worker himself Murugesan was part of the socialist faction that split with Periyar in 1934. The friendship between the two dated from the early 1930s. The two septuagenarians would address each other in the singular much to the amusement of this teenager. CS would chide Murugesan for one reason or the other, with Murugesan receiving the reprimands quietly with a bowed head. It did not take much to realise that the chiding really masked fondness and affection. On one such occasion, after the routine chiding, CS pulled out a book and handed it to Murugesan with the words, 'Here's our book!' It was an edited volume of Singaravelu's writings with their names appearing on the cover as editors: as in all their publications Murugesan's name appeared first, even if the book was in English, a language that Murugesan could barely read.

In the 1980s CS was researching M. P. T. Acharya, who belonged to the Mandayam family that supported Vivekananda, and published Subramania Bharati's *India*. After re-establishing *India* in Pondicherry when Bharati took refuge there, Acharya left for London and joined the revolutionary group of V. D. Savarkar and V. V. S. Aiyar. (Incidentally, CS also edited a volume of critical essays on the latter.) Following Sir Curzon Wyllie's assassination by this group Acharya fled to Turkey, France, and the USA. In 1919 he met Lenin and became a founding member of the CPI. Disillusioned with communism, following a bitter falling-out with M. N. Roy, he lived for over a decade in Berlin as an anarcho-syndicalist. Returning to India in 1934 with his Russian wife he died in penury, a bitter man, in 1953 in Mumbai. It was Acharya's role in the genesis of the Communist Party that interested CS, and he embarked on a full-length study of Acharya. The manuscript went through a long and tortuous process with the press before its eventual publication in 1996. The heavy hand of Rajani Palme Dutt's *India To-Day* is evident in the first chapter, indicating a major and abiding influence on CS's intellectual make up.

Through his contact with V. Subbiah, the labour leader and communist of Pondicherry, CS traced the 1908–9 volume of Bharati's *India* to P. Kothandaraman, a veteran Tamil writer residing in the Aurobindo Ashram. CS planned to compile the writings from this volume in the *Bharati Darisanam* series. The first two volumes, as noted above, pertained to 1906–7. The first edition being out of print, CS planned an expanded edition of the volumes. The *India* issues for the intervening year (1907–8) – the year of frenetic Swadeshi activity in Tamilnadu – remain to be traced to date. CS did not want to launch on the 1908–9 volume without filling the intervening gap. He hit upon a brilliant idea. The colonial government kept track of the native-owned press through its Criminal Investigation Department (CID). Official translators selected features and editorials and submitted translations to the government which were not only used to gauge public opinion, but also to sue editors for sedition. These translations are embodied in the Native Newspaper Reports (NNR). In the absence of the original, CS argued, the NNR provided an alternative version. He patiently culled out the translated extracts from the NNR volumes of missing issues of *India* and typed them out (as the largely damaged volumes did not lend themselves to photocopying). He entrusted me with the task of retranslating them into Tamil. Unfortunately the manuscript was not published and is now lost.

CS's work on documenting the history of the communist movement in south India continued. Amir Hyder Khan had penned a memoir on his experience of building the party in south India. The manuscript fell in CS's hands through G. Adhikari. CS had the memoir translated into Tamil, and prepared the manuscript with extensive appendixes and notes – a hallmark of all his editions. This too appeared after much delay, in 1989.

It was also at this time that CS readied the Tamil translation of the Singaravelu biography. As over two decades had passed since its original publication, CS had lost the notes and transcripts that went into it. To trace the original Tamil version of the translated appendices he sought my help which he once again acknowledged in his preface.

Reading his generous words of thanks is gratifying, but it is difficult to miss the inelegance of his Tamil phrasings and idiom. Much like the language of Christian missionaries – 'like the English people of the Salvation Army in Indian dress', as one early Tamil scholar caustically observed – the political language of Tamil communists is congenitally afflicted by a certain awkwardness, and CS's language stands as an exemplar of it. (Here one must add that he translated Aristotle's *Politics* into Tamil.) He was more comfortable speaking in English and often slipped into it in conversations.

After his wife's death CS relocated to his family house on Josier Street, Nungambakkam, in Chennai. The huge house was decrepit and in a state of perpetual disrepair, musty with cobwebs and piles of old papers and files. His elder sister shared the house and she fitted the stereotype of an old orthodox Brahmin widow – tonsured head and draped in a drab *narmadi* sari in the traditional manner, constantly snapping at everybody. CS didn't sport the 'sacred' thread, and must have thrown it away in the mid-1930s. The combination of an unconventional marriage and affiliation to the Communist Party ensured ostracism, and CS bore the brunt of it. It is said that his sister wouldn't touch the water he had drawn. A frugal man, not known for culinary finesse, he cooked his own meals. If there was any remnant of caste in him, it was unconscious. CS would have considered caste as part of the superstructure that would wither away sooner than the state after the revolution. He never evinced interest in theoretical debates, and it is likely that he had resolved all questions in the 1930s at the time of joining the party.

Reading Eric Hobsbawm's autobiography *Interesting Times* one cannot miss the contrast between English and Indian communists. If the English left intellectuals did not forsake the pleasures of life, an important strand among Indian communists aspired to a Gandhian austerity. I remember visiting a five-time communist MLA's home in Kovilpatti to find that there was not one proper chair to sit on. CS exemplified that tradition.

During the last year of his life CS was brought to Chennai and nursed in the hospital managed by the NCBH, his publisher where he breathed his last.

II
CULTURAL &
LITERARY FIGURES

8

IYOTHEETHOSS PANDITHAR
Anticipating Ambedkar

THE DEATH CENTENARY OF C. Iyotheethoss Pandithar (1845–1914) went a few years ago practically unnoticed. But some Tamil little magazines and Dalit intellectuals commemorated it. When I suggested his name to a scholar-administrator seeking nominations for a Ministry of Culture's scheme for celebrating the centenaries of leading Indian personalities, I had to write a follow-up mail outlining who he was.

Who was Iyotheethoss Pandithar? To put it simply he was an intellectual who anticipated Dr B. R. Ambedkar by two generations. In fin-de-siècle Tamilnadu Iyotheethoss forged a radical identity for Dalits arguing that they were the original Buddhists who were stigmatised as 'Untouchables' by Brahmins for resisting the caste system. At a time when Buddhism was in practical oblivion, and what little was known of it was mediated by Orientalist antiquarians, he reinterpreted Indian and Tamil history through Buddhism. His movement to revive Buddhism radicalised significant numbers of Paraiyars – especially among the working classes in the Kolar Gold Fields.

For long Iyotheethoss was little more than a footnote in the history of the Dravidian movement. One knew of him through intriguing references in the great Tamil writer and political personality Thiru. Vi. Kalyanasundara Mudaliar's classic autobiography. In the wake of Dr Ambedkar's birth centenary

the Dalit movement in Tamilnadu, for long subsumed within
the Non-Brahmin Movement, came into its own. In 1999, G.
Aloysius following his pioneering monograph on Iyotheethoss's
movement (*Religion as Emancipatory Identity*, 1998) published
an edition of his copious writings from *Tamilan*, Iyotheethoss's
weekly published from 1907 until his death. These volumes
have been the major ideological arsenal for the Dalit intellectual
movement in Tamilnadu over the last decade and a half. His
image is now emblazoned on Dalit banners. There has been a
stream of studies on his work by scholars such as Raj Gowthaman
and Stalin Rajangam.

India is notorious for not having a sense of history. The terrible
state of our archival repositories stands testimony to our apathy.
The dimension of caste – the mainstream disdain for lower-caste
histories – makes this historical apathy lethal. Not surprisingly
our knowledge of Iyotheethoss's life – 'Not much is known of
[Iyotheethoss's] life', reads a footnote in G. Aloysius's monograph –
especially until the launch of *Tamilan* in the last years of his life, is
particularly sketchy. Only two photographs have survived, one an
impressive portrait and the other, a hazy group picture.

Some tantalising new information has recently turned up. In
2011 the autobiography of Dharmanand Kosambi (1876–1947),
father of the great historian and polymath, D. D. Kosambi,
appeared in English (*Nivedan*). Translated and edited by his
granddaughter, the pioneering feminist scholar, Meera Kosambi,
the original Marathi had been serialised intermittently during
1912–16, and was published in book form in 1924. Reading this
fascinating text, unknown to scholars outside Maharashtra, I was
struck by his references to Iyotheethoss.

Kosambi's quest for Buddhism had taken him all over
South Asia. In 1903 he spent over six months in Chennai
where he encountered three important figures in the revival of
Buddhism in south India: M. Singaravelu Chettiar; Professor

P. Lakshmi Narasu (1860/1–1934), author of *The Essence of Buddhism* (republished in 1848 with Dr Ambedkar's foreword); and Iyotheethoss Pandithar. After reaching Colombo with Singaravelu's help, he joined the Vidyodaya Vidyalaya where he learnt under its founder, Hikkeduwe Sri Sumangala Thera, Kosambi returned to Chennai in late March 1903. Let us now hear in Kosambi's own words his encounter with Buddhism in Chennai and Iyotheethoss Pandithar.

> A Buddhist society called the 'Madras Mahabodhi Sabha' already existed in Madras, with Professor Lakshmi Narasu Naidu as president and Singaravelu as secretary. This Sabha did nothing other than celebrate Vaishakh Purnima…. A number of Pariahs (Ati Shudras) had embraced Buddhism in Madras city. Their leader was Pandit Ayodhidas. But he and the members of the Mahabodhi Sabha did not get along. About two months after I came to Madras, all these Buddhists united. They rented a small house in Rayapet [Royapettah], named it Bauddhashram, and installed me there.

After six months in Chennai, Kosambi was tired and felt like an exile, and decided to proceed to Burma.

> About the middle of October 1903 … I left for Burma. Pandit Ayodhidas and others came to the harbour to see me off. A Madrasi acquaintance of theirs was to go by the same steamer. Pandit Ayodhidas introduced me to him and told me that he would look after me during the voyage.

Brief as these two references are, they are valuable considering that they were written when its author had little inkling about the standing Iyotheethoss Pandithar would command a century later.

~

Let us now turn to a few documents in the colonial archive and a report in the *Hindu*, both dating to 1898, which present some new information on Iyotheethoss and his movement.

In mid-1898 the government noticed from occasional newspaper reports – it would add immensely to our knowledge if these reports could be traced – that 'certain persons of the Pariah caste' were attempting to establish that they were once Buddhists. The issue was referred to the commissioner of police who set the intelligence machine in motion. The police functionary who made the enquiries was right on the mark when he noted that caste disabilities rather than purely religious motives were behind the claim to a Buddhist identity. Even though he remarked pejoratively that they were 'posing as Buddhists' he rightly noted their desire to be 'free from all the intolerance of caste' and be 'liberated from the position of degradation in which they now are'.

The investigator also had 'a long conversation' with Iyotheethoss himself – we do not know if Iyotheethoss was aware that he was speaking to a CID policeman – but the results provide interesting gleanings that confirm and amplify the little that we know about his life. Iyotheethoss, according to this report, was born in Mylapore, Chennai. He acquired knowledge of Tamil and English apart from acquiring expertise in native medicine. He then moved to Ootacamund where he practised medicine for seventeen years before returning to Chennai in 1893 or thereabouts. At the time of the enquiry he was said to be earning between seventy and hundred rupees a month, not an inconsiderable sum.

Iyotheethoss stated that he had his first insight into the Buddhist origins of Paraiyars in an old palm-leaf manuscript titled *Narada Purana Sungai Thelivu*. Towards propagating his new discovery he had started 'a Buddha Sungum' in Ootacamund. (The police checked out this information in Ootacamund: while they could confirm that he was 'respected ...

as a skilful doctor and also as a Sanskrit scholar' no information was forthcoming about the Sangam itself.) At this time he came into contact with Colonel Henry Steel Olcott (1832–1907), co-founder of the Theosophical Society and its first president, and a high-profile convert to Buddhism who was based in Chennai then. Through Olcott he interacted with two Buddhist scholars from Sri Lanka. One was Anagarika Dharmapala of the Maha Bodhi Society of Ceylon, who forged a Sinhala–Buddhist majoritarian identity in Sri Lanka. The other was an old Sinhala priest 'Gunaratnaswami' (Gunaratne).

Iyotheethoss organised a meeting in Chennai on 8 June 1898. Colonel Olcott and the two Buddhist priests spoke, and an appeal was made to support Iyotheethoss's movement. On the same day Iyotheethoss issued a public appeal to Colonel Olcott, making a plea to support the movement. '[I]t was our heartfelt desire to return to our old Buddhist faith only in its primitive purity.' 'For thus alone, we believe, can we hope to restore our self-respect and to gain that right, to win by our exertions, domestic comfort and untrammelled personal liberty of action, which are denied us in the Hindu Social System of caste, under the weight of which, we are now, and for many centuries have been, crushed into the dust.' The plea, 'A Unique Petition', was carried by the *Hindu* (14 July 1898) – the title most certainly the handiwork of a subeditor.

The report of the 8 June meeting was printed in English with the title 'The Revival of Buddhism in Southern India: A Great Event'. It is not clear if the two other pioneers of Buddhism in India, M. Singaravelu and P. Lakshmi Narasu, were present on the occasion. Probably Iyotheethoss's involvement in Buddhism predated their interest, and in any case the trajectory of his movement took a more radical turn rather than remain bookish.

Iyotheethoss soon started a Dravida Buddha Sangam, which at this time, according to the police, had a modest membership of fifty. More than a month after the meeting, towards the end of July 1898, Iyotheethoss accompanied Olcott and the Buddhist priests to Sri Lanka, addressed some meetings at Colombo and Kandy, before returning to Chennai on 5 September 1898.

As the Indian nationalist struggle progressed in the twentieth century Iyotheethoss's loyalist position was confirmed. He saw in the colonial state an agent that would create the necessary conditions for the uplift of Dalits. An uncompromising critic of the INC – he dubbed it 'the Brahmin Congress' – he wondered what self-rule under the Brahmins might mean for the lower castes, a position articulated after his death by both Periyar and Ambedkar.

After making this enquiry the Government of Madras seems to have hardly worried about Iyotheethoss and his movement, and there are few reports of his activities in the colonial archive. The enquiry smugly concluded that 'The movement is scarcely likely to have any political significance as it is extremely unlikely to succeed'.

Writing in 1898 the police inspector may be pardoned for not sensing the momentous significance that Iyotheethoss was to have for the Dalit movement. Historians have fared worse.

9

SUBRAMANIA BHARATI
Tamil Bard

IN THE EARLY 1980s the playwright and public intellectual, the recently deceased Gnani Sankaran (1954–2018), plastered Chennai's walls with a poster: in Indian ink on a plain white background, all it depicted was a twirled moustache and piercing eyes. But even a child could identify it as Subramania Bharati. The poster was a teaser for his newly launched journal, *Theemtharikida*: an onomatopoeic word suggesting apocalyptic fury, drawn from a poem by Bharati.

Bharati is *the* cultural icon of modern Tamil culture. Except for a thin fringe of the Dravidian and the ultra-left movements, Bharati is universally acclaimed. Now, nearly a hundred years after his death, the turban, the piercing gaze, and the twirled moustache are easily recognised by people across the Tamil world. Looking for a nom de plume? Suffix 'Bharati' to your name. Want a name for your new journal? You could do no better than pull out a phrase from his poetry. A slogan for a cause? A line from his poems will eminently do. Even M. Karunanidhi, whose sympathies may lie more with the Dravidian movement's poet laureate, Bharatidasan (interestingly, a pen name that means 'the disciple of Bharati'), drew the title *Nenjukku Needhi* for his multivolume autobiography from Bharati. Contemporary writings are replete with allusions to his writings. Tamil writing, nearly a century after his death, continues to flourish in his penumbra.

How did this come to happen?

Modernity was ushered into India under colonial aegis. Under the impact of far-reaching social transformations all Indian languages experienced profound changes. Described erroneously as 'renaissance', this change, in each linguistic region, threw up fascinating literary figures. Few of them however have contemporary relevance. Subramania Bharati (1882–1921) is exceptional, an abiding influence on modern writing in Tamil.

The poet began his career as a journalist. First as subeditor of Tamil's only daily then, and later as the editor of a women's magazine. For his writings as the editor of a nationalist weekly *India*, he had to flee British India. His journals and some of his books were proscribed by a repressive government geared to crush the rising wave of mass nationalism. The first to publish political cartoons in the vernacular, Bharati's journalistic prose was both informed and incisive.

But Bharati was essentially a literary man, a poet – it is hard not to use the cliché, of inspired genius. Tamil has a long literary history with great poetical riches that could weigh down poetasters. Bharati's achievement lay in forging an old language steeped in tradition to voice contemporary concerns.

His early poems, written from the barricades at the height of the Swadeshi movement following the partition of Bengal, demonstrated the potential of language for political mobilisation. Bharati was the earliest to write of land and language, and the pain of their subjugation to an alien power. He employed popular tunes from older songs and filled them with new content for a larger, inclusive, democratic public. The songs dealt with patriotic themes: the glory of the motherland and its current fallen state; colonial exploitation; eulogies of nationalist leaders. Bharati was the earliest to write exhortatory poems in Tamil, and these became ammunition in the nationalist arsenal through the decades leading up to Independence. More than a century later lines and phrases from these poems have passed into common language, and many of them will live as long as a quest for freedom remains.

Even as he wrote patriotic verse the grave social inequities – of caste, class, and gender – were very much in the forefront of his mind. 'Without social reform,' he remarked in one of his early writings, 'our political reform is a dream, a myth, for social slaves can never really understand political liberty.' *Pudumai pen* (the new woman) was his coinage, as are such terms as *puratchi* (revolution) and *poduvudamai* (communism). Bharati's imprint on the Tamil language is palpable.

Of an all-too brief life of less than thirty-nine years Bharati spent more than ten in exile in Pondicherry, then under French rule. In the poems written in exile, we find a more reflective poet extending the possibilities of language and confronting the larger questions of life.

For someone who declared that 'Poetry is my occupation' Bharati's output was substantial, but not staggering. For all his complaints about the poetic muse deserting him often, when in its embrace, his verse was unfailingly superb. Bharati was aware of Whitman and the haiku, and experimented with free verse, thus becoming the founding father of New Poetry in Tamil.

Bharati had a wide range. He wrote some sixty stories – of varying length – which do not conform to accepted forms of the novel or short story. He wrote a commentary on the Bhagvad Gita, and translated some Vedic hymns. As a journalist he introduced column writing to Tamil journalism and commented extensively, if fitfully, on contemporary affairs. Humour, an unknown commodity to Tamil literature, was his forte – his prose brims with satire, sarcasm, irony, and parody. He was also the forerunner of the autobiographical form in Tamil. In short Bharati touched nothing that he did not adorn.

In the high noon of Indian nationalism and Tamil cultural efflorescence Bharati's writings were an essential component in the formation of a new Tamil identity. It was in this context, immediately after Independence, that a demand for making his writings public – free of copyright – was made. And for the first time in global literary history the copyright of a writer was taken over by the state and put in the public domain.

Why then is Bharati not celebrated outside Tamilnadu? Why is he not as well-known as Tagore? The Nobel Prize? Part of the answer, but not the whole.

Despite the Indian nation state's heavy investment in Hindi, Tagore continues to be a celebrated figure in Indian literary culture. The interested English reader is spoilt for choice if she were to go looking for books on and by Tagore. There is but one road and a nagar named after the Tamil poet in New Delhi, and it is usually misspelt, without an 'a', as Bharti. The only books an English reader will find on Bharati would be some *sarkari* publications.

As an academic travelling beyond the Tamil land, when faced with the question of how to introduce Bharati, I have often swallowed Tamil pride and described him as the Tamil Tagore. Analogous, but inadequate. To historically sensitive intellectuals my opening gambit has been to say that Bharati was born twenty years after Tagore (a little sleight of hand here; he was born twenty-one years after) and predeceased him by an exact twenty.

Bharati and Tagore are not apples and oranges. They are more like mangoes. But Indian mangoes come in all shapes, sizes, and levels of sweetness. Comparison is difficult and fraught.

~

But before we attempt a comparison the first question that comes up is: Did the two know each other? Did they ever meet?

Bharati went to Calcutta for the annual Congress session in 1906, a session Tagore had 'ran away from ... tired and disappointed'. In March–April 1919, Tagore travelled extensively in the Tamil country, but the two never met despite being in the same city, Chennai, giving talks at about the same time.

In spite of being a keen follower of Swadeshi politics in Bengal, Bharati came to know of Tagore only after the Nobel. But after the prize he followed Tagore closely, translated many of his essays and stories into Tamil – a compliment that Bharati bestowed on few – and commented extensively on his work and activities. Bharati had nothing but unalloyed admiration for Gurudev. It is therefore a fitting coincidence that Bharati's last published piece was on Tagore's European tour of 1921, appropriately titled 'Sri Ravindra Digvijayam'.

> If one attains fame it should be like that of the great Ravindrar. Is it only in Bengal? Is it just in India? Is it in Asia alone? His fame has spread across this world, from Germany, to Austria, to France. This despite the fact that his songs are available only in Bengali.

In Bharati's view the praise won by Tagore did not belong to him alone.

> Can the fame that is gained for one's own sake ever be called fame? Fame is that which comes from garnering glory for an entire nation. Ravindrar has established to the world that India is the *loka guru* [the preceptor of the world]. May the flowers at his feet be praised!

More fulsome and unconditional praise is yet to be heaped on one poet by another. For Bharati, Tagore's greatest achievement was this fame, a fame that redounded to a fallen nation. A fame that he never experienced in his own lifetime. And did not know that he would gain posthumously.

Was Tagore aware of Bharati? Despite outliving Bharati by twenty years there is no evidence to suggest so.

~

Tagore was a myriad-minded man with renaissance talents. Through his long life Tagore wrote poetry, novels, short stories, plays, essays. He wrote for children. He painted. Sang. Composed music. He was also a journalist. An educationist. An institution builder. Knighted, his stature was such that he could even return his knighthood. Born into a celebrated family he did not know poverty. Though riches didn't mean he was always a happy man.

In contrast Bharati's life was short. Of which over ten years were spent in exile in Pondicherry. (Bharati's desire to step on European soil, the seedbed of democracy, never came to fruition, while Tagore went to England even before Bharati was born.) At a time when Tagore was being feted, Bharati was pleading with the governor of Madras for justice. If the crowds at the time of Tagore's death caused near-riots, Bharati's cortège drew eleven persons and there was a confusion over who would light the funeral pyre.

A poet who relied on inspiration to write, in volume and variety, Bharati comes nowhere close to Tagore's staggering oeuvre. Bharati faced yet another constraint. Bengali literary history is short, not longer than four centuries in Tagore's days. Tamils can claim an unbroken poetic tradition of two millennia: this can extract a heavy price. Its richness can be a daunting burden, and to make a mark in such a rich field is, to say the least, most challenging. Bharati's greatest achievement was to be the harbinger of modernity in a strongly rooted literary tradition. A century after his death Bharati remains an inspiration.

The question recurs: Why then is Bharati so little known outside Tamilnadu?

Translation into English – its quality or its lack thereof – is the prime culprit. Little was done in Bharati's own lifetime to translate his poems. If about half of his original poetry remained uncollected or unpublished when he was alive can the lack of translation be bemoaned? When his posthumous stars rose stray translations made their appearance. After Independence it became a cottage industry. Many translators have tried their hands – Prema Nandakumar, P. S. Sundaram, K. Swaminathan, J. Parthasarathy, T. N. Ramachandran, Usha Rajagopalan – but Bharati's poetry simply refuses to work in English. Lyrical, reliant on sonic effect, and suffused with a romantic idealism the poems fall flat in translation. M. L. Thangappa's translations work to an extent, thanks to his limited and careful selection. Unfortunately A. K. Ramanujan attempted to translate only his prose poems. Frost's quip about poetry being what's lost in translation was never more true than in Bharati's case.

The Tagore translation industry is now a century old. Seen as doing little justice to the originals Tagore's own translations have faced much criticism. But at least it won him a Nobel Prize. Over the many decades some of the finest translators have turned their attention to Tagore. The most recent example is *The Essential Tagore*, published by Harvard University Press (2011), the work of Tagore scholars from Bangladesh, West Bengal, and the diaspora.

In music, one understands, Rabindra Sangeet is central to the classical repertoire. In the world of Carnatic music Bharati remains a *thukkada* (a sop thrown in towards the end of the concert).

The other reason for Bharati's oblivion is sociological. The Bengal bhadralok produced generations of bilingual scholars at ease in English and Bengali. The English-speaking Tamil middle class forsook Tamil, and has not surprisingly failed Bharati as well. Subramanyan Chandrasekhar's mother translated Chekov into Tamil, and his younger brother wrote both in English and Tamil. But did Chandra ever read Bharati or Thirukural? Bankim and Tagore are the staple of modern Bengali intellectual culture. A series of Bengali social scientists have written on Tagore. A quick list would include Amartya Sen, Sabyasachi Bhattacharya, Partha Chatterjee, Ashis Nandy, and Sudipta Kaviraj. These brilliant minds have interpreted Tagore for our times and made him relevant. Historians of such accomplishment as Ramachandra Guha, Sanjay Subrahmanyam, M. S. S. Pandian, Shiv Visvanathan, Sumathi Ramaswamy, Sunil Amrith, and Srinath Raghavan notwithstanding one cannot think of a halfway decent essay on Bharati.

Bharati is too important to be the monopoly of Tamils. As Bharati's death centenary approaches let us hope that this situation is redressed, and the poet gets his due.

10

PUDUMAIPPITHAN
Crazy about the Modern

IN THE 18 OCTOBER 1933 number of *Gandhi*, a nationalist journal, appeared a short article – *'Gulabjan Kadhal'* or falling in love with a gulab jamun. It was a humorous polemic on the notion of romantic love, love at first sight. Signed 'Pudumaippithan', it was the debut of the greatest writer of Tamil fiction. The pseudonym meaning 'one crazy about the new/modernity', with a manifesto quality to it, was most apt, for nothing captures what Pudumaippithan did to Tamil writing better and not without its irony: *pithan* (the crazed one) also refers to Lord Siva. Pudumaippithan's modernity was no rootless wonder – it was deeply imbued by a critical grounding in tradition, quite unlike most of his contemporaries.

In a brief life of forty-two years and a writing career spanning less than fifteen years Pudumaippithan (1906–1948) wrote short stories, essays, reviews, poems, political biographies, literary translations, and an incomplete novel – all this while being squeezed dry by the nascent newspaper industry and the emerging world of Tamil cinema. While the flash of genius is present in every piece of his writing it is in the short story that Pudumaippithan left his everlasting imprint.

Pudumaippithan was born on 25 April 1906 in the Saiva Vellala community, an elite landholding caste known for its accomplishment in religion, philosophy, and arts and literature. His family hailed from Tirunelveli in southernmost Tamilnadu, but as his father was in government employ as a tahsildar and was transferred routinely, Pudumaippithan was born in Thirupathiripuliyur in present-day Cuddalore district in north Tamilnadu. He was named Vridhachalam. Despite his close association with Tirunelveli and its culture Pudumaippithan's early life was spent in various parts of the Tamil districts of Madras Presidency. The family returned to Tirunelveli in 1918 on his father's retirement. Little is known of his mother Parvatham who died when he was young. But he held a deep respect for his mother, and when he started a film production in his later life he named it after her.

On his return to Tirunelveli Pudumaippithan completed his school education in St. John's High School. Later he joined the famed Hindu College, Tirunelveli, for his intermediate and undergraduate education. Indifferent in his studies Pudumaippithan managed to get a BA degree, in 1931, at the age of twenty-five. Pudumaippithan's strained relationship with his father, V. Chokkalingam, was further complicated by the presence of a stepmother. Chokkalingam had intellectual ambitions – he even authored a book on the origin and history of Indo-European races, a massive tome steeped in colonial ethnology – which perhaps aggravated the tension between father and son. Eventually the rift ended through a legal disowning by the father.

In July 1932 Pudumaippithan was married to Kamala. Though their marriage was punctuated with long separations, miscarriages, and impecunious circumstances the two made a devoted couple. Pudumaippithan encouraged her to write, and she published many short stories. The frequent and long separations resulted in a steady correspondence between the two. Kamala kept alive her husband's memory until her death, nearly half a century after his passing away. Their only daughter, Dinakari, was born in April 1946, two years before his death.

Much against his father's wishes to take up a government job Pudumaippithan, aspiring for a writing career, moved to

Chennai in 1934, where he was to spend most of his adult and professional life. He worked briefly as subeditor in the nationalist journals *Suthanthira Sangu* and *Ooliyan* (1934–5). In July 1935 he joined the daily *Dinamani* (edited by T. S. Chokkalingam; first owned by S. Sadanand and later bought over by Ramnath Goenka) as subeditor; this was the only time he had a regular job with a steady if low salary. In September 1943, along with a group of other subeditors, Pudumaippithan left *Dinamani* in solidarity when the editor resigned over a principled conflict with the management. He was associated briefly with another daily, *Dinasari*, launched by the protesting editorial staff. However, it was Pudumaippithan's close association with the journal *Manikodi*, considered the harbinger of modern Tamil literature, especially the short story, that brought him into his own.

Pudumaippithan spent his last years in the film world, working on a few film scripts and even making an abortive attempt at film production. He worked for S. S. Vasan's Gemini Studios on the script for *Avvaiyar*. From late 1947 he worked for the singing superstar M. K. Thyagaraja Bhagavathar's *Raja Mukti* at Pune. In already weak health, Pudumaippithan contracted tuberculosis, and undergoing acute suffering, died on 30 June 1948 in Thiruvananthapuram at his father-in-law's home.

SHORT STORIES

Pudumaippithan's first short story was published in *Manikodi*, in April 1934. Titled '*Aattrangarai Pillaiyar*', and carried in two instalments, it is an allegorical story: in narrating the story of a Pillaiyar (Ganesha) idol by the riverside Pudumaippithan constructs a critical narrative of Hindu/Indian society and culture through the ages.

Following this there was a flurry of stories, and in the first two years of his writing career (1933–5) Pudumaippithan published nearly fifty of them – constituting more than half of his entire oeuvre. Pudumaippithan's early stories are quite short but cover a wide range of themes. Even in his early writings he makes a clear break with the dominant strand of writing suffused with romanticist outpourings, and he shocks readers with stark portrayals of subaltern life – the life of mill workers, prostitutes, hotel waiters, plantation workers, political prisoners – not to speak of lower-middle-class life in the cities and a realistic depiction of caste-ridden and iniquitous life in the countryside.

Some early stories, set in the city of Chennai, explored bold themes. 'Kavandanum Kamanum' (puranic metaphors of hunger and lust personified, respectively) has a vignette in Chennai's nightlife, and begins thus:

> Have you looked around the city of Chennai after eight in the
> night? If you have, what I describe below will not shock you.
> Lights that catch the eyes. Civilisation that captures the heart.
> If you want to understand that this is no age of kali but the age
> of advertisement you should see the city's nights.

And then Pudumaippithan cuts to a dark corner. 'Did you see the wall around the corner? The act of creation is on. Are they humans or animals? Don't feign politeness and look away. Your poplin shirt and shell-frame spectacles are but stolen from what should have been their bread.' And then the story quickly turns to the streetwalker who accosts a novitiate client who runs away after thrusting money into her hands. She throws away the money swearing at him saying, 'Did you take me for a beggar?' And then bends down to search for the coins in the darkness.

'Puthiya Nandan' recasts the medieval story of Nandanar, an 'untouchable' devotee of Siva, for contemporary times where an 'untouchable' is discriminated despite converting to Christianity. One of the most reprinted stories is 'Ponnagaram' (ironically meaning, 'the golden city'). In it a horse-cart driver injures himself in a drunken stupor and his wife, a millworker, sleeps with another man to earn a rupee so she can make milk gruel for her husband. This brief story of all but three pages ends with the oft-quoted line, 'Ye, all those who rant about chastity, this is Ponnagaram'.

The 1930s were the years when the Tamil short story as an artistic genre was taking shape, and within a few years, achieved great heights. *Manikodi* was the primary vehicle for the short story. Within a span of a few years many major writers emerged, but even within this group of talented writers Pudumaippithan stood out, for many reasons. This was the idealist moment when nationalist politics was at its peak. Pudumaippithan introduced a strong dose of realism – much like in other languages, for example, Premchand. But more importantly he introduced humour in all its varieties into his narrative: wit, sarcasm, parody, and satire dominated his writings. In terms of writing style he fashioned a new prose – a staccato style heavily resonant to the cadence of English. Acutely self-conscious about this art he referred to it as a 'leapfrogging' style. All these elements made the literary world look up, and to this mix he also added a strong antidote to idealism. A classic example is a short story entitled '*Gopalaiyangarin Manaivi*' (Gopala Iyengar's Wife). The story is prefaced by a characteristic authorial note.

In his novella *Chandrikaiyin Kathai* (The Story of Chandrikai) Bharati describes the inter-caste marriage between Gopala Iyengar and Meenakshi, the housemaid of Veeresalingam Pantulu. The drift of the story is in conformity with the ideal – it can even be termed illusion – of 'love at first sight' that Gopala Iyengar holds. What transpires later Bharati may perhaps have intended for the unfinished second part of the story. 'For the sidelong glance of the beloved', a man may eat fire; but can he eat overcooked rice and stale sauce? I have continued the story in my own manner, which may not necessarily conform to Bharati's.

Pudumaippithan then proceeds to show how this marriage between an idealistic educated Brahmin youth and an illiterate Yadava girl ends in a fiasco with incompatibility in terms of food habits and lifestyle. Unable to put up with her husband's vegetarianism Meenakshi first begins by eating meat on the sly. Finding this too cumbersome she soon converts him to non-vegetarianism. Gopala Iyengar, on his part, disappointed by the failure of his ideal of a companionate relationship in his submissive wife, initiates her into alcohol. The story ends with their endearing words uttered in complete inebriation. Bharati's dreams of inter-caste marriage and casteless society lie in a shambles in the hands of Pudumaippithan.

In theme, context, language, and style Pudumaippithan fashioned a new sensibility that was self-consciously modern. With a sharp wit, sarcasm, and irony he punctured romanticist and idealist dreams – something that is striking given the fact that he wrote at a time when nationalist and social emancipatory movements were riding a crest of popular support. Criticism of the existing reality, but always coupled with self-doubt and irreverence, marked Pudumaippithan's writings.

Pudumaippithan handled a variety of themes in his stories. His long story 'Thunba Keni' is set in the tea plantations of Sri Lanka and explores the plight of indentured labourers in the harsh conditions of economic and sexual exploitation. While capturing large social processes his métier is clearly etching out characters who are real, made of the substance of life, not cardboard characters.

Pudumaippithan's life was divided between Tirunelveli and Chennai, and both are recurring locations in his stories, often taking on the character of metaphor. Pudumaippithan's Chennai not only talks of its big buildings, broad roads, and its then nascent airport, but also the dark alleys and the howling of the tram which he calls 'the modern *yaksha*'. In his short story '*Mahamasanam*' (The Great Burial Ground) a beggar, a Muslim one at that, dies in slow degrees, watched by a middle-class girl left behind by her father for a while as he goes across the road to buy some mangoes. For Pudumaippithan this epitomises city life – with its vastness, callousness, and indifference, yet not without its humanity.

Not surprisingly Pudumaippithan's city characters are forever dreaming about going back home, to the village, to Tirunelveli. However, Pudumaippithan anything but romanticises the countryside. His villages are deeply stratified by caste and wealth. It is an oppressive society where physical and symbolic violence is let loose on the lower castes and classes.

Deeply critical of the Hindu social order Pudumaippithan was at once sceptical of other emancipatory avenues. Given his upbringing in Tirunelveli he was also critical of the Christian missionary project, especially, its Protestant variety. All the major political movements of his time – Indian nationalist, anti-colonialist, Dravidian, and communist – make their appearance in his stories, but none meets with his complete approval.

Pudumaippithan's stories show deep sensitivity to women – whether it be widowed women, young wives married to older men, or credulous women leading mundane lives. Rarely does a woman get portrayed in poor light in his stories.

This brief mapping of his stories may evoke the image of a 'progressive' writer, even a social realist one. However, such a labelling is inadequate, for at least two reasons.

First, as he himself once remarked, his writings often have an undercurrent of pessimism, 'a drying up of hope'. While he is deeply, even violently, critical of the existing order he also doubts every emancipatory project. While he writes movingly about caste oppression, especially of the Dalits, he immediately counterposes the situation with a story about how Dalits beat up a Brahmin advocate of temple entry. In short, he is ever the healthy sceptic.

Second, his stories are not confined to social realism, some variant or the other of which dominated Indian writing in the high noon of Indian nationalism. He wrote fantasy, even pieces that can be called precursors to magic realism and science fiction. And he delighted in rewriting and reinterpreting literary classics, legends, and folklore. Some stories are deeply introspective, even philosophical, and may be called 'stories of ideas'. In his last published story, 'Kayittravu' (the title, 'Rope-Serpent', plays on one of Indian philosophy's enduring conundrums), as the 'protagonist' Paramasivam Pillai ruminates on time and being under the palmyra tree in the small hours of the morning as he defecates in the open he is bitten by a snake. The story ends there.

Few Tamil writers have indulged in as much parody as Pudumaippithan. His stories are experimental in terms of form, content, structure, and prose style, and the creative tools that he employs are those of wit, sarcasm, and irony. Digression is a weapon of frequent resort. His creative prose blends both literary Tamil and the colloquial dialect, and its structure resonates heavily to English prose. His leapfrog style is particularly evident in the early prose that he employed for realistic depiction and the exposure of hypocrisy.

Pudumaippithan was a noted figure and many of his stories provoked controversy, especially 'Sapa Vimochanam' (Redemption). A finely crafted story it is a reinterpretation of the Agaligai (Ahalya) branch-story from the Ramayana. The story begins with the redemption of Agaligai. However, as in much of Pudumaippithan's writings, life is not lived happily ever after by her or by her husband, Gautaman. A psychologically sensitive portrayal of Agaligai's post-petrification trauma follows, as she is ever conscious of her misadventure. If Gautaman cannot speak to her with an unblemished heart as his incendiary description of her as a harlot has scorched his tongue, Agaligai's plight is much worse. Both are in anguish, each wondering if they are suitable for the other. Agaligai tries to conduct herself in a way that no one would look at her through the prism of her past action. But this is precisely what makes her forget her natural manner. 'She agonises over even casual words that Gautaman spoke, wondering whether they contained underlying meanings?' and is rendered incapable of meeting even the ordinary glance of other people. In short the very business of living becomes one hell. In all this difficulty the presence of Rama and Sita is the saving grace. But their banishment to the forest leaves Agaligai devastated. Agaligai continues to pull along in the hope of seeing Rama and Sita. But here too she feels let down. On their return from the forest, when Sita narrates her fire ordeal, an outraged Agaligai asks, 'Even if he asked you how could you undergo it?' Here she slips from the horrific plural to refer to Rama and addresses him instead in the singular. 'One law for Agaligai, quite another for Rama?' asks Pudumaippithan. With her last hope shattered her heart hardens into stone. And she turns into stone again.

This is a provocative interpretation of the Ramayana branch-story. Pudumaippithan himself, conscious of this, states teasingly at the very outset: 'Those who are familiar with Ramayanam may not grasp – nor even like – this story. I remain unconcerned about that.'

In 1940 he published his first collection, *Pudumappithan Kathaigal* (The Stories of Pudumaippithan), a most uninspired title, even lazy, from today's perspective. But it was an audacious literary statement much like his pseudonym. It exuded a supreme confidence of the author's own abilities and was very much in

keeping with his enfant terrible image. No author, least of all a
fledgling one, in an emerging literary public sphere, had given
his own name to his book until then. What was innovative at
first became passé later.

Pudumaippithan attempted one novel titled *Anna Itta
Thee*. Two draft chapters have survived. It has a strong
autobiographical element, especially about his relationship with
his overbearing father. The canvas is vast, and evidently it was
planned as a big novel.

TRANSLATIONS

Like all his contemporaries in the emerging modern Tamil
literary world Pudumaippithan was steeped in English literature,
the staple of modern Western education in India. In addition,
through English, writers accessed European, Russian, and
American writing, and to a limited extent from other parts of the
world. His friends have recorded his interest in reading which
was avid, extensive, and eclectic. Pudumaippithan's surviving
book collection also bears testimony to this.

An early influence was the French writer Guy de Maupassant.
Using various pseudonyms Pudumaippithan translated, or rather,
adapted and published seven stories from Maupassant in the first
year of his writing career.

From late 1935, Pudumaippithan began to publish translated
stories regularly. On the whole he translated about sixty short
stories, retold three Shakespearean plays (*Timon of Athens*,
The Tempest, and *Hamlet*) and one each from Henrik Ibsen
and Molière, abridged Mary Shelley's *Frankenstein*, and made
an incomplete translation of Alexander Kuprin's *Yama: The
Pit*. Each story contained a short note on the author and a few
glosses. Probably he made some extra money by translating,

but there is no doubt that the stories were chosen consciously reflecting his own artistic and social interests. A keen awareness of the literary milieu in which they were being read is also evident. His first published book was *Ulagathu Sirukathaigal* (Stories from Around the World), in 1939, a year before his own collection of stories was published, an indication of his literary investment in translation. This volume of twenty-four stories from around the world included a combative preface where he stated his credo: his purpose was to shake Tamil people out of their hidebound existence, unaware of life in other climes and cultures.

However, in his later life, in desperate financial need, he tried to put together stories translated earlier, and new ones hastily translated, between covers. Evidently, his choice of *Yama*, set in the brothels of pre-Tsarist Russia, satisfied both his interest in the critique of bourgeois decadence and the demands of the market. (It is worth recalling that Premchand translated *Yama* in Hindi.)

Stories that he translated included those written by Guy de Maupassant and Anatole France (France); Franz Kafka (Germany); R. L. Stevenson, E. V. Lucas, and John Galsworthy (Britain); Jack London, William Saroyan, Nathaniel Hawthorne, Edgar Allen Poe, Sinclair Lewis, and Thomas Wolfe (USA); Anton Chekov, Ivan Turgenev, Maxim Gorky, Mikhail Sholokhov, and Ilya Ehrenburg (Russia); Grazia Deledda (Italy); and Selma Lagerlof (Sweden). He also translated six stories from Japanese of which the author of only one story is identified. (Needless to add, the translations were made from English.) Strikingly, Pudumaippithan explored literature from outside England, which he considered lacking in experiment, and looked for more artistically daring writing from Europe, Russia, the USA, and Japan.

However, despite his heavy investment in terms of time and energy in translating there is no evidence to suggest that Pudumaippithan's efforts had any lasting influence on contemporary literary trends.

POETRY

Pudumaippithan, unlike his fellow writers in the *Manikodi* camp, was deeply interested in classical Tamil poetry and its traditional forms. Some of his early essays focus on the aesthetics of such poetry. However, he himself did not write any poems, except one or two parodies, until the 1940s. During this time modernists were dissatisfied with the restrictions imposed by prosody and the conservatism of the themes handled in traditional poetry. Influenced both by Vedic hymns and Whitman, Bharati had experimented with prose poems. From the 1930s, Pudumaippithan's fellow writers, Ku. Pa. Rajagopalan and Na. Pitchamurthy, began to write prose poems. Pudumaippithan ridiculed them and considered 'prose poems' to be an oxymoron. However, in the last few years of his life he wrote poems by taking great liberties with prosody. He also composed occasional and impromptu verses. Considering how little poetry he wrote many lines continue to be remembered.

CORRESPONDENCE

An avid and lively correspondent many of Pudumaippithan's letters written to two young writers, T. M. C. Raghunathan and M. P. Somasundaram, have survived. Views and opinions expressed in his letters have an even sharper edge than in his published writings. Given the circumstances of his life, where he was separated from his wife for long periods, he wrote many letters which were preserved by Kamala. The surviving letters, numbering over eighty, provide interesting insights on conjugal relationships in modern Tamilnadu.

PLAYS AND FILM SCRIPTS

Pudumaippithan wrote two one-act plays: *Bakhta Kuchela* and *Saar, Nichayama Nalaikku*. *Bakhta Kuchela* is a response to mythological films based on the Krishna myth where the god helps his childhood friend. Pudumaippithan recasts it in modern times and brings in the issue of birth control and labour in a modern industrial setting. *Saar, Nichayama Nalaikku* – about one day in the life of an aspiring writer – recasts his earlier short story into a play.

After the inauguration of the Tamil talkie in 1931, through the late 1930s and the 1940s Tamil cinema emerged into its own. As film producers looked for writing talent and writers looked for better incomes a stream of authors joined films. After his break with *Dinasari*, Pudumaippithan decided to enter the film world. He wrote dialogues for one or two films, and joined the Gemini Studios of S. S. Vasan to work on the script of *Avvaiyar* (the film was eventually released only in 1953; none of his inputs went into the final script, being considered too highbrow for a popular audience). He then made the mistake of venturing into film production himself, attempting a film based on the Tamil classic *Kuttrala Kuravanji*. He lost heavily. Finally, he joined M. K. Thyagaraja Bhagavathar at an inopportune moment when he was slipping from superstardom following his imprisonment and subsequent acquittal in a sensational murder case. The film was being produced in Pune, where he took severely ill and was diagnosed with tuberculosis. One surviving script was published as *Vakkum Vakkum*. (It was plagiarised and made into a film by A. P. Nagarajan – *Saraswathi Sabatham*, 1966.) A couple of incomplete film scripts have survived in manuscript form.

REVIEWS, JOURNALISM, POLEMICS

Pudumaippithan was a pioneer in book reviewing in Tamil. Until the 1930s book reviews in the Tamil press were in the nature of notices advertising and informing readers about a book and mostly lacked critical perspective. Pudumaippithan was conscious of a reviewer's duty towards readers and believed that it was his responsibility not to mislead the reader. Misleading reviews, he feared, would kill the fledgling publishing industry and the emerging modern literary world. In the early and middle part of his career, as a subeditor in *Dinamani*, he kept up a flurry of book reviews, both short and long. Many of his reviews were sharp, scathing, and even abrasive, winning him many enemies.

Working as a journalist in a leading daily, at the height of the Indian freedom struggle and World War II, Pudumaippithan was necessarily involved in political literature. He wrote two biographies – one of Adolf Hitler (jointly authored with his fellow journalist N. Ramarathnam) and another of Benito Mussolini. Based on easily available newspaper despatches and other writings in English these two books provide the Tamil reader with a clear picture of the dangers of Fascism and Nazism, and the threat that they posed to world peace. He also wrote an unpublished and incomplete manuscript on Stalin at the peak of the World War which is largely sympathetic to the Soviet Union. He also wrote a short tract for the times on the nature of political power titled *Adhikaram Yarukku?* (Power for Whom?)

As a writer with strong opinions and critical views Pudumaippithan was easily drawn to polemics. In 1937 he was involved in a debate with his fellow *Manikodi* writers on the nature of translation (as opposed to adaptation, both acknowledged and unacknowledged), eroticism in literature, and variant readings in Bharati's poetry. But 1943 was the year of polemics for Pudumaippithan. At the height of World War II the government introduced many restrictions on the use of raw stock in films, and decreed that no film be of more than 10,000 feet. What started as a debate on this between Kalki, popular writer and the editor of an eponymous journal, and Pudumaippithan quickly turned into polemics on literary creativity and plagiarism. Pudumaippithan accused Kalki of plagiarism and used sharp language to criticise him. Apart from the long rivalry between the *Ananda Vikatan* and *Manikodi* dating from the 1930s it was fuelled by differing ideological positions on the nature of art.

POSTHUMOUS REPUTATION AND INFLUENCE

Pudumaippithan believed that he was not adequately recognised. But his premature death resulted in a spate of tributes and obituaries. As he died in penury leaving behind a young wife and a two-year-old daughter, Tamil writers came together to raise a purse in 1951. His young admirer, T. M. C. Raghunathan, wrote a biography on the occasion that established not only his reputation, but enshrined the personality of the quintessential writer who is ahead of his times, and at odds with the society at large, and attains posthumous fame. From the 1950s, Tamil literary culture forked into two directions: the first, the popular press which catered to a large audience, and second, a self-conscious artistic strand which elevated art to a pedestal and decried the philistinism of popular art. The left-progressive stream was at odds with both streams. Pudumaippithan was appropriated as the icon of the artistic strand and the left movement underscored the progressive aspects of his writing.

In the 1950s there was a left reaction to Pudumaippithan when his so-called decadent aspects – of pessimism and non-realist modes of writing – came in for criticism. In a famous essay Thi. Ka. Sivasankaran wrote, '*Veeravanakkam vendam*' (Don't idolise him), in the left-progressive journal, *Saraswathi*. In the 1990s, in the wake of the Dalit literary movement and the influence of postmodernism, his writings came in for both criticism and adulation. His texts were subjected to deconstruction and read to reveal upper-caste proclivities. On the other hand, his metafictional forms were seen as the precursors for post-realist, non-linear, and postmodernist writings. In this climate of renewed interest his uncollected writings were published and this was followed by the publication of the critical, variorum, and chronological edition of his collected works.

Seventy years after his death, Pudumaippithan remains one of the two axes – along with Bharati – around which modern Tamil literature revolves. His erratic genius notwithstanding, his writings continue to challenge today's readers and writers alike.

11

SUNDARA RAMASWAMY
Arch Modernist

HOW MANY INDIAN WRITERS can claim to be recognised and celebrated as one of their own in two language cultures. If one discounts Hindi and Urdu, few if any. Sundara Ramaswamy would rank in the top of such a non-existent list. When this Tamil writer died in October 2005 the leading Malayalam daily, the *Malayala Manorama*, observed in its editorial that his death was a loss to two language communities. A more apt tribute could not have been paid to him.

How did this come to be?

Sundara Ramaswamy was born in 1931 in Nagercoil, then part of the princely state of Travancore. He was raised in Kottayam, then in central Travancore, until he was eight, when his family moved to Nagercoil. This was in 1939 just as the news of the World War was breaking out. (His third novel, *Kuzhandhaigal Pengal Aangal*, is set in immediate pre-war Kottayam.) Sundara Ramaswamy spent his life in the town of Nagercoil – until his death.

Situated barely twenty kilometres from the Indian peninsula's southernmost tip, Kanniyakumari, its district headquarters was described once as 'the last outpost of Indian literature'. It was not until 1956 that Travancore was reorganised as part of the modern Kerala state. The Tamil-speaking regions of south Travancore, present-day Kanniyakumari district, joined the then Madras state, now Tamilnadu, in the same year, after a hard fought popular struggle. (Some of these events find echo in Sundara Ramaswamy's first novel, *Oru Puliyamarathin Kathai*.)

Growing up in the cultural intersection of Tamilnadu and Kerala, Sundara Ramaswamy grew up 'half-knowing' Malayalam, Sanskrit, and English. An attack of juvenile arthritis and subsequent indifferent health (a recurring theme in his writings) saw him barely reach school final. Despite his intermittent attendance in school some of his evocative short stories are about school life – my favourite being 'Our Teacher'. Tamil, which he used with such consummate mastery and nuance, he did not learn until he was about eighteen.

This bilingual milieu is central to Sundara Ramaswamy's writing. As a young Malayalam critic observed, Sundara Ramaswamy was introduced to the pathbreaking writings of Malayalam's greatest writers 'at the first signs of the dawn of modernism in Malayalam literature'. His first literary endeavour was to translate Thakazhi Sivasankara Pillai's *Thottiyude Magan* (The Scavenger's Son) into Tamil. His translation of another of Thakazhi's novels, *Chemmeen*, continues to be in print half a century after its first publication. Sundara Ramaswamy was associated with M. Govindan, the offbeat Malayalam cultural critic, and maintained an intimate relationship with many Malayalam writers. Translating several Malayalam poems into Tamil he kept Tamil readers informed of cultural happenings in Kerala with his comparative commentaries. When the centenary of D. C. Kizhakemuri, the founder of DC Books, the pioneering Malayalam publisher, was celebrated he was invited to give the keynote address.

~

Sundara Ramaswamy made his literary debut in late 1951 with the publication of an edited volume in memory of Pudumaippithan, the fountainhead of Tamil modernity, and an undying influence on his work.

In the early 1950s, Sundara Ramaswamy was drawn to the (undivided) CPI and came to know P. Jeevanandam, its leader and litterateur, a charismatic personality and legendary orator. Another key influence was T. M. C. Raghunathan, progressive writer and biographer of Pudumaippithan. Years later he recalled with understated humour that he was initially drawn to Raghunathan in the belief that he was possessed by Pudumaippithan's spirit.

Sundara Ramaswamy's early fiction was published in progressive literary journals, making his mark with short stories in the monthly, *Shanthi* (1955–7), edited by Raghunathan. After *Shanthi* folded up he continued to write acclaimed short stories in another progressive literary journal, *Saraswathi* (1955–62). His first novel was also serialised in this monthly. *Saraswathi*, edited by the communist V. Vijayabaskaran, was an exciting journal marrying art with left politics. No accident that Jayakanthan too flowered in this journal.

But in the years following Khrushchev's secret address to Communist Party of Soviet Union's XX Congress, exposing the brutalities of Stalin's regime, and the crushing of the democratic Hungarian Uprising (1956), Sundara Ramaswamy distanced himself from the left movement. These were difficult times when, with a sectarianism characteristic of the left, he was isolated and subjected to calumny – this continued to colour the left movement's relationship with him until his death nearly half a century later.

At this time Sundara Ramaswamy came in touch with Ka. Naa. Subramanyam, a writer of the *Manikodi* group who had a controversial reputation as a literary critic for celebrating art and running down popular writing and agitprop. Despite many differences, stated with respect in an obituary, he maintained a lifelong esteem for him. As he moved away from the left movement, Sundara Ramaswamy increasingly identified himself with an avant-garde modernism which functioned through the little magazines. This moment also coincided with the growing hiatus between popular literature appearing in mass magazines and self-conscious art in little magazines, and a widening rift between progressive literature and the little magazines. The little magazines were also a reaction to a dominant strand of Tamil identity politics that had a strong non-, if not anti-, Brahmin streak to it.

Never prolific, however, Sundara Ramaswamy kept a consistent stream of some free verse (he is considered one of the most prominent poets of the literary monthly, *Ezhuthu*, edited by C. S. Chellappa), and critical and polemical essays. Employing the pseudonym Pasuviah for his free verse, his early poetry is memorable for its declamatory style. With occasional bursts of poetry he wrote a little over a hundred poems in his career, most of them short, but still recalled by readers. With the folding up of *Saraswathi* he published in the little magazine *Deepam*, edited by the popular writer Naa. Parthasarathy; it was under his editorship that he also published in the popular weekly, *Kalki*.

In 1966, Sundara Ramaswamy completed his first novel, *Oru Puliyamarathin Kathai* (The Tale of a Tamarind Tree). It combines oral lore and history to narrate the story of change in a small town. The tamarind tree is the central character until it falls prey to the machinations of local business and politics and is ultimately poisoned to death. The disillusionment of the post-Independence era is writ large over this novel, and it manifests an acute understanding of time and the changes its passage ushers in through human agency. In this narrative oral lore and folk traditions are skilfully woven. Characters are carefully etched with a clear sense of their social location. The narrative brims with humour and satire, and the dialogues convincingly capture the dialect of the region for the first time in Tamil literary history. One of the earliest dialect novels in Tamil, it successfully employed the demotic language of the region. Not surprisingly therefore Sundara Ramaswamy remains to this day an inspiration for young writers from this region. *Oru Puliyamarathin Kathai* remains a classic despite contemporary critics ignoring it. The publication of this novel marked the end of the first phase of his writing, a phase characterised by social criticism combined with artistic finesse.

This was followed by an interregnum of silence lasting seven years until 1973. A literary critic described this hibernation as *ezhandu thavam* (a seven-year *tapas*). But the silence was caused by rather mundane reasons. Sundara Ramaswamy's relationship with his father, who disapproved of his literary pursuits, was tense. In a bid to assuage him he took over the reins of the family business, a textile shop in the town square. For nearly twenty years after this father's death in 1973, he struggled to ride the twin horses of business and art.

Sundara Ramaswamy announced his return with a combative *Savaal* (Challenge) in the little magazine *Gnanaratham*, arguably one of the most quoted of modern Tamil poems. His short stories of the time, collected and published in book form *Pallakku Thookkikal*, by the pioneering new publisher Cre-A, reveal a tighter language and a conscious attempt to experiment with form and content, challenging new readers. His later oeuvre of short fiction alternate between the storytelling of the first phase and the experimentation of the second phase. In all Sundara Ramaswamy wrote some eighty short stories, and definite shifts in his writing style and a determination not to repeat his artistic successes are easily discerned.

Ever a stylist, employing a language consciously crafted, shorn of traditional rhetorical devices, but brimming with satire, parody, humour, and metaphor, Sundara Ramaswamy's enquiring perspective marked him out distinctly. By the 1970s he was the figure that the progressive literature camp loved to hate. Further, Sundara Ramaswamy developed an increasing dissatisfaction with the state of Tamil literature and culture.

Despite his artistic success with short stories what made him a literary hero of sorts was his second novel. *J.J.: Sila Kurippukal* (JJ: Some Jottings), in its form and content, the studied mastery and precision of its language, and the sensitive and provocative formulation of ideas, was a rupture in the narrative tradition of Tamil fiction. The novel, complete with footnotes and appendices, as the biography of a fictional Malayalam writer, Joseph James (J. J.), created a literary sensation.

The Tamils – like the English, but unlike the French – do not have the stomach for ideas dressed up as literature. *J.J.: Sila Kurippukal* is a single swallow in that Tamil literary–intellectual summer. Its literary brilliance notwithstanding, it is very much a novel of ideas.

Its appearance in 1981, impressively produced by Cre-A, created a literary sensation with its overt intellectualism. Since then, despite being initially poorly distributed, the novel is in its eighteenth edition – a considerable achievement by the standards of serious Tamil literature. Almost every reader remembers the shock and exhilaration the novel caused on its first reading. The clever way in which the novel is structured, almost a *Künstlerroman*, of the fictional Malayalam writer, left readers gasping. Of course, in this entire make-believe the author had probably strewn around banana skins, chuckling as readers and critics stepped on them and tumbled headlong. The detailed depiction of the Malayalam literary world, while being rather novel, simultaneously triggered the search for Tamil parallels. Unfortunately, many readers got lost in this wild-goose chase, missing the import of the novel. This was often followed by (mis)identifying themselves with one or the other character; the progressives with Mullackal Madhavan Nair,

Tamil enthusiasts with Thamaraikkani, women writers with Chittukkuruvi, and so on. Sundara Ramaswamy's masterful parody and caricature only added to this effect.

However, it is a loss to read the novel at this level. It is nothing less than a thoroughgoing critique of Tamil culture and society and, by extension, much more. With the pretext of talking about the Malayalam literary world the novel indulges in a deep introspection of Tamil culture. Wrestling with the pressing philosophical questions of its time, it provides insights into ideas, institutions, and individuals, and the souring of idealism.

Despite the generally adverse, if not hostile, reaction to it from fellow writers and critics, the novel has continued to capture the imagination of young readers and writers. Left intellectuals were particularly cross with him for the philosophical challenge that it posed. Sundara Ramaswamy was unique among his generation of writers, in being taken seriously by new readers.

J.J.: Sila Kurippukal represents Sundara Ramaswamy at one of his peaks of writing prowess. And as such represents a phase of his writing career.

Sundara Ramaswamy wrote one more novel. By some coincidence his three novels are separated by intervals of a decade and a half. After the dazzling *J.J.: Sila Kurippugal* readers wondered what he would offer next. In 1998 he published *Kuzhandhaigal Pengal Aangal* (Children, Women, Men), a tome compared to the slim volume of his earlier two novels. And, uncharacteristically, it was set in a family, within the four walls of a home. At a time when postmodernism was the rage in Tamil literary circles, and the death of realist writing being declaimed from rooftops, and writers were experimenting with non-linear narratives and metafiction, Sundara Ramaswamy opted for a deceptively direct narrative.

Set in the years before the outbreak of World War II in September 1939, it is transparently autobiographical with a large dose of intertextuality evident to a reader of his earlier work. The narrator of *J.J.: Sila Kurippugal*, the Tamil writer Balu, figures as a boy and a major character. The long novel narrates incidents and ruminations in a Tamil Brahmin family in Kottayam torn as it is by the cataclysmic changes unleashed from political and social forces from all over the world over which the characters have little control. Written in over a hundred short chapters, which can be seemingly dropped or interchanged, the reader can almost dip into the novel at any point. Underrated by readers and critics alike its artistry is deceptive, concealing great craftsmanship.

The novel is also not without great personal significance. Aware perhaps that it was his last major work, Sundara Ramaswamy visited his childhood haunts in Kottayam, and refreshed his memory before embarking on its writing. His complex relationship with his father is more or less resolved in dealing with the character of S. R. S., Balu's father.

~

Sundara Ramaswamy turned to writing essays only in mid-career. At the invitation of Ka. Naa. Subramanyam, in 1963, he wrote his first essay, on his engagement with Subramania Bharati. It is a demonstration that he had caught the knack of writing the personal essay. For the next two decades he wrote essays occasionally and during the 1970s, in the heyday of the little magazine, he also indulged in polemics. Though much of it has lost relevance, his devastation of Akilon's novel *Chitrapavai* when it received the Jnanpith Award (1975) is a classic. Akilon never forgave him for this, and Sundara Ramaswamy's relationship with his first publisher Gana. Muthiah soured as he was not only Akilon's publisher, but also related to him by marriage. Sundara Ramaswamy's eponymous first collection of essays, published in 1984, was a slim volume with just fifteen essays, and included a list of another ten. These numbers were to change dramatically over the next decade and a half, and his views would win him both cloying admirers and vicious detractors.

In the early 1990s, Sundara Ramaswamy withdrew from his family business, a retail textile shop started by his father at the time of World War II. Unsuited to the ways of business he was never a happy businessman. But he bore the difficulties stoically, juggling writing and work, entertaining literary friends who made a beeline to Nagercoil, and spent long hours talking and debating. In the early 1990s when his only son, Kannan Sundaram, returned to his hometown after studies, he handed over its reins. Sundara Ramaswamy's lifelong dream of devoting full-time to writing and contemplation was now a reality. Meanwhile, his eldest daughter was diagnosed with multiple sclerosis. The pain of this dreadful disease was somewhat offset by the success of his second daughter as a rheumatologist in the USA. From the early 1990s, Sundara Ramaswamy began to visit her annually, with his wife, in her home in Santa Cruz, California (later dividing his time at his youngest daughter Thangu's home in Connecticut), and spent his time reading and writing in near solitude.

This period also marked his emergence as a public intellectual. His early youth in the decade immediately after Independence had been spent in the public, attending cultural events, and a closeness to the left progressive movement. His distancing from the Communist Party in the early 1960s was followed by an immersion in a narrow literary world cut off from the larger public sphere. This changed dramatically at the turn of the last decade of the last millennium.

In February 1992, early in her first term as chief minister of Tamilnadu, Jayalalithaa visited the temple town of Kumbakonam during the once-in-twelve-years Mahamaham festival. Enjoying her new-found Z+ security her callousness in the midst of a crowded watershed led to a stampede. Over fifty pilgrims died and many more were injured, a tragedy worsened by Jayalalithaa's lack of remorse. An angry Sundara Ramaswamy shot off a searing op-ed article to *Dinamani*, terming it a *padukolai* (a massacre). *Dinamani*'s editor Kasturi Rangan decided to carry it in the literary monthly *Kanaiyazhi* rather than in the mass-circulated daily. From that time Sundara Ramaswamy maintained a steady stream of essays and reviews.

The early 1990s were a great time of churning in India. The fragmentation of polity, the economic crisis, and liberalisation of economy; Masjid–Mandal; the break-up of the Soviet Union and the crisis of the communist parties; Ambedkar's birth centenary; and the rise of Dalit literary movement underpinned this churning. The Tamil intellectual world was sucked into this.

As noted Sundara Ramaswamy was freed from his work and had begun to devote full time to writing. Never one to jump into bandwagons he critically engaged with new ideas and trends. Open to new ideas he was also ill at ease with regurgitation of undigested ideas, and questioned half-baked ideas that masqueraded as postmodernism. Unlike other contemporary writers – Jayakanthan being a prime example – he read the works of younger writers and commented on them. In the 1990s new journals emerged and he used these avenues to express his views. Using the newly opened up leader pages of *Dinamani* he expressed views which ruffled many feathers. For instance, criticising the hugely celebrated film actor Sivaji Ganesan for his theatrical histrionics, Sundara Ramaswamy wondered if he had ever factored in the powerful lens that stood between the actor and the audience! We can also recall that he had once described MGR as a clown.

In the 1990s he enjoyed robust health, something he said he was not used to during his entire life. He was a very active correspondent writing letters every day. Letters were drafted before being typed and mailed, and it was a pleasure to receive them. Readers and fellow writers treasured them. At one time he even maintained a steady correspondence with a Terrorist and Disruptive Activities (Prevention) Act (TADA) convict which drew unwarranted attention from the state, but he was not deterred.

Sundara Ramaswamy was legendary for being parsimonious with praise. Authors who sought his endorsement became angry when it was not forthcoming, and the enemy camp swelled. When he occasionally lauded the work of a young writer it only infuriated other writers.

In 1987 he had launched a literary review, *Kalachuvadu*, which folded up in two years, after publishing eight substantive quarterly numbers and a bumper signing-off number. In late 1994 his son revived *Kalachuvadu* in a different form. Within a year he had also launched a publishing imprint in the same name, primarily to publish Sundara Ramaswamy's writings as well as reliable editions of the collected works of Tamil modern greats such as Pudumaippithan and G. Nagarajan. Despite his reputation Sundara Ramaswamy had been unhappy that his works were out of print most of the time, and these developments gave him new energy to write anew and consolidate older work. For instance, his earliest first effort, the translation into Tamil of Thakazhi Sivasankara Pillai's *Thottiyude Makan*, was retrieved from old volumes of *Saraswathi* and published in book form. The response of readers, starved of his writings for decades, delighted his heart, and gave him the energy to crank up his literary production.

Not only nectar, but also poison turns up in churning the milky ocean. With his strong views and uncompromising stance Sundara Ramaswamy was the object of vicious and motivated criticism, complicated by the fact of some of his self-proclaimed protégés turning against him. The success of an international Tamil literary conference, Tamil Ini 2000, that *Kalachuvadu* organised in September 2000, widened the fault lines. Sundara Ramaswamy was forced to expend his energies writing rejoinders, clarifying his views, and correcting wilful distortions.

Not surprisingly he was passed over for many awards. Cheekily, he once observed that the Sahitya Akademi not give him the award posthumously – a writer's wife dressed in widow's white receiving an award did not make for a fetching sight! The only real award, despite the miniscule purse that came with it, was the Asan literary prize – the Asan Smaraka Kavitha Puraskaram – named for the Malayalam poet Kumaran Asan. In the last years of his life the University of Toronto conferred on him the inaugural Iyal award for lifetime contribution to Tamil; and the Katha Choodamani was awarded by the Delhi-based Katha. It is not incidental that none of these three awards came from Tamilnadu.

In February 2005 he published 'Pillai Keduthal Vilai', a short story about a resourceful lower-caste girl who gets educated and becomes a teacher. The resentful upper castes of the village charge her with seducing a student and physically assault her. She goes missing for many decades and returns as a recluse, giving the name to the village (and the story). Very much a vintage Sundara Ramaswamy story, it leaves the reader with a suppressed anger about the inequities of village life in a distant corner of the country early in the century. A most unexpected response came from fringe elements who accused him of insulting Dalits (in spite of the fact that no Dalit character figured in the story) and launched a campaign against him. Kumudam, a popular Tamil weekly, which Sundara Ramaswamy used as a metaphor for all that was crass in Tamil society, settled scores by calling for his arrest. Despite many prominent intellectuals rallying behind him Sundara Ramaswamy was devastated. In the summer of 2005 he went on his annual visit to the USA. He fell ill, was hospitalised, and died of pulmonary fibrosis in California on 14

October 2005. His diary jottings of the time make for painful reading. The spiteful attacks had hastened his death. The coffin was flown to Nagercoil and his funeral, without any religious rites, was attended by one of the biggest congregations of Tamils writers ever seen.

~

CODA

This essay would not be complete without a personal note.

It was in my fifteenth year, in the summer holidays after my eleventh standard examination (1983), I first read *J.J.: Sila Kurippugal*. J.J.'s mocking query, 'Has Sivakami Ammal yet fulfilled her vow?' still rings in my ears. (An allusion to the immensely popular historical romance of Kalki, *Sivakami's Vow*; this thousand-plus-page novel, originally serialised for many years in the weekly *Kalki*, revolves around the vow made by Sivakami, the danseuse and lady love of the Pallava king Narasimhavarman, when she is captured by the Chalukya king.) Like many readers of my, and subsequent, generations, I read *J.J.* in full many times over, and dipped into it at random in moments of gloom and emptiness. Being a curious amalgam of Cherthala Krishna Iyer, Thamaraikkani, Mullackal Madhavan Nair, and much else, I never quite agreed with much of what Sundara Ramaswamy said. But a running inner dialogue with him continued. One of the few writers I wished to meet in person, since my first meeting with him in 1986, the dialogue proceeded enriching me. I can claim that he was proud of my activities, especially the variorum edition of the collected works of his great hero, Pudumaippithan, to which he contributed a long and memorable introduction. In 2002, I translated *J.J.* into English – for me, it was a rite of passage, a coming to terms with my own intellectual development.

12

JAYAKANTHAN
Enfant Terrible

DANDAPANI JAYAKANTHAN (1934–2015) WAS not yet forty when he received the Sahitya Akademi Award in 1972. Quite unusual as Tamil writers are deemed worthy of awards only after the hair turns grey. Since then he did not miss a single honour due to any Tamil writer: Rajarajan Prize, the Sahitya Akademi National Fellowship, Padma Shri and later the Padma Bhushan – you name it. The one award that eluded him, some say for decades, was awarded in 2005: the Bharatiya Jnanpith. With characteristic self-confidence, or should we say, immodesty, he stated that the Jnanpith was 'not a recognition, but an endorsement'!

Jayakanthan's oeuvre is staggering, especially considering that he wrote little in the last few decades of his life after an active writing career of three decades or so. Some forty novels and novellas, hundred-and-thirty-odd short stories, over a hundred essays, memoirs, film scripts, columns, a few poems and songs, and translations.

This school dropout, born in Manjakuppam in 1934, Cuddalore in northern Tamilnadu, began his life as a volunteer in the undivided CPI, distributing clandestine pamphlets at street corners when the party was underground. Little wonder then that despite his many instances of volte-face and embarrassing public statements Jayakanthan continued to be the blue-eyed boy of communists. A self-taught man, he claimed that he learnt to write by proofreading the books of Pudumaippithan as they were being issued systematically after his death.

Jayakanthan published his first stories when barely in his teens. Left journals such as *Samaran* and *Saraswathi* published his early stories. Following the pioneering Pudumaippithan he wrote stark and evocative portrayals of lower-class life in urban settings. For the first time rickshaw pullers, pressmen, prostitutes, and other footloose labourers were convincingly and empathetically portrayed in Tamil fiction. Who can forget the pressman of his story 'Treadle' who prints marriage invitations but cannot himself marry. If his subaltern characters shocked readers his bold depiction of their sexuality evoked even more opposition. Jayakanthan realised early that nothing paid more than controversy; thereafter he assiduously courted it. Until his death he remained in the limelight.

The philistine Tamil popular press sensed ready saleability in Jayakanthan's shock strategy. For the first time self-consciously serious writing began to find a place in it. At a time when literary writing in Tamil was getting ghettoised in the little magazines, Jayakanthan made deft use of this space and wrote with little inhibition. After *Saraswathi* folded up the popular weekly *Ananda Vikatan* became the vehicle of his writings from the early 1960s. Jayakanthan's protagonists also changed with the forum. From subalterns he changed tack to talk of urban-middle-class Brahmin life and explored bold themes such as incest, Oedipus complex, pre-marital sex, and notions of privacy and individualism. It has been rightly said that few writers – Brahmins not excepted – captured the Brahmin dialect as well as this non-Brahmin writer.

Soon Jayakanthan graduated from short stories to novels. *Parisukku Po* (Go to Paris!), *Sila Nerangalil Sila Manithargal* (Some People on Some Occasions), and *Oru Manithan, Oru Veedu, Oru Ulagam* (A Man, A Home, A World) betray similar concerns, especially an individual at odds with a putatively hostile society. For a generation between the late 1950s and the early 1970s not a year passed without one of Jayakanthan's writings being in the news, seriously debated and discussed in the Tamil public sphere. It is difficult to imagine today the furore caused by the short story '*Agni Pravesam*' in which an orthodox mother condones her seduced daughter without moralising by pouring a few mugs of water on her head. Jayakanthan's women are strong and wilful even if they often spoke his words rather than their own.

Except for the time when he edited the little magazine *Gnanaratham* in the early 1970s and the monthly *Kalpana*, he stuck to mainstream magazines such as *Kumudam*, *Dinamani Kadhir*, *Idhayam Pesugirathu*, and *Kumkumam*. When he did not write fiction he maintained a steady stream of columnar writing that suited his style immensely.

If writers remained writers alone they would not be public figures in Tamilnadu. If Jayakanthan was a celebrity even after virtually ceasing to write for the last two decades and more of his life, he was from the very beginning of his literary career in active public life dabbling in film-making, politics, and journalism. *Unnai Pol Oruvan* (1965), a film he made based on his own novel, inaugurated in a sense the 'art' film in Tamil and went on to win a national award. In the mid-1970s the film adaptation of his *Sila Nerangalil Sila Manithargal*, directed by the veteran A. Bhimsingh, fetched a National Award for Best Actress for Lakshmi in 1976.

Combined with his strong views on commercial Tamil cinema and the star cult, especially surrounding MGR – recall his *Cinemavukku Pona Chitthalu* – Jayakanthan's forays into film-making and scripting remained the only alternative cinema for a long time. His negative views on Tamil cinema grew from his adversarial position vis-à-vis Tamil identity politics and the Dravidian movement. Along with K. Balathandayutham, the stalwart of the CPI in Tamilnadu, Jayakanthan campaigned consistently against the DMK from the 1960s and once even took on Periyar in a writers' conference in Trichy in 1961, who smilingly acknowledged the young man's diatribe.

Taking a humanist position he also articulated a variety of neo-Brahminism defending all that was Indian and Hindu. Expressing his admiration for Vivekananda's brand of Hinduism, Jayakanthan was also influenced by the philosopher J. Krishnamurti – for some time during the 1970s Krishnamurti was the rage among Tamil writers, who included Sundara Ramaswamy, Ashokamitran, Piramil, Kovai Gnani, and Sukumaran – and Jayakanthan was happy when friends referred to him, abbreviating his name, as JK.

Representing a stream within the Indian left movement that lays great faith in the national bourgeoisie, Jayakanthan was closely associated with K. Kamaraj, supported the Emergency, justified the IPKF's presence in Sri Lanka, and defended the infamous anti-conversion law introduced by Jayalalithaa. Once he even contested in an election, and lost very badly.

To his credit Jayakanthan stopped writing fiction in the late 1980s as he felt that he had run out of creative steam, switching to writing columns instead. His powerful, but humourless, prose cut him out for this task. He also penned memoirs: on his political life, his life in the world of arts and letters, and his experiences as an on-and-off journalist. Despite being self-serving they provide an insightful record of the times.

Voicing politically incorrect views kept Jayakanthan in the limelight. After a brief visit to the USA in the mid-1990s he called it a socialist state. If he wrote the novel *Jaya Jaya Sankara* in the 1970s to extol the Sankaracharya Chandrasekhara Saraswathi as the epitome of nobility and a fitting rebuttal to atheism, his *Hara Hara Sankara* (2004), at the time of the arrest of Jayendra Saraswathi on charges of murder by the Jayalalithaa government, was an unabashed apology.

Modelling himself on the great communist leader P. Jeevanandam, Jayakanthan was a forceful public speaker with the ability to hold the audience with his brilliant modulation and stentorian voice even when voicing unacceptable views. To say that his brilliant recitation of Tamil verse – of Bharati and of Kamban – is inspiring would be an understatement.

Jayakanthan's public presence in a culture starved of intellectual luminaries kept him in the reckoning. His public positions were frequently defined by his imagined rivals. His statement, 'A Mahabharata war is now on in Indian politics. I've sworn that I shall not bear arms in this war. But I will be the charioteer', reveals as much about his politics as his swagger.

Discarding the white kurta – for long the regulation attire of Tamil writers – he wore fashionable clothes and insisted on posing for pictures with a smoking pipe on his lips and a twirled moustache. He turned up in trousers for public meetings and sat cross-legged on the dais. He was probably as short as C. N. Annadurai, but people always thought of him as a giant. In a society where writers have been seen as only supplicants Jayakanthan created a new persona for the writer. Tamil writers should remain ever indebted to him for this even if the larger society had to put up with many toothless clones. The ink portraits at the time of his sixtieth birthday, by his friend, the great painter K. M. Adhimoolam, capture the personality of Jayakanthan even better than photographs.

At least two generations of Tamil readers and writers were raised on Jayakanthan's works; but it is a moot question if the present generation sees him as more than a meteoric moment in literary history. Critics have been even harsher. Being loud, argumentative, shrill is not the best route to literary acceptance these days. If talking through the characters with ubiquitous exclamation marks was not enough Jayakanthan delivered long homilies in his prefaces. Prapanjan, the Tamil writer, once reviewing his collected stories likened them to 'continuously listening to a public meeting from morning to evening'.

Jayakanthan was even more ill-served by translation. Though stories abound about his success in Russian translation, translations into English (by A. A. Hakim, K. Diraviam, and others), perhaps because they predate the present boom in Indian Writing in English and Indian literature in translation, failed to leave a mark. Recent translations by K. S. Subramanian and by his own daughter Deepalakshmi too have failed to make the cut.

Jayakanthan's last years were not good. Indulgence in tobacco and alcohol, and his advocacy of ganja for a chemical-free high took their toll. A man who refused to be a supplicant – stories float about how he confronted MGR and Karunanidhi on equal terms – was sadly domesticated. He accepted a solatium offered by the DMK for his medical expenses, and, in return, the lifelong critic of the Dravidian movement declared that he withdrew all his earlier criticism. When, at the time of his death in 2015, the popular film lyricist Vairamuthu produced Jayakanthan's endorsement of him as Tamil's greatest poet – later proved to be phoney – the denouement was complete.

13

ASHOKAMITRAN
Aesthetics of the Ordinary

ASHOKAMITRAN (1931–2017) IS THE most translated of Tamil writers. Over the last two decades a stream of translations of his writings – by able translators – has been published. Apart from being anthologised in Adil Jussawalla's *New Writing from India* (1974) decades ago, *Shoot at Site* (1980) was followed by *Water* (1993, 2001), *The Eighteenth Parallel* (1993), *The Colours of Evil* (1998), *A Most Truthful Picture and Other Stories* (1998), *Sand and Other Stories* (2002), *My Father's Friend and Other Stories* (2002), *Mole!* (2005), and *Today* (2008). Recently, in 2017, *Manasarovar*, *Still Bleeding from the Wound*, and *The Ghosts of Meenambakkam* appeared in the Penguin silver classics imprint along with his non-fiction book, *Fourteen Years with Boss*.

Few Tamil writers have been better served by English translation than Ashokamitran with two fine translators – the late Lakshmi Holmström and N. Kalyan Raman – giving him the best treatment possible. That he was a bilingual writer ('Personally, I am forced to struggle a lot merely because I think and write in two languages,' observes the narrator of *Mole!*) who could write nuanced English prose and was a regular presence on the Indian literature scene also helped familiarise non-Tamil readers with his work. He published original work in the *Illustrated Weekly of India* and used to submit work regularly to *Encounter*.

Interest in his work, however, predates the present boom in the translation and publication of Indian literature in English. This is most surprising considering that the choice of texts for translation is most often the exotic, while Ashokamitran's work is truly modernist, in the classical Western sense of the term, and is informed by his wide reading in modern Western writing, especially fiction. Perhaps this is the reason why his work apparently lends itself to translation into English with ease. Ashokamitran's stories are mostly set in Chennai, the city of his adulthood, and in the twin cities of Hyderabad/ Secunderabad, the place of his birth and early life. While the Tamil village rarely figures in his stories, people from other cultures are convincingly etched. Ashokamitran is exceptional in the world of Tamil letters in that many Muslim characters people his fiction. While many flounder even to capture the everyday reality of the neighbouring street, he accomplishes plausible portrayals of the faraway. Few Tamil writers can match Ashokamitran in this.

Ashokamitran's writing career spread over six decades and he wrote until the very end of his life. But for the fourteen years (1952–66) at Gemini Studio as a PR assistant, he was a full-time writer. Though he could write English with ease, he chose, early in his career, to be a full-time Tamil writer – a brave decision considering how difficult it is to make a living doing so. As editor of the middle-brow literary monthly, *Kanaiyazhi*, he could not have made much. He wrote predominantly short stories (nearly three hundred). He also wrote ten novels, but as he never tired of mentioning in his prefaces, his short stories are but parts of a novel and his novels a collection of short stories in a certain order. They are all set in the city, among lower-middle-class people. As a full-time writer he seized every opportunity to write. His non-fictional writing too is therefore substantial. As a voracious reader he commented extensively, if briefly, on world literature as well as reviewing contemporary Tamil writing. His one blind spot was his adulation of the critic Ka. Naa. Subramanyam.

It is difficult to write about Ashokamitran's stories because nothing much ever seems to happen. And his characters, almost mundane and quotidian, are even less memorable. As the Tamil writer Jeyamohan observed none of Ashokamitran's characters are memorable. There are no real protagonists. The names of the characters are nondescript. Their physical traits are rarely ever described. Dialogues and conversations are brief and matter of fact, revealing little emotion. Yet their life situations remain with us. For the most unlikely events take place in their lives which, however, never get dramatic treatment. Ashokamitran consciously, or perhaps by second nature, avoids the dramatic and the spectacular. Often the incidents strike one as absurd. This element of the absurd, coupled with prose stripped bare, apparently carelessly written, with no striking images, metaphors, or similes, make it possible to miss his true import. Ashokamitran's art can be termed the aesthetic of the ordinary. Precisely the aesthetic that makes him such an extraordinary writer. The overtly striking aspect of his writing is the wry, understated humour – a quality never absent, whether it is a story, novel, essay, or columnar comment. Understatement is not the Tamil language's forte. It is in Ashokamitran's.

A keen observer of the quotidian Ashokamitran is also the least ambitious of the great writers. His admiration of Tolstoy and Dostoyevsky notwithstanding he certainly cannot be compared to the Russian greats in terms of bulk. The recent spate of hefty Tamil novels made him shudder. Most of his putative novels are extended short stories or novelettes. Perhaps only *The Eighteenth Parallel* may be termed a real novel, in its relative breadth, scope, and wideness of canvas.

If all these aspects make Ashokamitran a modernist writer, his world view is profoundly informed by what can be described as a deeply Indian philosophical orientation. Perhaps this world is an illusion. Absurd at best. Despite which the men and women are real, in their actions and their suffering. His depiction of women is deeply moving and sympathetic, and in this he reminds the Tamil reader of Pudumaippithan. Ashokamitran portrays human travails with a paradoxical combination of deep empathy and studied detachment. Pessimism, if not fatalism, pervades his creative world. There is little cause for celebration in his stories. At the end the reader is often left feeling disturbed. But the understanding delivered by his stories, of the human predicament, is only liberative.

Ashokamitran's Tamil prose has but little root in Tamil tradition. Often, on close examination, the syntax appears to be a translation of sentences thought out in English. (Ashokamitran often translates the English conversation of his characters into formal written Tamil with a parenthetical reference to it.) With his almost absolute equanimity in handling the conundrum of life and a carefully nurtured but deceptive craft, consistency was the hallmark of his writings. If his work did not cause rapture, it did not disappoint either. Such a verdict fits neatly with his world view and his approach to the art of writing. A particularly cantankerous Tamil critic, Venkat Swaminathan, once derisively likened Ashokamitran's writings to the habitual making of *kai-murukku* (the great Tamil savoury) by old women. But would the gourmet not walk miles to eat a delicacy that never disappoints?

Despite Ashokamitran's considerable, if not staggering, output, critical attention was late in coming. Apart from a 1993 special number of the little magazine, *Kanavu*, and an extended essay as part of a series on modern Tamil writers by Jeyamohan, I cannot think of any other considered writing about Ashokamitran's work. There have of course been journal reviews; and Gnani Sankaran, journalist and theatre personality, who edited an Ashokamitran reader, was a consistent champion of his works. On the other hand, he was often the target of some vicious criticism. When he was given the Sahitya Akademi

Award (1996), a prominent personality of the CPI (M)'s literary front, Tamilnadu Progressive Writers and Artistes Association, condemned the Akademi. The then DMK government went one step further: its Tamil development minister is said to have written to the Akademi's president, U. R. Ananthamurthy, questioning why 'a pessimistic writer' was being honoured.

Many reasons can be discerned for this unhappy situation. The understated and muted quality of his writings is not particularly amenable to loud appreciation. Rather, it calls for quiet absorption and introspection. Perhaps he did not receive sufficient critical attention because he straddled both worlds – of commercial publishing and of literary little magazines – and had fallen between the two. As a full-time writer Ashokamitran could have never afforded to write only in little magazines. It is also surprising that Ashokamitran's writing was published so widely in the largely philistine Tamil commercial magazines, in the 1970s and 1980s, especially in their annual Deepavali festival numbers. Other than discerning readers Ashokamitran also captured the imagination of many, then, young and promising writers. Writers as diverse as Prapanjan, Jeyanthan, Dilip Kumar, Subramania Raju, Devaki Gurunath, and Era. Murugan – some of whom were to acquire a significant presence in the Tamil literary scene later – solicited Ashokamitran's forewords for their first collections of short stories, even in the 1980s. Particular mention must be made of Narmadha Pathippagam's publisher T. S. Ramalingam who persisted in publishing him unmindful of limited sales.

Things changed dramatically in the early years of the millennium. A serendipitous review of his short novel, *Water*, by the noted Malayalam writer Paul Zacharia in tehelka.com caused a literary sensation and triggered critical interest in Ashokamitran. A decade later Ashokamitran caught the fancy of Aravind Adiga, who came to meet him more than once in

Chennai, and went on to write a fine essay in *Outlook*. In the
last decade of his life he became somewhat of a literary star,
and despite not being a public speaker at all – he addressed, if
that is the word, the audience in a conversation style – became
somewhat of a star personality.

OBSERVER OF TAMIL CINEMA

What first drew Adiga was a slim volume of Ashokamitran's
essays on his years at the Gemini Studios, *My Years with Boss*
(now expanded as the slightly longer *Fourteen Years with Boss*).
Let me here consider his Tamil essays on cinema (anthologised
as *Iruttilirundu Velicham*, 1997). Ashokamitran evokes the
ambience of the studio which played a decisive role in the
formation of the cinema industry, not only in Tamilnadu. Despite
his characteristic understated and wry style he can barely conceal
his admiration for the boss, S. S. Vasan. He provides fascinating
details about how Gemini worked: the army of employees, the
various specialised departments (story, dance, stunts, etc.), the
ruthless editing that Vasan practiced, the planned PR exercise. It
is an insider's account which is at once detached. Ashokamitran
also records Tamil/Gemini cinema's close interaction with the
Telugu and Hindi films of those days. His account of the making
and marketing of *Avvaiyar*, and how Rajaji willingly let himself
be used to suit an anti-Dravidian movement agenda, is my
pick of the essays. Apart from an insightful section of the star
system – where he retrieves the achievements of yesteryear
actresses in the face of great adversity – his elaborate account of
the studio system is set in an all-India context. No historian of
Indian cinema of the 1960s can afford to ignore Ashokamitran.

Ashokamitran was unlike other Tamil intellectuals of those
times who turned their nose on popular cinema, preferring the
art circuit (of which he was not unfamiliar). (The tide has now

turned: present-day Tamil intellectuals are obsessed with the popular.) His appreciation of Vasan's film-making is evident. 'Like all Gemini films, *Mr Sampath* had an easy-paced storyline and was interesting.' 'A film by Gemini was received with acclaim not for individuals: actors, actresses, music composer or cinematographer. In a Gemini film all these aspects would always be up to the mark. That this was what the audience expected was known to Vasan…. The wholehearted cooperation of all concerned was what contributed to the excellence of Gemini films. Even a person who appeared for a single moment on the screen would execute his job as though it was his life's mission.'

Well, with such a wonderful beginning, what went wrong with Tamil cinema? 'A film called *Parasakthi* [scripted by Karunanidhi], a skinny, egg-eyed, loud-voiced V. C. Ganesan – a youth who came to be known as Sivaji came to act in that film.' In Ashokamitran's view, 'In the twenty years [before *Parasakthi*] Tamil cinema, right at the moment when it had slowly freed itself from the Parsi theatrical beginnings and had begun to come to grips with "a [visual] language" unique to cinema, was pushed back to the old drama style.' In an uncharacteristic passage, a real giveaway, he employs a powerful metaphor to drive home his point. 'No doubt *Parasakthi* is a milestone in Tamil cinema. But it pushed the cinematic approach to the background. Like a monstrous insect that kills the male after mating and itself dies after laying the eggs, *Parasakthi* pushed cinema to the background and left Tamil theatre fighting for its very life.'

Many of the essays are interspersed with such observations on how Tamil cinema came to be distorted by the Dravidian movement. Ashokamitran goes so far as to state that even in communist Bengal and Kerala this kind of cultural change ushered in by a social reform movement did not take place. Ashokamitran anticipates criticism in his typical understated manner. 'Examples of sublime excellence in Tamil are always different from those held in other states and countries. To state that such examples are of doubtful quality is now generally believed to be against ideas opposed to social justice.' The sting is in the tail and it often landed him in trouble. An insensitive comment on drawing Jewish parallels with the lot of Tamil Brahmins put him in a spot. Like Borges it is better that Ashokamitran is not judged by his political views.

MOLE!

Among Ashokamitran's works *Mole!* is my favourite. Though the original Tamil edition described itself as a novel the text defies easy slotting in any genre. It could as well be described as a work of non-fiction, a travelogue, a memoir, an autobiographical narrative, or a collection of short stories. In fact, two of the chapters of the Tamil original set aside by the publisher to keep the book under two hundred pages were later published separately as short stories.

Mole! has its origins in the year that Ashokamitran spent at the University of Iowa's International Writing Program (1973–4). Ashokamitran was in his early forties when he was invited as the first Tamil writer to join the programme. This invitation came when it was still not common for Indians, especially language writers, to travel to the West. Therefore, even if travelogues were a staple of the Tamil commercial magazines, sensitive accounts of foreign travels were absent. (The travelogues of A. K. Chettiar, the renowned maker of the first documentary on Gandhi, who wrote more like an ethnographer in participant observation, were exceptions.) As Ashokamitran observed shortly after his return from Iowa:

Scores of people, on their return from the US, have written about the American cities, and its roads, cars and buildings, and hamburgers and ice creams. If I had been one such tourist, I too might have written on similar lines. But as one who has lived for months amidst Americans and developed some intimacy with them, I am unable to talk about them in such terms.

And then in his typical style he adds, 'A journey like this remains important for a lifetime. I strive to clarify this in my writing.'

Ashokamitran's work is strongly located within the coordinates of a certain physical space and a specific social class – a milieu, of mostly lower-middle-class Brahmins, he portrays with a unique combination of empathy and understatement. His world view is also largely determined by this materiality and is suffused by a particular stream of Indian monist philosophical tradition. But it is the ability of his writings to transcend these limits that makes Ashokamitran a great writer.

Mole! is structured like a travelogue. It begins at an immigration queue and ends on the day the narrator leaves Iowa City for his home. The narrator is the author himself. While this is not stated expressly, neither is it concealed in fictionalisation. At various points in the novel Ashokamitran's real name J. Thyagarajan, a common upper-caste Tamil name, is mentioned. The narrator constantly complains, in mock seriousness or in good humour, about how his name is mispronounced by writers from dozens of other countries. Of one person he says:

Distorting my name in a way that was possible only for him.... My name remained a riddle, not amenable to the grasp of the people from both eastern and western countries. To eliminate any difficulties on this score, I wrote my name down in large, block letters and showed it to them. That did not help, either. They were able to read and pronounce clearly certain truly

odd permutations of letters, but none could pronounce my
name properly.

Consequently, he gets called variously as 'Tagarazan', 'Takka
Rayan', and so on.

On a cold afternoon, on a boat on the river Mississippi,
he wonders:

I reproached myself for having been so reckless and insane.
How foolhardy of me to have travelled abroad like this! I could
not get proper food, and there was no one around to help me
learn the ropes here. There was not a soul with whom I could
share the ups and downs of my days. This cold was choking my
very breath....

What is such a person, all lost, doing in a country thousands of
miles away? Adherence to strict dietary preferences is significant
to the narrator's orthodox Brahmin background. He can only eat
cereal, milk, fruit juice, and coffee for most of his stay. Even garlic,
not to speak of meat, is taboo. However, in an extremely sensitive
chapter, which centres on garlic, the narrator demonstrates his
ability to transcend the narrow limits of his own genesis. The
smell of the garlic used by his housemate – Choe, a Korean
writer – envelopes the whole apartment. Everything, every bowl
and dish, smells of garlic. Complaints are of no avail for the
roommate does not even recognise its presence. The pervasive
presence of garlic drives the narrator to obsessive preoccupation,
while it is an unobtrusive part of life for his roommate. Choe is
one of the few persons at whom he shows anger. (Once again
it is expressed in characteristic understatement: 'I knocked my
friend's door. The third time, you couldn't have called it a mere
knock.') Choe is no doubt alien to the writer-narrator. As he

overhears Choe's telephonic conversation he notices that, 'A lot of words in his language began with "ha" and ended in "ha". From his conversation, I could not even make out whether the news was good or bad.' The news *is* bad: Choe is shattered to hear about his mother's death. We find him in the narrator's embrace with scarcely a word spoken. A good writer would have stopped at that – a demonstration of humanity, across cultures, in times of adversity. But not Ashokamitran. The chapter ends with the lines: 'I haven't forgotten how I had sat next to him in that apartment in Iowa City, ten thousand miles away from either of our two countries, holding him tightly in my embrace. Even then, a faint smell of garlic was coming off him.'

The episode of the Italian girl, Ilaria, who is in the university to study creative writing, is one of the finest. Ashokamitran's ability to depict tricky human situations with almost effortless ease is best demonstrated here. Nowhere does he state that Ilaria is depressed. Nor is her developing affection for the narrator expressed clearly, or for that matter his subtle attempts to ward off her emotional clinging. But no sensitive reader can be left untouched by the subtlety of Ashokamitran's craft.

Finally, on the title and the translation. Ashokamitran titled his Tamil novel *Otran!*. Literally it translates as 'Spy', but N. Kalyan Raman has appropriately preferred 'Mole'. While it is indicated in chapter ten that it is the title of a novel by an Ethiopian writer Abie Gubegna (Ashokamitran goes a step further, naming another chapter 'Supermole', after a novel by a Latin American writer!), one cannot think of a more apt title. But who is the mole? By constantly judging and understanding one society/culture in terms of the other, whom is he informing on? Is he informing on American culture to a Tamil audience? Or is it the other way round? While the narrator interprets details of American life to his Tamil reader he also betrays the interstices and deep secrets of his own lived culture. Ashokamitran plays on this ambiguity (suggested also by the exclamation mark in the title) with awareness and skill.

Translation only adds to the complexity and fuzziness of the Tamil text *Otran!*. Ashokamitran's prose is deceptively simple and is heavily influenced by English syntactic structures and expressions. Paradoxically this makes translation into English difficult. Slipping into banality is a pitfall difficult to avoid. Kalyan Raman's translation (all quotes above from the novel draw from his translation) retains the subtlety of the original and is a good read in English.

LAST NOVEL

Ashokamitran never lost his touch. *India 1948*, his last novel, his ninth, was published a few years before his death in early 2017. Few authors write when they are past eighty. Fewer still write well. Ashokamitran was a rare exception. Consistency was the hallmark of Ashokamitran. That recognition was late in coming might explain his longevity.

India 1948, written after he was well past eighty, does not fail to impress. In many ways this is vintage Ashokamitran. 'India 1948' would be a most unlikely title for a work of fiction. But, not unlike the titles of many of his other works, it is simple, direct, and yet apt. Most of his few hundred stories have single-word titles.

Probably because he was born and spent his youth outside Tamilnadu Ashokamitran revelled in choosing non-Tamil locations, and often even non-Tamil actors, and yet succeeded in evoking the milieu and the characters with great conviction. In one of his novellas the protagonist is a failed Argentine film-maker.

India 1948 begins with the first-person narrator making the long journey from Detroit to Mumbai. The protagonist's name is

Sundar – something that is revealed to the reader only in the latter part of the novel when his mother addresses him by name. The experience of the long journey on a hopping flight is described in some detail. Amidst these details the careful reader can sense that something is amiss – a fact that is grasped immediately by his widowed mother on his unannounced arrival in the small hours of night.

Sundar, married to his cross cousin – not by choice, as the reader understands as the narrative unfolds; in fact, the predicament of most of his characters is that they find themselves in situations not of their making – has found a new wife on his two-year assignment in the USA to train as a motor engineer. The woman is from a rich Gujarati family; widowed young, but now studying in Harvard. As in many of his stories the first encounter occurs by chance: Sundar misreads her name (Lakshmi) as a Tamil one, and attends her talk. Soon a relationship develops as Lakshmi takes the initiative to build it into a conjugal one, though it appears to lack any romantic touch. Sundar lets himself be led and yet remains honest and true to himself. He is however wracked by guilt for a choice that could emotionally hurt his long-suffering wife and damage his family's social standing. The year is 1948 when bigamy was not only legal, but also common. But Sundar neither wants to hurt nor deceive his dear ones. This predicament creates the tension that underlies this novel.

The novel is set during 1946–8. It soon becomes clear that it is not an arbitrary time frame. Rapid social and political changes have transformed the country in these momentous years. Sundar had left a placid world – a country ruled by the British – to return two years later to a changed world, a new nation run by brown sahibs. Characteristically, Ashokamitran indicates and suggests these changes rather than describe them. The visible external changes and the protagonist's inner turmoil provide another axis for the unfolding of the narrative.

The novelty of a Tamil family living through difficult times in the faraway metropolis of Mumbai provides a backdrop that cast the characters in a contrasting light, their deeply held values and mores challenged by apparently alien customs. The mobility – spatial and social – of an impoverished Tamil Brahmin family from Palghat to Chennai to Mumbai to the USA, and the family's life set in Mumbai forms a scaffolding for the characters' wrestling with changing values and mores.

As in much of his other works, it is impossible not to empathise with Ashokamitran's women. Put in the most disturbingly adverse situations, in circumstances not of their own making, his women act with grace, refusing to be cowed down. The last lines when Sundar's mother and his Gujarati wife hug each other are a fitting denouement – Indian men with any sense of honour can only hang their head in shame on reading them.

14

M. L. THANGAPPA
Classic Translator

TAMILS ARE JUSTIFIABLY PROUD of being the inheritors to one of the longest unbroken traditions of poetry writing in the world. But surprisingly they have not adequately celebrated, until his death, someone who translated this tradition and took it to a larger world.

'Hiding your light under the bushel' is an old-fashioned saying. But it comes immediately to mind when one thinks of M. L. Thangappa (1934–2018), the distinguished translator of Tamil poetry into English (among other things). I cannot recall the last time a seventy-five-year-old man's first real book was published by a major publisher and went on to win the Sahitya Akademi's translation award. Until *Love Stands Alone: Selections from Tamil Sangam Poetry* was published in 2010 (followed a year later by *Red Lilies and Frightened Birds*) he was unknown in the world of Indian English writing.

In the Tamil literary world Thangappa had a different, if niche, status. Known largely as a writer of traditional verse and a critic of free verse, he kept up a steady stream of poetry over half a century and more. An early member of the editorial collective of *Thenmozhi*, he was a great champion of *thani* Tamil (pure Tamil) and eschewed the use of all non-Tamil words. An activist in the cause of language, he once returned an award given to him by the Government of Puducherry (Pondicherry) for its perceived anti-Tamil stance. Never one to privilege intellectual work over activism, he gave equal time to whatever cause demanded his attention. In the last years of his life his time was taken by editing *Theli Tamil*, a little magazine championing pure Tamil. Thangappa wrote many essays reflecting on human life and was an avid correspondent. A man of few words, his views and feelings found expression in long letters. He was a pioneer of environmental activism, taking up ecological issues when it was unfashionable to do so.

In the last decade of his life Thangappa found new fame through his translations. Traditionally the English language is the bugbear of Tamil teachers – there is still an undergraduate degree in Tamil (BLitt) offered by universities in Tamilnadu which can be acquired without knowing a single word of English.

Born in Kurumpalaperi, a village in Tirunelveli district in the deep south of Tamilnadu, not far from the mythical birthplace of Tamil, the Pothikai hills, Thangappa came from a family of Tamil pandits. Thangappa was a somewhat precocious child and when barely a boy he could recite scores of Tamil poems. (This immersion in Tamil verse at an impressionable age had a very peculiar effect on his prosodic skills. His keen ear could always detect even minor variations or improvisations in metric forms even when not being able to actually name them.) When Thangappa went to the then venerable St. John's College, Palayamkottai, his grasp of idiomatic English, already imbued from reading English fiction, was buttressed by reading the Bible and the Romantic poets taught by learned teachers, including European clergymen who lectured there.

In the late 1950s his friendship with a fellow Tamil poet, Tha. Kovendhan, made a deep impact on his life. At his egging Thangappa began to translate classical Tamil poetry into English. This was a decade before A. K. Ramanujan discovered Tamil poetry in the dark corridors of the University of Chicago's Harper Library. These were the years of the rise of

Tamil identity politics. Proclaiming the glory of Tamil culture
to the larger world, through the medium of English, informed
these attempts.

Inspired by English poetry, especially the romantics,
Thangappa's early translations were set in rhyme and had a
quaint ring. But soon he gave this up for free verse. In 1970, three
years after A. K. Ramanujan's *The Interior Landscape*, Thangappa
published *Hues and Harmonies from an Ancient Land*. Despite
not having the benefit of an editor and being privately published
the slim volume saw much purchase among Tamil enthusiasts.
Hues and Harmonies signalled his genius for translating classical
poetry. In this phase we can discern his habit of not translating
stock epithets and formulaic phrases, and a penchant to explain
and paraphrase a bit – a desperate sign of wanting the non-Tamil
reader to understand. By the 1980s, when I had begun to work
closely with him, he was already moving towards terseness and
brevity. It has been said that great works of literature should be
translated anew for every generation. In a manner of speaking
Thangappa has done that himself revising his translations (for)
every generation.

There is a long tradition of translating Sangam poetry into
English and, to a certain extent, other European languages.
It began with the Orientalist interest in Tamil, largely as
counterweight to the Sanskrit bias of Indology. Even by the
end of the nineteenth century, as the Sangam classics went
into print, G. U. Pope had identified *Purananuru* as 'heroic
poetry' and had begun to translate from it. In the post–World
War II period American academic interest in India had taken
considerable proportions. A. K. Ramanujan stepped into
the scene, publishing *Fifteen Poems from a Classical Tamil
Anthology* (1965) followed by the celebrated *The Interior
Landscape* (1967) and the more substantial *Poems of Love and*

War (1985). The directness of the poems broke the Western stereotypes, based on an exclusive focus on Sanskrit literature, that Indian poetry could only be ornate. Ramanujan made classical poems read like contemporary ones. His reflections on translation and scholarly afterwords fed into the academic fields of postcolonial and translation studies. If Sangam poems are now found in anthologies of world literature the credit goes to Ramanujan alone.

Thangappa had only a nodding acquaintance with this tradition. But when I first met him in the early 1980s, as a high-school student, it was clear to me that he wanted his translations to be contemporary and to be read by a non-Tamil audience. But given his personality and his milieu he had little knowledge of the English publishing world. Over the years his draft translations accumulated in his chaotic study, finding occasional publishing avenues in little known Tamil magazines.

I was fascinated with the manuscripts he shared with me. From the late 1980s it became my mission to get his translations published. I began to act as his typist, secretary, editor, collaborator, and PR person all rolled into one. A skilled translator of poetry Thangappa was unconformable with writing English prose and did not feel up to writing a framing introduction to the poems. I decided to write the introduction. Reading, interpreting, comparing, composing, editing, circulating his translations, and knocking on the doors of publishers for a quarter of a century was a rewarding exercise even if it had been often punctuated by frustration.

By the late 1980s, I had a clean manuscript ready. Penguin was the first to reject it. Further rejection slips came at a furious pace over the 1990s. In 2007, R. Sivapriya who had edited me at Orient Longman (Orient BlackSwan) joined Penguin and took charge of the Black Classics. I promptly submitted sample translations. The reaction was incredible. Facing rejections for decades I was little prepared for the enthusiasm with which it was received.

The first questions everyone asked were: Who is he? Where was he until now?

The bigger challenge was the cult status of A. K. Ramanujan. Ramanujan was not just an acclaimed poet, but also a scholar with a named chair in a famed American university. He had inaugurated a new approach to translating Indian classical poetry in contemporary American English resorting to modernist techniques such as idiosyncratic typographical arrangement. Was there a place for another translation by an unknown translator?

Arvind Krishna Mehrotra, and the University of Chicago philologist, Whitney Cox – both of whom provided endorsements for *Love Stands Alone* – raised this question and still found it worthy. Every reviewer unfailingly asked this question. A young poet, reviewing the book, said that she compared Thangappa and Ramanujan poem by poem, and gave up saying, 'this goddamn Thangappa can stand on his own'.

So what accounts for Thangappa's success?

Thangappa is an accomplished Tamil poet. As a teacher for over twenty-five years lecturing at various colleges of the Puducherry government, Sangam literature was the staple of his teaching, parsing and interpreting the terse poems for generations of students. His mastery of Sangam vocabulary and prosody is such that he has even written a modern 'guide poem' in Sangam Tamil: *Iyarkai Attrupadai* mimics the *attrupadai* genre to guide an urban youth to the pleasures of nature. Here was tradition encountering talent at its best. Sundara Ramaswamy's words in his novel *J.J.: Sila Kurippugal* about one Cherthalai Krishna Iyer – 'I could barely even begin to imagine his scholarship in Sangam Literature. I fancied that he could probably go through a novel written exclusively in Sangam

TAMIL CHARACTERS

vocabulary, as one reads the daily *Dina Thanthi*' – has often
reminded me of Thangappa. It is this thorough immersion in
Sangam poetry – its language, vocabulary, style, and content –
that makes Thangappa an enviable translator. His understanding
of the poems is more intuitive than erudite. Not for him the
second-hand interpretation of Sangam poems through mediaeval
and modern commentators. Led by intuition, he invariably came
up with the right interpretation of complicated texts. Surprisingly
for someone who barely read anything new – I can swear that he
had never read Salman Rushdie or Amitav Ghosh; he even gave
up reading English dailies many years ago – he had a keen ear
for contemporary English. He constantly revised his translations
and appreciated editorial changes, his face brightening up when
the translation was improved.

Nabokov is said to have listed three unbreakable rules for
a good translator: intimate knowledge of the language from
which one translates; experience as a writer of the language into
which one translates; and 'that one knows, in both languages,
the words designating concrete objects (natural and cultural,
the flower and the clothing)'. Thangappa fitted the bill perfectly.
Though his English was not half as good as his Tamil it is saying
an enormous lot. Regarding the third of the Nabokovian rules,
Thangappa was a nature enthusiast who bicycled long distances
and could identify many a flower and plant by its Sangam
nomenclature.

Steeped in Tamil literature Thangappa tried his hand at
every phase of the two-millennia long poetical tradition. His
translations ranged from Tamil bhakti poetry, the iconoclastic
Siddhar poetry, Kalingathu Parani, the nineteenth-century
Vallalar Ramalinga Swamigal, and not to mention the twentieth-
century greats, Bharati and Bharatidasan. Some years ago he
finished a translation of the Tamil didactic text, *Naladiyar*. An

anthology of 2,000 years of Tamil poetry can easily be compiled from his draft translations.

After *Love Stands Alone*, as Thangappa's 'literary agent', I receive a steady stream of requests for permissions for inclusions in anthologies and demands for new translations. To whom will I now turn to?

15

PERUMAL MURUGAN
Chronicler of Kongu

IN 1983 A SEVENTEEN-year-old student of Chikkaiah Naicker College, Erode, inspired by a dictionary of the *karisal* (black cotton soil) region of southern Tamilnadu, resolved to prepare a similar lexicon for the Kongu region. With the zeal of a recent convert he collected dialect words from friends and relatives, and from oral traditions. The historical Kongu region, covering the districts of Coimbatore, Erode, Tiruppur, Salem, and Karur in western Tamilnadu, with its hostile agricultural environment and hardy peasants would hold an undying fascination for this young man.

The Kongu region's achievements in modern literature are about as low as its water table. But for R. Shanmugasundaram, the author of the classic novel *Nagammal* (1942), few had fathomed the rich life in the region. From 1991 a stream of novels, short stories, poems, and essays were to flow from the young man's pen. Almost single-handedly he would put Kongu on to the literary map of Tamilnadu.

Modern Tamil fiction had for long been obsessed with village life in the rice bowls of Thanjavur and Tirunelveli, and urban-middle-class life in the city of Chennai. In the fiction of this young man the hardy peasants of Kongu came into their own. Who can forget Marimuthu of *Kanganam* or Muthu of *Alandapatchi*. The latter is also the saga of frontier peasant life narrated through the migration of Kongu Vellalar Gounder peasants to the east, towards Attur. But his admiration for the hard-working peasants did not mean the neglect of the life of goatherds and other lower castes. Rich ethnographic portraits of non-sedentary and lower-caste life animate his work.

A scholar with a rich sense of history, he unearthed writings on the region by earlier authors and published two volumes – one, a collection of shorts stories on the Kongu region, and another, a collection of short stories on Dalit life in the region. The early attempt at lexicography would be published seventeen long years later, in 2000. He also retrieved and republished a long-lost book on the history of the Kongu region by T. A. Muthusamy Konar. In sum his over thirty-five books provide a veritable cultural map of the Kongu region.

It is this great literary chronicler, Perumal Murugan (b. 1966), who was virtually banished from his beloved Kongu region from 2015. At the centre of the controversy was his fifth novel, *Mathorubhagan*.

Mathorubhagan was published in December 2010. The novel marks the second phase of Murugan's fictional explorations. If his earlier novels revelled in ethnographic detail, narrated in a controlled naturalist voice, *Mathorubhagan* poignantly tells the story of a childless peasant couple set in a time about a century ago in the temple town of Tiruchengode. Ponna and Kali rejoice in their conjugal love, but they are childless. The pain of being childless is accentuated by the taunts of neighbours and insults at domestic rituals and religious occasions. Tiruchengode, the abode of Siva in the form of half-woman half-man, Ardhanareeswaran, is the sacred town to which childless couples flock to this day hoping to extend their lineage. Over 125 years ago Chinnathayammal and Venkata Naicker of Erode circumambulated the *varadi kal* at Tiruchengode resulting in the birth of Periyar, the great rationalist!

After exhausting all means, many childless couples in that tract sought what from a modern perspective is an exotic, even 'immoral', solution. Every year, at the Vaikasi Visakam car festival, in the darkness of pre-electricity times, childless women engaged in consensual sex with men they did not know – strangers – in a carnivalesque atmosphere. The lucky were able to conceive. Children born of this socially sanctioned ritual were referred to as *sami kodutha pillai* (god-given children). Such practices are by no means unique. Anthropologists attest to similar practices in many premodern societies with no access to assisted conception. Classical Hindu traditions refer to this practice as *niyoga* – it is even termed *niyoga dharma*, an indication of its religious sanction. Noted scholars such as A. Sivasubramanian, A. K. Perumal, and S. Theodore Baskaran have vouched for the existence of such practices in other parts of Tamilnadu.

It is this section of the novel that provoked the ire of Hindu fundamentalists and caste purists. Portrayed as a slur on Hindu/Kongu Vellalar women Murugan was pilloried for denigrating Tiruchengode and its people. The dominant middle-caste Kongu Vellalars, who have experienced considerable economic mobility in the past few decades, and are now seeking commensurate political power – the last decade has seen the emergence of separate political outfits claiming to represent them – became assertive and took issue. The virtual sweep by the AIADMK in the legislative assembly elections in May 2011 was underpinned by this community's support. In the 2016 elections this community formed the single largest caste bloc among the legislators; and, after the death of J. Jayalalithaa, a member of this community, Edappadi K. Palaniswami has become the chief minister. Not surprisingly, caste assertion has been accompanied by renewed oppression of Dalits and the strengthening of patriarchy. In the wake of the sweeping success of the BJP in the Lok Sabha elections the Sangh Parivar, seeking a toehold in Tamilnadu, sensed an opportunity and joined hands with the casteists. Hindutva-in-office is the context in which the controversy played out.

For four years nobody was offended by the novel. Quite the contrary. Discerning readers identified themselves with Ponna and Kali. Their intimacy, described in loving and sensitive terms, easily struck a chord. The novel has a fuzzy end. After he wakes up from a long night of drinking Kali realises that Ponna has left for the carnival, having been deluded into believing that she has his consent. As he collapses onto the ground, a rope slipping from the hayrick presses his back, and he espies the *poovarasu* tree. Readers badgered Murugan with questions on Kali's fate. The author responded creatively – with one, no, two sequels: *Alavayan* and *Ardhanari*. The sequels follow two different trajectories in *Sliding Doors* fashion, where two different events occur in two parallel universes. *Alavayan* narrates the story of Ponna after Kali's suicide, and *Ardhanari* of the tension between the two after Kali's attempted suicide is thwarted by his mother.

Evidently the advocates of burning books do not understand literature. And in a worrying scenario they were joined by other sinister interests. Murugan is not only a novelist. With a doctorate in Tamil literature he has been teaching in government colleges for over two decades now, transforming the lives of many underprivileged students. Over the years he has written scathing essays on the commercialisation of education. Namakkal, the town adjacent to Tiruchengode, specialises in two forms of poultry farming: hatcheries produce broiler chicken and eggs, while schools churn out high-scoring students! Murugan has pulled no punches in exposing the many unethical, even illegal, practices of such factory-like schools. He has written in support of U. Sahayam, the crusading bureaucrat, who, as collector of Namakkal, brought many environmental culprits to book. The whole gamut of local vested interests joined hands in the witch-hunt.

All this came as a shock to Murugan. Murugan was at the height of his creative powers. Brimming with creativity he was looking good to deliver more worthies. Despite publishing primarily in alternative and little magazines recognition has been steady in coming. Three of his novels had been translated into English, and one each into Polish and Malayalam. In the wake of the controversy more translations were in the offing. *The Season of the Palms* was shortlisted for the prestigious Japanese Kiriyama Prize. His name was tipped for the 2014 Sahitya Akademi Award. *One Part Woman*, the English translation of *Mathorubhagan*, was published to rave reviews a year earlier, in 2013.

Ironically, this author who shunned the limelight came into public glare. On 1 December 2014 Murugan returned from Bengaluru after a fortnight in the Sangam House's residency programme. The quiet of the residency had given him the respite from his teaching duties to put final touches to the two sequels. He arrived at his Namakkal home flush with fulfilment, and was looking forward to seeing the books hit the stands at the annual Chennai Book Fair.

Murugan's nightmare began immediately. For two days his phone barely stopped ringing. Initially the calls were polite asking him for details about *Mathorubhagan*. There was a pattern to the calls: the callers had apparently not read the novel and were parroting questions fed to them. Soon they became abusive, accusing him of being a Christian, an anti-Hindu, and an anti–Kongu Vellalar. At first Murugan maintained his calm and tried to explain what the novel was all about. But when physical threats were issued something in him crumbled.

On 26 December an illegal assembly paraded through the streets of Tiruchengode, burnt copies of *Mathorubhagan*, and slippered his picture. It demanded a ban on the book and the arrest of its author and its publisher. A local RSS functionary led the assembly that burnt the book. Later, Hindu outfits began to work from behind the scenes giving a free reign to caste mobilisation.

Murugan and his family were intimidated and feared for their lives. On the evening after the book-burning incident he lodged a complaint with the district superintendent of police giving the specific numbers from which threatening calls were received. But there was complete inaction on the part of the police.

Meanwhile provocative posters were plastered all over Tiruchengode. Violent views were expressed in a series of unauthorised meetings even after Murugan's complaint to the police. One vigilante threatened to cut off the hand that dared to write lines insulting the community. (That it was no empty threat became frighteningly clear when he was arrested later in the year on the charge of murdering a Dalit youth who had the audacity to fall in love with an upper-caste girl.) Over the next few weeks thousands of the supposedly offending pages, ripped out of context, were reprinted and distributed to devotees flocking the temple. A call for a total bandh in Tiruchengode on 9 January 2015 was announced.

Murugan deeply loves his town and his people. And he has prided himself on having given literary immortality to the community and the region. He was therefore pained not only to see his writings being distorted, but the normal life of his people being disturbed. On the evening of 27 December he issued a long clarification. Murugan is known for his controlled prose and is not given to exaggeration. In what must be utterly humiliating for a writer he explained the art of fiction, and described how fiction is an artistic amalgam of fact and imagination to portray reality and understand the human condition. The teacher in him also explained the context of the novel, the motivations of its characters, and the semantics of the words attributed to them. Murugan expressed his confidence that anyone reading the novel in full, rather than being offended, would actually like it. However, in a bid to resolve the controversy he apologised if, in their reading of the text, anyone was offended. In a conciliatory gesture he also offered to revise the text in all future editions so that Tiruchengode and its people could not be identified.

Meanwhile the two sequels, *Alavayan* and *Ardhanari*, were launched in Chennai on 3 January 2015. Releasing the books, the noted writer Ambai (C. S. Lakshmi) composed a song in the manner of one of Murugan's characters and even sang it, wherein she expressed her envy at Murugan's artistic brilliance. Murugan had quietly revised the text of the two sequels. Paring away all identifiable markers he now called the locale Karattur (literally, 'the rustic/unrefined place'), deleted references to caste, and in true style added a cheeky disclaimer:

> O Sirs, let me submit a petition to your august presence. Not only in this novel, but in all my writings, the setting is not any place in Tamilnadu. In fact, I don't write about this world at all. I write only about the world of asuras. All my characters are asuras. They belong to the asura caste. And they speak the asura language. If it appears as though any particular caste or place is being referred to, it is but an illusion. Therefore, please free yourself from that illusion.

But the controversy refused to die down, with the adversaries baying for blood. As the day for the total bandh approached, on the night of 8 January, on the pointed advice of the police, Murugan left his hometown with his wife and children. A day later Tiruchengode, the town that is now part of the Tamil literary landscape, thanks to him, observed a total shutdown condemning the novel.

In parallel, protest meetings in support of Murugan and freedom of expression were organised all over the state. The national media also turned its attention. But the district administration, which had thus far kept quiet as law and order was being flagrantly challenged, either at the instance of the government or with its tacit support, now began to intervene. It called for 'peace talks' on 12 January at the Namakkal district collector's office. The term 'summons' was used to call Murugan to the meeting.

The so-called summons was also issued to the publisher, Kannan Sundaram of Kalachuvadu Pathippagam, who did not heed it. Against the best advice of his friends, well-wishers, legal experts, and especially his publisher, Murugan, in a desperate bid to end the controversy, decided to attend the meeting. He reached Madurai on the morning of 12 January, and accompanied by an influential lawyer with experience of handling human rights cases reached Namakkal. Ominous signs greeted them as they entered the town. The police directed the car to take a circuitous route to the collector's office. The atmosphere was charged. An intimidating mob had gathered on behalf of those who wanted to silence Murugan.

The so-called peace talks were held in the presence of the revenue divisional officer who was intent on 'resolving' the issue so that the tension could be diffused. Scant respect was shown to constitutional guarantees regarding freedom of expression. Murugan's lawyer was cold-shouldered and shown his place. The two contending parties did not meet face to face as Murugan was confined to a back room. At first Murugan was willing to express regret, but it was not accepted. In a situation that could only be called duress Murugan's hand was forced and he signed an unconditional apology, promised to withdraw all copies of the novel, and never to republish it.

By the time the meeting ended it was late evening. Late that night the following post, in Tamil, appeared on Perumal Murugan's Facebook page. It was prefaced by the note:

> Friends, the following posting will be on this Facebook page for two days. After that Perumal Murugan will withdraw from all social media. My thanks to all those who have supported him on the social media.

This is P. Murugan writing for the person called Perumal Murugan.

Writer Perumal Murugan is dead. He is no god. So he will not rise from the dead. Nor does he believe in resurrection. Hereafter only the lowly teacher P. Murugan will live. Thanks to all the magazines, organisations, readers, friends, writers, and people who supported Perumal Murugan, and fought for his freedom of expression.

The controversy is not going to end with *Mathorubhagan*. Other organisations and individuals too may take issue with any of his other writings. Perumal Murugan has therefore taken the following decision. He announces firmly that:

(1) All books – novels, short stories, essays, poems, and other writings – by Perumal Murugan, except those compiled and edited by him, now stand withdrawn. His books will no more be available for sale.

(2) The publishers of Perumal Murugan's books such as Kalachuvadu, Nattrinai, Adaiyalam, Malaigal, Kayal Kavin are requested not to sell his books anymore. P. Murugan will fully compensate them for losses incurred.

(3) All those who have bought his books are free to burn them. If anyone claims that they have suffered any loss they may approach him and they will be compensated.

(4) Perumal Murugan requests that he be not invited to any literary events.

(5) As all his books stand withdrawn he requests organisations based on caste, religion, or party not to indulge in any further agitation.

Leave him alone.

My thanks to everyone.

P. Murugan
for Perumal Murugan

By signing the apology Murugan may have felt that he had broken the unwritten covenant between reader and writer, and had therefore no option but to give up his calling. But this pained note of literary suicide galvanised the country. People who were unmoved by constitutional logic were now overtaken by emotion. Support gathered from all over. In a rarity the national media bent over backwards to report on a vernacular writer. The international media was not far behind. The *New York Times*, *Guardian*, and *Washington Post* reported on the controversy. The electronic media provided extensive coverage.

In a context where publishers continue to buckle under pressure Murugan's publisher, Kannan Sundaram of Kalachuvadu Pathippagam, backed the author unconditionally and was ready to battle it out in the courts. But his hands were tied by Murugan's wishes, and he stopped further publication. However, even as the book was freely floating on the Internet and, in a first for a Tamil book, was even being pirated, Kannan turned a Nelson's eye.

Meanwhile the literary front of the CPI (M), the Tamilnadu Progressive Writers and Artists Association, filed a writ petition in the Madras High Court pleading for the annulment of the agreement. At the instance of the court Perumal Murugan and his wife were transferred to Chennai. While Murugan himself filed an affidavit Kannan Sundaram, a respondent, represented by the National General Secretary of the PUCL, V. Suresh, responded with a detailed supporting affidavit.

In July 2016 the High Court's first bench, consisting of Chief Justice S. K. Kaul and Justice Pushpa Sathyanarayana, delivered a blow for the freedom of expression. In a detailed verdict it told those who claimed hurt, 'If you do not like a book, simply close it. The answer is not its ban.' Observing that our 'tolerance level seems to be on the decline. Any contra view or social thinking is met at times with threats or violent behaviour' it emphatically asserted that 'India is not endangered by someone writing about social practices, real or unreal, more so qua a childless couple'. Exposing the mala fide on the part of the novel's opponents, Chief Justice Kaul stated, 'The incident, if examined, can be said to be an orchestrated and stage-managed one, by a small group of people. The dates and events suggest it to be so'.

In a stirring appeal the judgement ended with the words, *Let the author be resurrected to what he is best at. Write.*

Coda: Soon after the court order Perumal Murugan announced his comeback with a book of poems titled *Kozhaiyin Padalgal* (The Songs of a Coward) – pained poems scrawled during the harrowing days. In a sense the learned judges were prescient: 'If we may say so, such antiques [referring to the opponents of the novel] have only given hype to the novel and possibly garnered more publicity and readers than it had earlier.'

During the Chennai Book Fair 2017 sixteen books of Perumal Murugan were republished (with changes that obscured all specific references to place and people). He also wrote a novel, *Poonachi allathu Oru Vellattin Kathai*, ostensibly the life story of a she-goat.

Since then translations of his works have appeared with steady regularity in many languages both in India and abroad. For the first time in Indian publishing history the English language rights of an Indian language novel, for *Poonachi*, were auctioned. His novels will appear in the American market as well.

Perumal Murugan is now a widely sought-after writer in literary festivals in India and abroad.

Despite all this success it is not status quo ante. Perumal Murugan is a changed man, and the controversy has left a wound. It can at best become a scar. It cannot go away.

16

CHO. DHARMAN
Peacock on Black Cotton Soil

'WHEN KOVILPATTI SNEEZES,' IT was said, 'the Tamil literary world catches a cold!' Located in the dry 'black cotton soil' (karisal) region of southern Tamilnadu this small town with a population of barely one hundred thousand is perhaps the most unlikely place for a modernist literary renaissance. Kovilpatti, the town and the taluk in present-day Tuticorin district, stands in for the entire karisal region covering the Kovilpatti, Ottapidaram, Ettayapuram, and Vilathikulam taluks of Tuticorin district, Sattur and Sivakasi taluks of Virudhunagar district, and a few marginal areas of Tirunelveli and Ramanathapuram districts. It is bereft of rivers. Only wild streams carrying flash floods and brackish brooks flow here. The perennial Tamiraparani river skirts this region and, ecologically and culturally, marks it out from the wet zone. The soil, though fertile, does not let water percolate, and consequently there are few wells. The abandoned wells of saline water that dot the often-desolate landscape bear witness to the ruin of the topsoil. To bring further woe the karisal region falls in the rain-shadow region of both monsoons, the southwest and the northeast. Scarcely mentioned in ancient and medieval historical narratives, this region itself came under the plough only with the advent of Telugu-speaking agricultural castes from the north – 'a new force in the agrarian system', in the words of the pre-eminent historian of Tirunelveli, David Ludden – along with the Nayaka chieftains following the fall of the Vijayanagara Empire in the late sixteenth century.

But just a spell or two of rain can turn the black soil bountiful, yielding a rich harvest of a variety of millets, pulses, and groundnut. Well-suited to the growing of cotton, it is often called black cotton soil in English. In the early nineteenth century a new variety of cotton, called 'tinnies' after Tinnevelly (Tirunelveli), the name of the erstwhile composite district in which the region is largely located, flourished and was the cornerstone of an economic upswing. When the American Civil War broke out in 1861 cotton supply from the American South was disrupted, resulting in a cotton boom in the Kovilpatti region, illustrating the popular saying in the countryside, 'The scorpion stung the coconut tree and the poison shot through the palm tree'. Cotton carding, ginning, and spinning mills mushroomed, effecting major economic and, in its wake, social transformations. This history is still visible in the not-inconsiderable cotton mills that survive. The dry and water-starved climate is also particularly conducive to the development of match and firework industries. Sivakasi (popularly called 'Little Japan'), the town in which much of this industry thrives, is globally recognised. Not far off, Sivakasi also became a major centre for offset printing, and the brightly coloured calendars produced here can be seen on many a wall across India. The name of Kondiah Raju, a local legend, crops up whenever one talks of calendar art in India.

The peasant here is a cursed being. The contrast with the adjoining rich rice-growing culture and the temples spawned by the Tamiraparani river basin is too stark to be missed. The precarious nature of agriculture, especially since the 1960s, has provided a steady supply to the workforce for the mills and match factories – the first of Cho. Dharman's two novels, *Thoorvai*, captures this social transformation evocatively while many of his short stories provide poignant vignettes of life inside these sweatshops. The nimble hands of young boys and girls were especially suited for stacking the matchsticks on the frames. Busloads of children being picked up from their homes in the wee hours to work in the factories to return only late in the night was a common sight. And for many a decade towards the fag end of the twentieth century Kovilpatti was notorious for employing child labour and drew considerable media attention, and consequent state and NGO activity.

The unrelenting blackness of the karisal landscape, broken only by the straggling *udai* trees, can occasionally light up with the dancing of peacocks. The great modern classics of Tamil, the fiction of Pudumaippithan and T. Janakiraman, were nurtured in the Tamiraparani and Kaveri basins, respectively. But until the latter part of the twentieth century there was little to show by way of a literary crop from the karisal. Subramania Bharati was indeed born in this region. But his literary career had little to do with the karisal, and one would be hard put to find any trace of it in his writings. In the 1940s the emergence of G. Alagirisamy as a part of literary modernism was certainly exceptional. Many of Alagirisamy's best short stories – for some inexplicable reason the short story has seen towering achievements in the hands of Tamil writers – are set in the karisal region.

But it was with Ki. Rajanarayanan that karisal literature came of age. Poomani, the distinguished novelist, aptly described him metaphorically as *munnathi aer* (the first plough that breaks the soil). Born in 1923, Rajanarayanan took part in the freedom struggle and was involved in the Communist Party. Despite being in the thick of the literary world through his friendship with Alagirisamy he was a late bloomer. It was only in the mid-1960s that he began to write stories. Originally published in the literary journal of the Communist Party, *Thamarai*, his stories were immediately recognised by the literary vanguard as strikingly new. With Rajanarayanan the dialect and the demotic announced their coming into the literary world. Tamil, linguistically speaking, is a diaglossic language with distinct written and spoken registers. The spoken register is the vehicle of fiction, and Tamil writers, with some distinguished exceptions, were not entirely comfortable with handling it. Rajanarayanan's writings marked a break with his bold usage of the karisal dialect, and unlike earlier writers, who narrated in the formal register reserving the dialect for capturing conversation, Rajanarayanan ingeniously brought the dialect into the narrator's voice. The strong romanticist streak underlying his stories seduced his readers. I remember my initial ecstasy on reading, at the age of fifteen, his short story collection, *Vetti*, and the resultant intense desire to visit the karisal land. (Such was my fascination for his writing and the milieu in which it was set that I read from cover to cover, headword by headword the karisal dialect dictionary that Rajanarayanan compiled!)

His short story '*Kathavu*' (The Door) is a poignant portrayal of the door, the children's only plaything in an impoverished peasant home. The children swing on it daily and decorate it with matchbox labels, until one day the bailiff takes it away in settlement of a debt. If this story can be said to have opened the door for karisal literature, Rajanarayanan's *Gopalla Gramam* (The Village of Gopalla, 1976), by defying all known forms of the Tamil novel, was another enabling moment. Drawing on a wide range of oral traditions and folklore, *Gopalla Gramam* etched the 200-year history of the Telugu-speaking peasant caste's migration to karisal country and striking roots there.

Parallel to the steady stream of writings from Rajanarayanan's pen through the little magazines larger social and political transformations were making their presence felt in the distant karisal region. The peasant uprising of Naxalbari and its attendant movement had its resonances here. Even though the Naxalite movement was confined to a few pockets in Tamilnadu and was soon crushed ruthlessly by the MGR government – V. S. Naipaul provides a brilliant account of it in his *India: A Million*

Mutinies Now – it had a lasting influence on Tamil literary writing. The left movement in Tamilnadu has had a chequered political history; but of its literary influence the less said the better. Squeezed by Tamil identity politics and the Dravidian movement the left had little influence on art and literature. That there was no representation from the Tamil region in the famed Indian People's Theatre Association is largely symptomatic of the non-existence of a cultural left in Tamilnadu. Left literature bloomed in Tamil only in the wake of Naxalbari. The pent-up creative energies that had few avenues for expression in the mainstream found sluice gates opened in the 1970s through leftist little magazines. It was a decade that triggered heated debates on the function of literature: the debate on 'art for art's sake' or 'art for people's sake' raged for years yielding ever-diminishing returns, but its effect in animating discussion and inspiring writers was enormous. Socialist realism was the dominant informing ideology and to say that a work was artistic amounted to damning it.

The first major break in literary writing in post-Independence Tamilnadu emanated from this moment. The karisal region was arguably the epicentre of this literary efflorescence. The fiction of P. Jeyapragasam and Poomani marks a new beginning in modern Tamil writing. Traditionally the writers of the Kaveri delta and the Tamiraparani basin had dominated modern Tamil writing. Kovilpatti marked a shift. It brought in its wake a very different social (read, caste) profile of writers with a different culture and lived experience. If the conscious Naxalite politics of Jeyapragasam foregrounded class differences expressed in a romanticist vein and alluring language, Poomani entered the field with a bang: the first line of his acclaimed novel, *Piragu* (Later), 'Hey, you *chakkili* mother-fucker', was the literary equivalent of a bomb going off, and caught the Tamil literary world by the scruff of its neck.

Many writers followed in their footsteps – Tamilselvan, Konangi, Melanmai Ponnusamy, S. Ramakrishnan, Suyambulingam, Veera. Velusamy, Gowrishankar, Vidyashankar, the poets Devathachan and Abbas, and the brilliant designer Maris. Birds of passage who spent some productive years at Kovilpatti as their job transfers stationed them in Kovilpatti, such as Yuvan and Samayavel, were part of this formation. If one cast a stone in Kovilpatti, it was said, the chances were it would hit a writer. The atmosphere was thick with writing and debate, and the memories of it so strong that already there is a clutch of memoirs recollecting those heady days. By 1984 this rich crop of writing prompted the publication of an anthology of stories by karisal writers. *Karisal Kathaigal* (Karisal Stories; its publisher Annam Pathippagam, founded by the poet Meera, had divined the talent of Ki. Rajanarayanan, and subsequently published most of the karisal writers) appropriately commemorated Rajanarayanan's sixtieth birthday, together with a companion volume, a festschrift of sorts, *Rajanarayaneeyam* (a collection of essays on his work by the leading critics and writers of the new generation, including M. A. Nuhman, G. Kesavan, A. Marx, and Raj Gowthaman). The twin volumes (to which may be added the aforesaid dictionary of the karisal dialect) announced the arrival of karisal literature as a distinct field in the Tamil literary world.

In the following decade fresh winds blew over this dry region. Translations from the Soviet Union – apart from the nineteenth-century Russian greats, Soviet writers such as Chinghiz Aitmatov of Kyrgyzstan, especially his *Jamila* and *Farewell Gul'sary*, had a great following – published at throwaway prices by Progress Publishers and Raduga Publishers from Moscow as part of a propaganda blitz in the Cold War opened new worlds and offered alternative, richer models of social realist writing for storytelling (not to speak of exemplary book production). Already with the first tentative baby steps taken by offset printing into Tamil book publishing, experiments were being made with book production.

It is difficult to imagine the awe and wonderment that Latin American writers – especially Gabriel García Márquez – evoked among Tamil writers. The confluence of social realism and magic realism created a literary sensation. Konangi published two bumper numbers of his irregular journal *Kalkuthirai*, one each on Dostoyevsky and Márquez. In the latter number an experiment in language – upsetting conventional Tamil syntactic structures to mimic Márquez's Spanish – triggered innovative uses of language. Non-linear became the buzzword. Magic realism was recreated, mimicked, and aped – choose your word.

Simultaneously, a bigger political storm was brewing. The turn of the last decade of the twentieth century was testing times for the Indian nation, state, and society. A one-party rule based on the Congress consensus was crumbling. The economic crisis of 1991 led to liberalisation and the consequent opening up of the Indian economy. The collapse of the Soviet Union left the communist parties of India to think for themselves. The acceptance of the Mandal Commission recommendations for reservations to backward castes let loose unprecedented social forces. The Babri Masjid–Ramjanmabhoomi controversy turned out to be the cutting edge of an ascendant Hindu fundamentalism. The centenary of Dr Ambedkar fuelled the rise of Dalit assertion. Periyar, who had until then been reviled by a discourse dictated by Brahmins and Marxists (proving Periyar's tongue-in-cheek comment that the two were one and the same), was discovered anew by Tamil intellectuals. This mix made for an explosive brew. A bliss it was in that dawn that intellectuals of my generation can scarce forget.

Caste, which was unspeakable despite the long years of Periyar's uninhibited anti-caste campaigns, was now out in the public sphere. The ugly truth began to be consciously realised that what had passed for the long and rich literary heritage of the Tamils was essentially the product of Brahmin and Vellalar upper castes. Few writers from lower castes, not to speak of Dalits, had a place in the Tamil pantheon. The caste question was complicated in Tamilnadu. The most radical of non-Brahmin movements had functioned here for well over a century, drawing sustenance from an even longer heterodox tradition. The Dalit question being subsumed within a larger non-Brahmin political movement, there had been no independent or autonomous Dalit movement – say, as in Maharashtra – to speak of. There was little of self-conscious Dalit literary writing – once again the contrast with Marathi or even Kannada was striking.

The Dalit movement – both literary and political – arrived at this moment. Autonomous political parties such as the Dalit Panthers of India (now the Viduthalai Chiruthaikal Katchi) and the Puthiya Tamilagam were born. A new generation of Dalit writers debuted with a strong and shocking language and vocabulary resulting in a rich outpouring of writing about Dalit lives. This creative outpouring was accompanied by a large volume of critical writing that foregrounded caste as a foundational element of both material and cultural spheres. In its wake also came debates about who could represent Dalits. Could non-Dalits write credibly about Dalit lives? On occasion these debates evoked memories animating left and socialist literature. Upper-caste writers had their first taste of the guilt of caste privilege. Instructive was a brash young non-Dalit writer's fear of being beaten with 'a Dalit stick' if he voiced the usual platitudes.

The fall of the Soviet Union and the freeing of the communist parties of India from the need to serve Soviet cold war interests paradoxically had a liberating effect on the left movements in India. Left intellectuals jumped into the Dalit movement: now that there was another cause to fight for. In literary terms socialist realism that had made for some appallingly stereotypical writings soon stood exposed as a bankrupt artistic creed. Writers seized the alternate models of writing emanating largely from Latin America.

CHO. DHARMAN

Cho. Dharman is a product of this milieu. Born in 1953 he hails from the village of Urulaikudi – a recurrent place name in his fiction, including *Koogai*. At the times in which *Koogai* is set in Urulaikudi was barely a dozen kilometres from Kovilpatti's town centre, but has now been nearly absorbed into the town. Dharman was born into the caste of Pallars, or Devendrakula Vellalar, as they call themselves. After finishing his school Dharman trained at an industrial training institute and worked for a few years in a fireworks factory before joining the workforce in one of Kovilpatti's many textile mills. After working for about a quarter of a century, like many contemporary writers, he took voluntary retirement in 2000 to pursue a full-time writing career.

Details about the formal education of the most distinguished Tamil writers, especially from subaltern classes, tell us little about their making. So is it with Dharman. Dharman's father spent his life on pursuing his passion, of being an *oyil kummi* (a popular folk dance form Tamilnadu) artiste. As Dharman recollects colourfully, as a young boy he had sat on the shoulders of Rama, played with Lakshmanan, and dozed off on Sita's lap. Dharman's many relatives were part of the troupe, and he grew up in a world animated by such dramatis persona. However, this is no innocuous recollection of his childhood, but an account suffused with an invisible politics. Dharman reacts to a dominant narrative, both well-meaning and adversarial, that thrives on portraying Dalits as victims and without resources, material or cultural. Mention here should be made of Dharman's pioneering attempt to document the life and work of a folk songster, the *villupattu* (bowsong) exponent, Pichaikkutty.

Here a note on the historical sociology of Dalits in Tamilnadu is in order. Dalit inter-caste dynamics is writ large in Dharman's fiction, and speaks for his courage in addressing an issue that many would prefer to sweep under the carpet. Three communities – Paraiyars, Pallars, and Chakkiliyars – account for the overwhelming majority of Dalits in Tamilnadu. Their geographic distribution is also distinctive. While Paraiyars largely inhabit the northern parts, they are also distributed more or less evenly across the state. Proximity to the administrative capital, Chennai, and access to colonial modernity has given them a lead and subsequently they have cornered much of the benefits accruing from modernity. Engagement with Christianity also impelled the emancipatory urge. Positive discrimination has tended to make the Paraiyars more politically assertive and enabled them to get a near-exclusive hold over Ambedkarite formations. The crumbs of political tokenism have usually accrued to Paraiyars, and until the present time, Dalit intellectuals usually were Paraiyars. Iyotheethoss Pandithar, for instance, hailed from this caste and his rediscovery as an iconic Dalit thinker dates to the early 1990s. Pallars are concentrated in the southern districts with small pockets in the western region. If Paraiyars had some access to colonial modernity the Pallars were distinguished by their access to landholding, even if it was limited. Political consciousness arrived late. If Paraiyars have been in the forefront of politics throughout the colonial period the first rumblings of Pallar assertion were not heard until the 1930s and really hit the headlines only with the infamous Mudukulathur riots of 1957. Their political presence is now an acknowledged fact, in the wake of the mid-1990s violence that rocked southern Tamilnadu. The few Dalit writers of the earlier period were mostly Paraiyars by caste. Not surprisingly Pallars have resisted the identification of all Dalits with Paraiyars. They have been particularly wary of being subsumed within the stereotypical representations of Dalits in popular as well as in socialist realist literature. In fact, the political party Puthiya Tamilagam of the Pallars demand that Pallars be removed from the list of Scheduled Castes.

The third significant Dalit community is the Chakkiliyar, or Arundhatiyar. Largely Telugu-speaking the Arundhatiyars migrated to the Tamil country after the sixteenth century. Traditionally involved in leatherwork, in colonial times, a section of them were recruited into municipal conservancy work that is the primary source of social stigma attached to them. In the Western regions of Tamilnadu they form the majority of the landless workers in an oppressive feudal-like situation. Lagging far behind even other Dalit castes, not surprisingly their voice is yet to be really heard in the Tamil literary or political worlds.

To the great chagrin of most Dalits the distinctions between these various communities are blurred and tend to be homogenised into a single identity. Cho. Dharman has especially reacted strongly against such oversimplification and collapsing of distinctions, and has gone to the extent of rejecting the Dalit tag. This rejection is shared by many Pallar writers and intellectuals. A powerful strand in this community contends that they were historically a ruling class; and a recent attempt to write such a history has been met with sedition charges and the book itself proscribed by the Government of Tamilnadu. Dharman's intellectual position, as stated below, can be situated in this politics. He writes:

> Some term my writings as Dalit writings. By birth alone I am a Dalit, not by what I write. I am not drawn to any of the so-called Dalit writings. This is perhaps due to the fact that I'm a Dalit, and that I've an acute understanding of Dalit society and culture. A

great writer who can artistically portray Dalit narratives, Dalit distinctiveness and Dalit social reality is yet to be born. I can only give it a try. The Dalit portraits presented to us thus far are one-sided; they portray Dalits as reeking in filth and smelly, their women as prone to immorality, as drawn to violence, as unlettered, as footloose workers with no landholding, as slavish, and as people who only struggle for food and wages. Much of it is a result of a warped leftist perspective. Ironically some Dalit writers too are mouthing them.

Dharman entered the world of letters somewhat late, in his mid-twenties. Like all young Tamil men drawn to reading he initially aspired to be a poet. It was not until 1980 that he was exposed to serious literary writing. Used to reading popular magazines he once went to his maternal uncle, the writer Poomani's home looking for something new to read. In Dravidian kinship terms a maternal uncle is as close as a relationship can get: often the horoscope of the newborn is matched with the uncle's not to mention that, for a girl, the most preferred form of marriage is with her maternal uncle, age difference notwithstanding. Poomani's home was filled with books and magazines of which Dharman had no clue. If Dharman had had little inkling of his uncle's stature as a writer – by then he had published many short stories and his novel *Piragu* to much acclaim – Poomani in turn did not know that his nephew was an aspiring writer. In the event he lent him two of Ki. Rajanarayanan's books. Reading his stories opened a new world. 'If this is real writing then I can write a hundred stories a day!' Dharman had said to himself.

But then writing like Rajanarayanan is not easy. Dharman discovered himself and the surrounding world of karisal through Rajanarayanan. Rather than indulge in the fantasies of cloud cuckoo land he began to process his lived experience and set it in a milieu that he knew well. Rejecting ready-made models offered by socialist realism, he kept a steady pace of short stories in the 1980s, especially to *Thamarai*. Despite being well crafted his stories largely fit in with the evolved models of karisal writing though the caste identity of his characters marked them out distinctly. For instance, Ki. Rajanarayanan tackled only Telugu-speaking landholding characters to the near exclusion of other castes, especially Dalits. Many of Dharman's stories were set in match factories and the firecracker industry, and etched sensitive portrayals of the unorganised workers who had migrated from the countryside. Such stories as yet did not fully upend the narratives peddled by leftist discourse. By the turn of the 1990s this changed with the rise of Dalit politics and other attendant factors delineated above. This should not make us oblivious to other trajectories present in Dharman's writings. His stories demonstrate a rare sensitivity to ecological issues, and the natural world forms an integral part of his stories. This is at the root of his celebrated stories such as '*Iravin Maranam*', which narrates a night's outing into the wilderness with an itinerant *kuravan* tribal, and '*Vanakumaran*'.

Like most serious writers of his generation little magazines were the primary vehicle of Dharman's expression. Recognition came slow. '*Nasukkam*' – published in the middlebrow monthly *Subhamangala* which acted as a new forum for literary writing in the turbulent early 1990s – first received the Ilakkiya Chinthanai's annual award, and later won him a Katha prize as well. Two years later, in 1994, Dharman repeated his Ilakkiya Chinthanai success, one of a very few to do so, with '*Ahimsai*'.

Despite some extraordinary artistic success with the short story few of the karisal writers have tried their hand at the novel. After waiting a dozen years to publish his first collection of short stories Dharman published his novel *Thoorvai* in 1996, and its publication was immediately noticed. *Thoorvai* captured the social transformation of the karisal countryside in the 1970s as agriculture became increasingly unviable and the impoverished rural folk migrated to work in the mushrooming factories producing fireworks and matchsticks. This transformation is traced through the life story of a Pallar couple Madathi and Minukki over two generations. The novel has many great passages and some subtle humour, and it announced the arrival of a major voice in Tamil writing.

KOOGAI

Koogai is Dharman's most ambitious work to date, and poses a challenge to current typologies of Dalit writing. It can only be compared to *Koveru Kazhudhaigal* (translated as *Beasts of Burden* by Lakshmi Holmström); published in 1993, Imayam's stunning debut boldly narrated the story of Arokkyam who belongs to a caste providing traditional washing services to Paraiyars and thus is a doubly marginalised community. Both novels are a treasure trove of Dalit oral lore and traditions which have found few chroniclers.

Koogai is a nocturnal bird. A member of the owl family, koogai bears close resemblance to the barn owl. A number of poems in classical Tamil literature evoke a common perception that this bird is an ominous creature. The eerie hoot of the owl is particularly inauspicious, and in popular parlance it is even called *sakkuruvi* (the sparrow of death) – its hoot is said to foretell death. Bharatidasan, the great poet of the Dravidian movement, derisively dubbed fatalist Hindu philosophy as *sakkuruvi vedanta*. The distinguished translator M. L. Thangappa, in writing a long poem titled '*Aandhai Pattu*', was producing a counter narrative of this reviled bird.

Dharman was therefore making a bold statement in titling his novel *Koogai*. Seeni, an old Pallar man, deifies the koogai, fashioning it into a kind of a totem or guardian angel of his community. This invites ridicule, as the obsession of an old man. But koogai is much more than that: it is an evocative symbol that stands for all oppressed communities, and especially for the Dalits. Koogai is a giant, but can display its prowess only at night when it seeks prey. At other times, and especially when the sun shines, it is helpless, and is endlessly pecked and teased even by smaller birds. In Dharman's hands koogai becomes a particularly apt metaphor for the Dalits. In a section of the novel, which aspires to Márquezian heights of magic realist imagination, koogai wins the respect of the upper-caste Gengaiya Naicker. The community falls when they neglect the owl-temple.

Set a generation earlier than his first novel, *Koogai* portrays the lower-caste social reality of the karisal region with aplomb and demonstrates an understanding of social reality that would do a sociologist proud. The novel begins with an arresting account of the beatings Muthukkaruppan and Mookkan receive at the hands of the Thevar village watchman for their audacity in going to town dressed in spotless white, and relishing a meal of white rice (rather than inferior grains) sitting on a bench (rather than squat on the floor) at Nachiyaramma's newfangled eating joint. It is only Seeni's tactical surrender that saves the day. Seeni's reverence for koogai is the fulcrum on which the story now turns. Soon the Pallars of Chithiraikkudi turn against their oppressors who have been routinely violating their women's bodies. This results in their migration to the slums of Kovilpatti. But they see that the mill and factory owners come from the same caste of their rural oppressors. They are empowered by the makeover of agricultural lands by the Brahmin landowner-lawyer, Nataraja Iyer. This is a shrewd depiction: this is no benevolent gesture on the part of the Brahmin landlord, but demonstrates the contradictions between Brahmins and intermediate castes as well. Dharman also brings in other contradictions, especially those between the various Dalit castes. Paraiyars embrace Christianity as a form of protest, while Chakkiliyars succumb meekly. Many such strands are woven into the novel, and there are many breathtaking myths and brilliant passages in this novel. *Koogai* is not a flawless novel, but, apart from offering sheer reading pleasure, it is certain to trigger a rethink not only of Dalit fiction, but of existing models of novel writing as well.

III
CULTURAL QUESTIONS

17

NON-BRAHMIN MOVEMENT
A Hundred Years

TOWARDS THE END OF 1907, Victorian Britain's foremost war correspondent, Henry W. Nevinson, arrived in India to report on the growing Indian nationalist movement. When he travelled south he saw 'a simple factory among the palms of the north of Madras', which ventured to manufacture swadeshi handlooms, following the lead of the extreme nationalists who advocated the boycott of foreign goods and the manufacture of indigenous products. The 'wealthy Hindu' who ran this factory was Pitti Theagaraya Chetty (1852–1925), the same man whom the Congress was to dub as 'anti-national' less than a decade later, for the crime of issuing the Non-Brahmin Manifesto.

Anti-national was not the abuse hurled at Theagaraya Chetty personally. His party, the South Indian Liberal Federation, or the Justice Party after its flagship newspaper, was also debunked as collaborationist, serving British colonial interests, for the fishes and loaves of office. But Theagaraya Chetty turned down the chief ministership of the Madras Presidency when his party swept the 1920 elections. So much for being collaborationist and anti-national. Calling one's political opponents anti-national is apparently no new weapon.

In this movement of so-called anti-nationalists and collaborationists Theagaraya Chetty was joined by Dr T. M. Nair (1868–1919), an Edinburgh-trained doctor. Associated with the grand old man of Indian nationalism, Dadabhai Naoroji, during his London days, Dr Nair was a regular at the annual gatherings of the Indian National Congress. But when these two nationalists, Nair and Chetty, their accomplishments and commitment to the national cause notwithstanding, realised that they were being sidelined by the behind-the-screen machinations of a Brahmin-dominated Congress, they launched a new organisation.

When the British, who looked at educated Brahmins with suspicion, provided through a series of administrative enquiries, the figures and numbers that demonstrated the fact of Brahmin domination in every sphere of public life – education, the professions, and official positions – it only confirmed their lived experience. As the nationalist movement gathered force, with a demand for some form of Home Rule, the non-Brahmin leaders wondered what might be in store for them in a free India.

These fears were articulated in the Non-Brahmin Manifesto, issued at the historic meeting in the Victoria Public Hall, Chennai, on 20 November 1916. The manifesto, articulated in a language that would do credit to any liberal intellectual, pointed out that though 'Not less than 40 out of the 41½ millions' of the Madras Presidency were non-Brahmins, 'in what passes for the politics in Madras they have not taken the part to which they are entitled'. Arguing that a government conducted on 'true British principles of justice and equality of opportunity' was in the best interests of India, it declared, in words reminiscent of the early Congress, that 'We are deeply devoted and loyally attached to British rule'.

The Justice Party won the first elections under the Montagu–Chelmsford reforms. Within the limits of dyarchy – the political arrangement under which the bulk of powers remained with the (British) executive and only the less important 'transferred subjects' were handled by elected (by a limited franchise) ministers – the Justice ministry had many landmark achievements to its credit.

The so-called 'communal government orders' of 1921–2 introduced reservations on the basis of caste and opened new avenues for backward caste mobility. Starting from government jobs, reservations soon encompassed education. This form of positive discrimination became the model for the rest of India, manifesting itself in the Mandal Commission recommendations a good seven decades later. The first amendment to the Constitution of India that secured reservations in the face of an adverse Madras High Court verdict (*Champakam Dorairajan vs Union of India*) was the result of an agitation centred in Tamilnadu. Even as north India continues to grapple with the mechanics of reservation it works with clockwork precision in the south. The profile of south India's higher education must warm the heart of every champion of social diversity. The fruits of reservation enjoyed by the other backward castes across India are in no small measure due to the demand articulated in the Victoria Public Hall during a monsoon evening a hundred years ago.

The Hindu Religious Endowments Act, 1925, at one stroke kick-started the secularisation of the administration of religious institutions. The numerous well-endowed temples, marred by maladministration and reeling under the control of locally dominant castes, now came under the state. That ninety years later Hindutva forces continue to clamour for its abolition speaks for the foresight of this legislation.

Why are these far-reaching moves of such great import so little known outside of Tamilnadu?

T. M. Nair's premature death in 1919 in London, and Theagaraya Chetty's death in old age in 1925 at a historic juncture, deprived the party of a sagacious leadership. But this loss was also an opportunity. The hitherto English-using Non-Brahmin Movement now took a vernacular turn with the rise of its new

leader Periyar. In an age of democratic politics, from the late
1920s, Periyar shaped the organisation into a movement – the
Self-Respect Movement – and took it from chamber halls to the
streets. This had the effect of sidelining the Westminster-tuned
English-speaking non-Brahmin elite – much as Gandhi had done
for Indian nationalism. It was this elite that M. N. Roy tried to
tap into when he spearheaded the Radical Democratic Party
in the 1940s. However, he soon forsook the likes of S. Muthiah
Mudaliar, 'Sunday Observer' P. Balasubramaniam, and T. A. V.
Nathan, all Justice Party stalwarts, and tried to forge an alliance
with Periyar.

The vernacular turn also meant the loss of advocates who
could articulate the Non-Brahmin Movement's programmes and
defend it against the calumnies heaped on it. Not until the rise
of Area Studies scholarship from the American universities did
reasoned analyses of the Non-Brahmin Movement's case reach
outside audiences.

The Justice Party functioned within the colonial public sphere,
using the language of liberalism and constitutionalism. Periyar
rejected that idiom and challenged the roots of inequality by
attacking caste, religion, and patriarchy. This campaign led to a
direct confrontation with a socially retrograde nationalism which
compromised with feudal values. One of the high points was the
anti-Hindi agitation (1937–9) launched against the compulsory
study of Hindi in schools. Periyar's movements in the 1950s – the
breaking of Hindu idols, the burning of the images of Ram, and
the torching of pictures of Gandhi, the Indian Constitution, and
the national flag – chipped away at the monolithic conception
of a nation based on a single language, a single religion, and an
upper-caste leadership.

Periyar eschewed electoral politics, preferring to play the
role of an unhidden persuader. Yet his impact on Tamil politics
continues to remain palpable. The DMK, which broke away from

him under C. N. Annadurai's leadership, pulled the carpet from under the Congress and scripted the political empowerment of backward castes. And consequently, one or the other Dravidian party has ruled Tamilnadu for a half a century now. On the other hand, Periyar's movement also triggered the de-Brahminization of the Congress party, and his support bolstered the chief ministership of K. Kamaraj. That Annadurai and Karunanidhi, both from stigmatised castes, have been chief ministers is an achievement – the contrast with, for instance, Bengal is striking, which to date has had no non-bhadralok chief minister.

Though the English-speaking elite remained ignorant of Periyar's radical programmes his imprint is discernible in backward caste movements across India. His leadership of the Vaikom Satyagraha in 1924 won him the support of the Ezhavas of Kerala. And their leaders such as Sahodaran Ayyappan remained in conversation with him all through his life.

Periyar's initial recognition of Dr Ambedkar as the sole spokesperson of India's Dalits strengthened his hands at a time when the Congress and Gandhi refused to acknowledge his leadership. Tamil was the earliest language to translate Ambedkar's landmark text *The Annihilation of Caste*. Not surprisingly, the history of the Dalit movement in Tamilnadu is intertwined with Periyar. Periyar's north Indian tours in the 1950s and 1960s kindled the hopes of backward castes. It was therefore appropriate that Kanshi Ram should invoke his name when he mobilised the Bahujan Samaj in the late 1980s.

Though derided as populism Tamilnadu has been an exemplary welfare state in relation to other parts of India scoring high on all human development indicators. These achievements have been built on the bedrock of the Non-Brahmin Movement.

Other parts of India too have seen non-Brahmin movements – for instance, Maharashtra. (In Karnataka it took the form of a backward caste movement.) But the movement in Tamilnadu remains unique. It encompassed within itself demands based not only on equality of castes, but also challenged the hegemonic hold of Brahminism over Hindu religion, articulated pride in language, and defied the imposition of Hindi, and struck at the root of a monolithic conception of a nation.

18

CLASSICAL LANGUAGE
The Chimera

'A LANGUAGE', THE YIDDISH linguist Max Weinreich is said to have remarked, 'is a dialect with an army and a navy'. To extend this cynical definition, a classical language would be any Indian language that is so notified by a weak-kneed central government in a fractured polity. For the first time in world history a language was designated as classical when, in 2004, the Congress-led UPA government declared Tamil as a classical language. This opened the floodgates for similar demands by other languages. And the government then conceded the same status to Kannada and Telugu, and later to Malayalam.

ORIENTALISM AND THE HIERARCHISING OF LANGUAGES

Orientalism, born out of the colonial encounter, profoundly mutated our attitude to language(s). Out of this, for instance, was born the notion of 'mother tongue' which concretised a new emotional relationship to one's own language and led to large-scale social movements. Similar to this is the category of 'classical languages' – the word for this term in any Indian language has to be a neologism. In Tamil, it is termed *semmozhi* (the refined language).

In the Middle Ages the recognition of Greek and Latin as classical languages paralleled the growth of various European languages, now recognised as modern, which were then designated as vernaculars. The Orientalist discovery of the Indo-European family of languages altered the status of Sanskrit. Given its newly discovered linkages to Greek and Latin, Sanskrit came to be recognised as classical – even though I am yet to find an official document specifically granting this recognition. So much so that Sanskrit's putative position as the fountainhead of Indian civilisation now seems to be taken for granted in the popular mind. The colonial government granted titles to scholars as part of its annual New Year honours. Invariably such titles were cornered by Sanskrit scholars even though Pali, Arabic, and Persian were not exempt. Rare indeed was a Tamil scholar (the exceptions were U. V. Swaminatha Iyer and M. Kathiresan Chettiar) who got the Mahamahopadhyaya title for his linguistic achievements. And I doubt if scholars from the languages which later came to be included in the eighth schedule of the Constitution of India were ever so honoured.

The longstanding rivalry between Tamil and Sanskrit was reconfigured during the colonial encounter. The formulations of William Jones and the Calcutta school of Orientalism which argued that all Indian languages were offshoots of Sanskrit was challenged within a generation by scholars based at the College of Fort St. George, Madras, led by Francis Whyte Ellis (the subject of Thomas Trautmann's path-breaking monograph *Languages and Nations: The Dravidian Proof in Colonial Madras*, 2006). This theory of a distinct family of south Indian or Dravidian family of languages was intellectually fleshed out by Robert Caldwell, with all its political implications, in his magisterial *A Comparative Grammar of the Dravidian Family of Languages* (1856). Neither linguistics nor politics have been the same since. Aryan and Dravidian came to be defined antithetically, and linguistic difference came to heavily influence political mobilisation. The rediscovery of Tamil Sangam classics in the late nineteenth century and their canonisation fuelled this process.

The demand for recognising Tamil as a classical language was made quite early – even at the turn of the twentieth century – by scholars such as V. G. Suryanarayana Sastri, Tamil pandit at Madras Christian College, in his history of the Tamil language (1903). This demand, antagonistically posed in relation to Sanskrit, was articulated in the context of education. The University of Madras, as the apex body of secondary and collegiate education in south India, in the examinations it conducted for matriculation, intermediate, and graduate studies, classified languages into baskets of 'classical' and 'vernacular'. Grouped together with Greek, Latin, and Hebrew Sanskrit in effect became compulsory as students (predominantly Brahmin; and in the early twentieth century, forming over 70 per cent of graduates) opted for it. Tamil, coming into the vernacular list, was given the go-by.

The demand for a recognition of Tamil as a classical language was rooted in this context, and was reiterated continually at many academic and intellectual forums. In the post–World War II context, in global scholarship, when Area Studies began to replace Indology, Tamil countervailed against Sanskrit in many American universities. Tamil offered a view of India that was different to the one seen through the lenses of Sanskrit. Even though the world of scholarship had recognised Tamil as a classical language, a persistent demand from Tamilnadu was made on the Indian state to give this an official stamp. The clamour for being classical is most certainly a colonial hangover, marked by an anxiety to be recognised by the world (read, the West). This popular and political demand for what was really an academic fait accompli can be understood only in the context of politics in post-Independence Tamilnadu.

Over the last few decades, as Tamil identity politics grew even as political parties simultaneously accommodated themselves with a strong union government, the demand for official classical status to Tamil became strident. Status took the place of substance. This was especially so after 1989 when the DMK and the AIADMK began to have a say in the formation of governments at the centre. In the wake of the unprecedented electoral sweep of the DMK-led alliance in the 2004 parliamentary elections in Tamilnadu, the classical language status to Tamil was one of the more easily conceded demands made by an assertive DMK, through a Ministry of Human Resources Development (MHRD) notification dated 12 October 2004. Notwithstanding the genuine claim of Tamil for the recognition of such a status this move was a political one. While the DMK went overboard in claiming credit, the AIADMK, then heading the government in the state, was tight-lipped. Subsequent developments only reinforced the political character of this concession.

Many interesting facts emerged during the process leading up to the MHRD notification and after. This was the first time in history that a language had been designated a classical language by the writ of the state. Despite repeated assertions by Tamil enthusiasts that the UNESCO had clearly laid out the criteria – of antiquity, seniority, idealism, universality, humanism, and so on – for identifying classical languages it became clear that no such document existed. Further, no earlier order of the Government of India which recognised Sanskrit, Pali, Arabic, and Persian was found. In fact, in a strange inversion, Sanskrit was officially notified as a classical language only after Tamil, even if for all practical purposes Sanskrit enjoyed state honours and preferential treatment. The irony that the Tamil demand had originated as a competitive demand in relation to Sanskrit was missed.

More disturbingly, the nature of the notification lent itself to manipulation. The perception that norms had been diluted to accommodate future claims of other languages that emerged from even a simple reading of the notification was not without substance. While the widely accepted scholarly criterion for antiquity was the existence of 2,000-year-old texts, the 2004 notification watered it down to only a thousand years. After M. Karunanidhi intervened, it is said, this was revised to 1,500 to 2,000 years (a wide window indeed). Clearly the Government of India had prepared to undermine the question, much like the way the Mandal issue and reservation had been handled in the past.

The whittled-down criteria should be seen in context. Over the last couple of decades, largely as a reaction to Tamil claims, Karnataka and (undivided) Andhra Pradesh have been demanding the status of classical language for Kannada and Telugu. Unfortunately, Karnataka's response to Tamilnadu's matters are coloured by the Kaveri dispute, and everything is seen as a zero-sum game: Tamilnadu's gain is seen as Karnataka's loss. Its positions remind one of the Biblical story of the contested child in Solomon's court. In such a politically charged situation truth has been a casualty. For example, the renowned epigraphist, Iravatham Mahadevan, a global expert on the Indus and the Brahmi scripts, expressed concern that his comments were distorted by the Government of Andhra Pradesh when putting forward Telugu's claim. As for the Government of Karnataka it accused Tamilnadu of trying to sabotage the Government of India's move to confer the status on Kannada.

Before long the classical language issue crossed the portals of the scholarly world. A writ petition was filed in Madras High Court against granting classical status to Kannada and Telugu, but was finally disposed off. The UPA government, in keeping with its consistent policy of appeasing every voluble group, went ahead and notified Kannada and Telugu as classical languages. The response of the Kerala government was interesting. V. S. Achuthanandan, then chief minister of Kerala, while stating that Malayalis did not grudge this status being given to Sanskrit and Tamil, demanded that Malayalam not be left out were Kannada and Telugu to be notified. Interestingly, the *Hindu*, which had

largely kept silent on this matter, published an edit-page article
by M. A. Baby, Kerala's education minister, putting forward
Malayalam's case. Following this Malayalam too was granted
classical language status.

It might not be long before every scheduled and unscheduled
language becomes classical provided the respective linguistic
state can sufficiently threaten the central government.

THE CENTRAL INSTITUTE OF
CLASSICAL TAMIL

What has classical language status meant on the ground?

In the run up to the battle for classical language status many
benefits were unreasonably anticipated or unknowingly promised.
For instance, it was said that all the world's big universities would
host a Tamil chair. At the least all Indian universities would teach
Tamil. Nothing of that sort could of course materialise.

The only concrete outcome was the formation of the Central
Institute of Classical Tamil (CICT). Incubated in the Central
Institute of Indian Languages, Mysuru it was later relocated to
Chennai. Unsurprisingly, the CICT was very quickly sucked
into narrow politics. In an ill-advised move Karunanidhi had
ensured that the chief minister of Tamilnadu was the ex-officio
chairperson. At his instance, two bodies – Aimperumkuzhu and
Enperayam (names derived from old Tamil polity), with five
and eight members, respectively – which had no foundation
in the statutes were constituted. (A member of the Enperayam
resigned when she was denied the DMK ticket to contest the
2006 elections!) The CICT's library was shifted to the state
secretariat in Fort St. George after the DMK government moved
the legislative assembly to a new complex.

Everything was undone when J. Jayalalithaa returned to
power in 2011. As ex-officio chairperson of the CICT, she refused

to convene its governing council, and therefore no decisions could be taken. The library housed in the legislative assembly was emptied and the books dumped in sack loads. The CICT office itself had to be shifted from the state-Government-owned premises, Palar Illam (appropriately, perhaps, named after a river that is legendary for carrying no water!), to the central government's Institute for Road Transport in Taramani. The only construction now completed in the land allotted for the CICT is a peripheral compound wall.

Nearly a decade and a half after its constitution the CICT has not had a single regular director. Professors, with no training in or understanding of Tamil, from central-Government-run institutions such as the Indian Institute of Technology Madras and the National Institute of Technical Teachers' Training and Research were given additional charge of the position. No regular appointments have been made to date. Academic fellows were appointed on a consolidated pay. Some badly conceived and produced books have been published. Grants for research projects and the conduct of academic workshops and conferences were sanctioned – that too has now come down to a trickle. The only regular activity is the annual award for scholars. In 2017 a proposal was mooted to relocate the CICT within the Central University of Tamilnadu in out-of-the-way Thiruvarur. Due to political opposition the proposal was shelved. Thus hangs the fate of a potentially world-class institution.

~

We need to remind ourselves that classical language status is not a matter for the state to decide. It is best left to scholars, even though they are not immune to politics, to identify what is classical and what is not. Further the assignation of such a status based on accepted scholarly standards to any language should not also mean the inferiorisation of other languages. This should be kept in mind in a context when the world is speaking of the death of languages. India is in a peculiar situation where 'tribal' languages are newly experiencing literacy and writing, and are in a sense being reborn.

Apart from its symbolism, on the ground, classical language status translates itself into substantial funds and awards. The solution to vexed claims and counterclaims for classical language status may therefore rest to an extent in the Government of India giving up its partisan patronage of Sanskrit and Hindi, and providing resources to all languages. Respective state governments can easily fund any amount for language and cultural development without depending on the central government. Surely revamping our universities and research institutions is more important than chasing the chimera of the classical. Unfortunately, the classical language claims have only served to sidestep the real issues plaguing linguistic scholarship in India.

In an informed intervention in the classical language debate Sheldon Pollock, the distinguished American Sanskritist, pointed out how many linguistic scholarly traditions are dying in our country. One can only extend this worrying diagnosis. How many scholars are there, say, who are proficient in both Tamil and Sanskrit, or in more than one Dravidian language? Is it possible now for a scholar in one Indian language to negotiate another Indian language without the mediation of English? Do we have a new generation of epigraphists to continue the task of deciphering inscriptions being discovered every other day? Surely these are signs of a serious epistemological and pedagogical crisis.

Ultimately, languages, classical or not, are the storehouses of human knowledge, and constitute the heritage and patrimony of humanity as a whole.

19

AGAINST HINDI
A Language That Doesn't Make the Cut

Let there be a solution not necessarily by us. We are not the last scions of India. Perhaps we are confused. We have more political rancour. In future times a proper solution may be arrived at…. It is my request, it is my pleading and I would say that on a solution of this issue depends the entire political future….
– C. N. Annadurai, Rajya Sabha, May 1963

IN A BOOK OMINOUSLY titled *India: The Most Dangerous Decades* (1960), US political analyst Selig Harrison was very much the prophet of doom when he warned of 'the risk of India being split up into a number of totalitarian small nationalities' – if not 'a million mutinies' as an even more bleak commentator would remark some decades later. A seedbed of discontent he identified was the Tamil south. Even though the rising DMK had formally forsworn secession from the Indian Union in the wake of the Chinese aggression of 1962, this was one prediction of Harrison that was not too far off the mark.

Language was a chink in the nationalist armour throughout the long anti-colonial struggle. Even from the turn of the twentieth century attempts were made by well-meaning nationalists from south India – the poet Subramania Bharati, for instance – to popularise the teaching of Hindi. But Hindi zealots were not particularly helpful with their endless debates, and resultant confusion, on defining Hindi and Hindustani, and its relationship with Urdu and north Indian Muslims. However, when the provincial Congress committees were reorganised in 1920, it was clear that for the national movement to succeed it had to accept the reality of the diversity of languages – Hindi could not be a binding force.

The seeds of language conflict were present even in the founding moment of the Indian nation state as its constitution was being drafted by a Constituent Assembly elected by a limited franchise. With the boycott by the Muslim League representatives the assembly was little more than a Congress legislature party. The most acrimonious debates in the Constituent Assembly were, interestingly, not on a common civil code, but on the question of the official language of the Indian Union. The arguments demonstrated that both sides viewed language as underpinning national unity – only that if the Hindi zealots saw Hindi as a unifying force, its opponents saw its imposition on an unwilling south as the cause of discord. In the event, Hindi nudged its nose at the finishing line by the casting vote of the president of the assembly, something that did little to legitimise Hindi's new constitutional status. The fifteen-year deadline for English to be an associate official language only postponed the day of reckoning.

The force of sentiment against Hindi could not have been lost on the members of the Constituent Assembly. Barely a decade earlier the Congress government in Madras Presidency had faced a most popular agitation against the teaching of Hindi compulsorily in schools. Interestingly, Tamil-speaking Muslims (who outnumbered Urdu-speaking Muslims in the Tamil region by a wide margin) joined the agitation in large numbers. The Congress's use of the same brutal colonial methods they had earlier condemned added to the force of the movement. The anti-Hindi agitation of 1937–9, it became clear, had strengthened a Tamil regional identity that continues to thrive. And it made a Periyar ('the venerated one') of E. V. Ramasamy, who led the movement.

Subramania Bharati is presumably known to every educated Indian, even Hindi zealots. Not so his childhood friend Somasundara Bharati. Somasundara Bharati was V. O. Chidambaram Pillai's associate in his great anti-British swadeshi shipping venture; his daughter Lakshmi went to prison for the cause of India's freedom and his son-in-law, L. Krishnaswami Bharati, was a member of the constituent assembly. But, in 1937, to protest compulsory Hindi in schools, he left the Congress to join the anti-Hindi agitation. This is how Hindi zealots, ostensibly for the greater good of the nation, actually end up driving nationalists away.

Their case is usually made in Hindi, resulting in a dialogue of the deaf. From Subramania Bharati to Periyar to Rajaji, Tamil leaders promoted, in good faith, Hindi language teaching in Tamilnadu to foster better integration. Only to give it up as counterproductive, the arrogance and insensitivity of Hindi advocates contributing in no small measure to their disillusionment.

In 1948, soon after Independence, there was another anti-Hindi movement, but of much lower intensity when the government attempted again to reintroduce compulsory Hindi in schools. This provoked a re-enactment of the earlier agitation. Significantly, the movement was suspended briefly when the government was engaged in the so-called police action in Hyderabad, only to be revived again. At the intervention of Kamaraj, the popular Congress leader, the government backtracked and consequently the movement was withdrawn.

With the promulgation of the Constitution, the debate shifted to the question of the official language of the Indian Union. The years leading up to 26 January 1965, when Hindi would become the sole official language, were marked by continued arguments and debates. The 1950s were marked by minor agitations such as the tarring of Hindi letters on boards at railway stations. In the various DMK conferences organised during this period the imposition of Hindi was a recurrent theme. Matters came to a head as the date approached. The DMK spearheaded the decisive anti-Hindi agitation of the 1960s.

Paradoxically nobody strengthened the case against Hindi more than the Hindi fanatics themselves. Consequently, new converts were won. P. Subbarayan, who had at best been evasive in the Constituent Assembly, and Suniti Kumar Chatterji, arguably the most distinguished of Indian linguists, both wrote notes of dissent to the report of the Official Language Commission (1955–6). The most spectacular convert was the sagely Rajaji. The man who had borne the brunt of the 1937–9 anti-Hindi agitation had a change of heart, and gave much legitimacy to the movement.

As the pitch of the pro-Hindi camp became more and more shrill its every argument continued to be effectively nailed. Countering the Hindi-is-the-majority-language argument Anna quipped that, in that case, the common crow, and not the peacock, would have to be India's national bird. Adverting to the case of national unity Rajaji pleaded, 'Let us not make the sixty million people in the South seditious, by one stroke'. If Anna's distinct Tamil rhetoric on stage and in the press enthused the newly mobilised masses of Tamilnadu, his forceful arguments in English in the house of elders, and the coldly reasoned articles of Rajaji in his journal *Swarajya*, left Hindi zealots fumbling for rational answers. Nehru's legally-not-binding assurance that English would remain as long as the south wanted did little to solve the problem. In fact, every successive move by the state to resolve the issue – for instance, the Official Language Act, 1963 – was seen as pandering to Hindi demands rather than assuaging southern fears.

With the DMK declaring Republic Day 1965 as a day of mourning the stage was set for unprecedented turmoil. If even the moderate Rajaji suggested that 'Part XVII of the Constitution', containing the section on the official language of the Union, 'be heaved and thrown into the Arabian Sea', the DMK preferred its burning. Thousands were arrested and top DMK leaders incarcerated, lending them an aura which was to be converted into electoral power in a few years. The near-spontaneous uprising of students – many of whom were first-generation literates and graduates – marked the changing social base of politics in Tamilnadu. Students who cut their teeth in that agitation – K. Kalimuthu, M. Natarajan, Inquilab, Naa. Kamarasan, P. Jeyaprakasam, and numerous others – played a prominent role in Tamil public life later.

Self-immolation as a form of protest swept the state resulting in the creation of scores of martyrs for the cause. An expression of subaltern commitment and despair, it was a favourite stick to beat Dravidian politics with until upper-caste protestors resorted to it during the anti-Mandal protests. The brutal repression let lose by the state – compounded by overzealous district officers such as T. N. Seshan – ensured that the Congress lost power in the 1967 elections. Symbolic was the defeat of K. Kamaraj, 'the kingmaker', at the hands of a young student leader. The unintended consequence was the emboldening of Indira Gandhi to decimate the Congress syndicate.

It is over half a century since the anti-Hindi agitation of 1965 and Delhi's assurance that English will continue to be the associate official language until non-Hindi-speaking states so desire. Since the days of the constituent assembly no intellectual argument has been made for why the south should accept Hindi.

What has changed in the fifty years since the 1965 anti-Hindi agitation?

If anything the case for Hindi has weakened. Over the last many decades, south India has made rapid strides in the social, political, and economic spheres. The social transformation triggered by Mandal was modelled on a caste-based reservation system fashioned in Tamilnadu. The rapid strides in education in the south have underpinned the software revolution and the leap in the service sector. On the other hand, the unending stream of uneducated and unskilled labour from the north flocking southwards selling pani puri on the streets and manning security gates is poor advertisement for the much touted employability potential of the Hindi language.

The vitality of the little and middle magazine tradition in Tamil outstrips anything remotely similar in Hindi. Despite the billions of rupees spent on official language commissions, government largesse, and the appointment of Hindi officers in every central government office only sarkari Hindi – which is about as fecund as a mule – has thrived. On the contrary, with little or no government patronage, Tamil and Malayalam constitute a far more vibrant presence in the virtual world. Unserviceable technical terminology coined in government offices and gathering dust in musty tomes does not make for a scientific language.

Such inadequacies apart Hindi's trajectory in modern India has been inflected – or rather, infected – by Hindu communalism. Hindi zealots have, on the one hand, been intent on Sanskritising their language and, on the other, erasing its rich dialectal variety, leading to separate movements such as those to protect Maithili and Bhojpuri. In the hands of a majoritarian government, with utter contempt for the cultural plurality and diversity of our great nation, the pipe dream of making Hindi the sole official language takes on nightmarish proportions.

Paradoxically, as the Hindi zealots realise it to be a lost cause, they have become even more vociferous in their demands. State patronage to Hindi continues unabated, a process that has gained momentum since 2014. Prime Minister Narendra Modi's insistence on speaking Hindi, a *shudh* (pure) variety at that, even in non-Hindi-speaking regions, has caused further bitterness. All this has fuelled renewed resentment. Recently it has gained unexpected traction in Karnataka: Bengaluru's Namma Metro was forced to take down Hindi signboards.

But perhaps what politics could not solve globalisation and technology have mitigated to an extent. The continued retreat of the state in many walks of life has made the official language question often irrelevant.

Hindi simply does not make the cut.

20

NATIONALISATION OF COPYRIGHT

'THERE IS POPULAR FEELING that the works of Sri C. Subramania Bharati, the great Tamil poet of Modern Tamil Renaissance, should be acquired by the Government and made available for the use of the public generally at as cheap a cost as possible.' When T. S. Avinashilingam Chettiar, Education Minister of Madras, announced the government takeover of the copyright of all the works of Subramania Bharati with these words on the floor of the Madras Legislative Assembly on 12 March 1949 he would have little realised that it was a unique moment in literary history.

A distinguishing sign of the nation has been its claim over everything including literature. But the above constitutes an unprecedented instance where the nation state staked a claim over the writings of its citizen, acquired the copyright, and put it in the public domain. Such an initiative of the state is unheard of. The government's executive action to divest copyright of certain literary works from individual owners and make it public property is unique. Acquisition of land, mines, minerals, and industries is not unfamiliar. In the immediate aftermath of Independence, when the new citizenry looked to the state for a variety of public needs and demands, it seems literature too came within the ambit of the state.

Like all events this move too has a history. As we saw earlier Bharati died at a young age under particularly indigent circumstances. Even though he died unsung his writings achieved iconic status, especially in the context of fervent Indian nationalist mobilisation and Tamil cultural awakening. By the time of Indian independence there prevailed the anomalous situation of some private individuals (not the writer's family, as copyright had been alienated in distress) possessing proprietary rights over what was becoming the cultural patrimony of a larger community. Copyright laws were invoked by its owners to restrict the use of Bharati's works in books, films, music, and theatre. This triggered a popular movement, in which cultural forces across the ideological spectrum – Indian nationalists, Tamil nationalists, communists, non-partisan cultural activists – took part and demanded that the newly independent nation state 'nationalise' the works of the poet. It is quite striking that the demand for 'nationalisation' of intangible assets was made even before similar demands on material resources, such as mines and industries, were made. A contemporary pamphlet made this demand with great emotional charge:

> … Leaders such as Rajaji had unanimously declared … that people should proudly sing Bharati's songs.
>
> But how is one to sing out the songs? And where to sing these songs? Are not individuals claiming them as 'It's my property! I own it!'…. Is it right … to let the immortal poet of Tamilnadu to be locked up in an iron safe and being made a matter of business?
>
> … [W]e have every right to ask the people living in a free country 'Who owns Bharati?'.
>
> Why should the Madras government not issue a proclamation that 'Bharati's poems and writings are the property of Tamilnadu. No individual has any right over it.'

The government yielded to popular pressure and after much legal wrangling and hair-splitting acquired the copyright by paying Rs 15,000 to one copyright holder and Rs 5,000 each to the poet's widow and his two daughters. A. V. Meiyappa Chettiar, the movie baron who owned broadcast rights, thought it better to transfer copyright gratis rather than antagonise the government. The government, however, held on to the copyright for over a decade until it brought out what were called 'authorised editions' before putting all the works in the public domain for free and unrestricted use.

The Government of Tamilnadu's style of handling this issue is in marked contrast to the way in which the Government of India and the Government of West Bengal responded in relation to a similar case: the works of Rabindranath Tagore. Not only was no state effort taken to put Tagore's works in the public domain, but when, in 1991, the copyright was to have legally expired after fifty calendar years of the author's death, the Government of India took the extraordinary step of issuing an ordinance to extend copyright by another ten years – a move that was subsequently granted legislative sanction through an amendment to the Indian Copyright Act of 1956. This legislation gave legal sanction to Visva-Bharati's stranglehold over Tagore that effectively curtailed innovative new editions and translations of Tagore not to speak of the manner in which the creativity of musicians was strangled. (The publishing boom following the lapse of copyright in Tagore's works in 2001 speaks volumes – pun intended – for the pent-up potential in his works.)

The Tamilnadu government's action to directly intervene in the intellectual property rights of a poet was no one-off move. Thirty-one years after the nationalisation of Bharati's works the writings of his prime follower Bharatidasan, the poet of the Dravidian movement, was nationalised by the DMK government to mark his birth centenary. Once again this was the culmination of a long struggle in civil society. It was generally believed that the delay in the nationalisation of Bharatidasan was not for lack of will on the part of the state or the seriousness of the public demand, but the bickering in the poet's family and the unreasonable pecuniary expectations on their part. In the event the copyright was acquired for a sum of Rs 10 lakhs. Despite the wrangling over the exact monetary compensation the act of nationalisation was seen more as a great cultural and national honour that endorsed the standing of the honoured writer with the stamp of the state's authority. This aspect of cultural policy and politics soon changed.

This change became manifest with the next acquisition that came a few years later. J. Jayalalithaa, who had become the next chief minister, was facing a mid-term crisis. In the face of strident criticism that she was swerving off Dravidian ideology, in a tactical move, she announced the nationalisation of the writings of C. N. Annadurai. Pictures of Jayalalithaa handing over a cheque of a staggering sum of seventy-five lakh rupees to Anna's ailing widow went some way towards saving face to her Dravidian apologists. As a sop to the communists Jayalalithaa also nationalised the works of Pattukkottai Kalyanasundaram, the film lyricist and communist songster.

The subsequent DMK government under M. Karunanidhi, realising the populist appeal of such state takeover of copyright that also proved to be a windfall to the family members of the writers in question, nationalised the works of about twenty writers during his five-year term (1996–2001). While the literary worth and centrality to the cultural world of some of the writers such as Thriu. Vi. Kalyanasundara Mudaliar, Maraimalai Adigal, and Va. Ra. were beyond question the nationalised writers included V. O. Chidambaram Pillai and V. V. S. Aiyar whose copyright had long expired! Interestingly some writers such as Va. Ra. and A. S. K. Iyengar had no legal heirs; no solatium was therefore paid making the whole move of nationalisation unnecessary. In one instance, that of V. Swaminatha Sarma, the gratuity was paid to the copyright holder rather than to the heir against the express state policy of only rewarding family members and not compensating non-family copyright holders. In cases such as that of Kavi Ka. Mu. Sheriff it was clearly a case of state patronage for an indigent writer and had nothing to do with literary importance.

By the 1990s the state takeover of literary copyright degenerated into competitive patronage and a veritable race for gaining cultural mileage. The acute financial crisis that confronted the Jayalalithaa government in 2001 did not deter the state from continuing with the policy of takeover of literary copyright – though at somewhat reduced monetary rates with a cap of five lakh rupees per litterateur! Once again this included such historical writers as the first Tamil novelist Mayuram Vedanayakam Pillai who had died in 1889! The only instance which actually bucked the trend was the nationalisation of Pudumaippithan which was more the result of petty literary politics than sincere demand for nationalisation – the end result being that the family of Pudumaippithan was given a solatium far less than the market value of his writings. Added to this was the ignominy of being equated with Ku. Pa. Sethu Ammal, a nondescript writer, whose writings were also nationalised at that time.

The DMK government, which took over power in 2006, continued with this policy at an accelerated pace with another twenty writers being the beneficiaries of this state largesse. At the last count the writings of over a hundred writers have been nationalised.

The future scenario looks somewhat comical. A bedridden Rajam Krishnan pleaded with the government that her works be nationalised! And it was accepted in 2009 for a compensation of three lakh rupees: thus giving her the distinction of having her works in the public domain when she was very much alive.

Consequently, the family of every ailing and dead writer is stalking the corridors of the Fort St. George hoping to receive a purse. It has become a routine in every obituary and in every centenary celebration to make a demand for nationalisation.

~

The Government of Tamilnadu's intervention in the sphere of literary production and intellectual copyright has been novel and unprecedented. What began as a unique and solitary instance where the works of an outstanding writer who decisively shaped the modern Tamil language and achieved iconic status was freed from the shackles of private individuals (who were not even heirs) took on completely different proportions. In a modern society where the individual and his unique creative abilities are privileged and accorded legal sanction in the form of copyright and intellectual property rights (which the state is expected to uphold) the state upturned this principle. This was due to popular demand that emphasised the social claim over the works of an individual. The fact that Bharati was long dead and the beneficiaries of the market for his works were not his family added a tremendous legitimacy to the demand for nationalisation and its eventual acceptance by the state. Further, in the immediate aftermath of Independence where the state was expected to work wonders and fulfil every public demand, and in the prevailing zeitgeist that favoured a socialist understanding of property rights, copyright over literary works was seen as being well within the ambit of state intervention.

However, there is no predetermined-ness to this: 'national' poets are by no means rare in the various languages of India which became modern languages under colonial aegis and through anti-colonial struggle. But the centrality of the cultural figures to that particular society, the accident of age (that is, early death in dire circumstances: a recently alive figure would be less amenable for such takeover by the state especially in the absence of uncontested and consensual social demand), the level of politicisation of the society, the democratic impulses active in the civil society, and so on, are some contingent factors that could make for the success of such efforts. It is instructive to remember that such demands were not made even in relation to such nationalist colossus such as Gandhi and Nehru.

A crucial factor that has contributed to the success of the nationalisation of literature has been the narrowness of the literary market. The acceptance of solatium by the family and heirs of the dead writer in lieu of copyright is predicated upon the abysmal monetary returns that would accrue from actually publishing these works. It is said that the family of the Tamil writer Akilon (Jnanpith award winner) refused the government takeover of copyright on the ground that the loss of royalties would far outstrip the one-time payment made by the state.

In the budget speech of 2009 when the Government of Tamilnadu announced on the floor of the legislative assembly its intention of nationalising the works of, among others, Mu. Varadarajan, Kannadasan, Sundara Ramaswamy, and Lakshmi, their families rejected the offer. The attempt to acquire the copyright of Sundara Ramaswamy was an act of political vendetta – to throttle the publisher/copyright owner Kalachuvadu for its criticism of the DMK.

The combination of honour and monetary advantage that nationalisation of literary works bestows undoubtedly underpins this particular state intervention in the literary sphere. The post-Independence Indian state, certainly its Tamilnadu variety, has played the role of royal patron in the way it has supported literature. However, the indiscriminate and liberal use of this measure has undermined the honour. The pressures of democratic electoral politics have tended to let the honour component fade before the glistening of gold.

21

EELAM, TAMILS

Is there an authentic Eelam narrative in Tamilnadu since 2009?
Since 2009 there has not been a single unilinear or monolithic
Eelam narrative in Tamilnadu. The first response to the end of the
civil war and the annihilation of the LTTE was one of disbelief as
few believed that the LTTE would or could be militarily defeated.
The LTTE was thus a victim of its own image of invincibility.
The myth that one section holds, that Velupillai Prabhakaran is
still alive, stems from this disbelief. That the final days of war
coincided with the parliamentary elections and the subsequent
formation of the UPA II government paused the immediate
emergence of a new narrative.

The first few months following the LTTE debacle was attended
by the DMK government and Karunanidhi's desperate bid to
shore up his lost image as the leader and protector of Tamils
worldwide. The MPs' delegation to Sri Lanka and the World
Classical Tamil Conference were part of this move. So one crucial
element of the narrative has been the loss of legitimacy suffered
by the DMK and Karunanidhi. The Congress party's historical
image as a formation opposed to Tamil interests was solidified
in this process. Evidently the Congress was a millstone that took
the DMK with it in the 2011 elections.

The Tamil press has consistently reported on Sri Lanka.
A dominant element in this reportage is the confirmation of
the Sri Lankan state's malafide intentions vis-à-vis the Tamil
people. Three periodicals – *Ananda Vikatan*, *Junior Vikatan*, and
the daily *Dinamani* immediately before, during, and after the
war – rode the wave of this perception. Even a cursory reading

of the reports would indicate the popular inability to come to terms with the defeat of the LTTE, and the anger against the Sri Lankan state for its treatment of its Tamil citizens. There have been extensive reports of the plight of the Tamil people in the Sri Lankan government's rehabilitation camps. The pro-China tilt of Sri Lanka and the attendant dangers for India's geostrategic interests have been stressed.

A disproportionate share of attention (measured by the yardstick of actual strength on the ground) has been cornered by Tamil nationalist fringe groups, who have occupied the space opened up by the elimination of the LTTE, the perpetrators of the assassination of Rajiv Gandhi, for the articulation of views unable to find a voice since 1991. The shift in J. Jayalalithaa's stand – to take up the Tamil cause in a bid to undermine the legitimacy of the DMK and Karunanidhi – radically altered the playing field.

The UN resolution provided the proximate cause for the simmering discontent in Tamilnadu to boil over. There was a steady undercurrent of resentment against the Sri Lankan government and the way the UPA government provided support to Sri Lanka. The documentation provided by international agencies such as the Channel 4 documentaries, or books like Gordon Weiss's *Cage* and Frances Harrison's *Still Counting the Dead* have given a new dimension to what were seen as only pro-Eelam propaganda.

But the protests are still largely inchoate. There are no clearly defined objectives or aims. Now that the UN session is over and the state government is beginning to take a tougher stance, student protests will die inevitably. But the roots of discontent will remain.

Has Mullivaikal and the delayed rehabilitation of the Tamil refugees had real resonance in Tamilnadu? When Prabhakaran was killed and the LTTE wiped out, there did not seem to be much reaction in Tamilnadu, so why has the anger over Sri Lankan Tamils come back?

There were at least seventeen cases of self-immolation in Tamilnadu in the months leading up to May 2009. The self-immolation of K. Muthukumar, a journalist, in January 2009, made a deep impression on the Tamil public mind.

The singular absence of an outburst in the wake of the bloodbath – contrary to the threat of some Tamil nationalist leaders that 'rivers of blood would flow' if the least harm were to befall Prabhakaran – can be adduced to the following factors. First, the LTTE was a victim of its own image of invincibility, an image bolstered by smaller political forces like Vaiko, P. Nedumaran, Seeman, and others who still maintain that Prabhakaran is alive. Another aspect to the containment of the situation was the role played by the then DMK government – for which the UPA government and the Congress in particular should be eternally grateful to the DMK. Karunanidhi's self-cultivated image as the leader of Tamils was exploited to deflect the mounting protests even though by the end of 2009 that image had worn thin.

Who are the authentic voices with influence in the Tamilnadu discourse on the Sri Lankan Tamil question?

Here it is appropriate to examine what Tamil Eelam means in the Tamil context. It means different things in different discourses. In the mainstream English discourse Tamil Eelam is secessionist, with a clear political, territorial, nationalist, and sovereign dimension to it. In the Tamil popular discourse, however, Tamil Eelam encompasses a whole range of issues of which an independent sovereign state for Tamils is only one part, perhaps a very crucial part. In the Tamil imaginary it has to do with cultural sharing, and evokes a social resonance and an emotional response – a distinction not to be lost sight of. And even within the Tamil imaginary there are various shades of opinion. There is an entire spectrum of Tamil opinion, ranging from fringe Tamil nationalist groups to the other end of the spectrum encompassing moderate and liberal views.

Is there a relationship of the Eelam concept to the larger ongoing Dravidian movement?

Tamil identity politics has a complex history, and it is necessary to trace its trajectory before analysing its relationship to Eelam. Tamil identity politics has its intellectual genesis in the work of nineteenth-century European Orientalists and the rediscovery of the Tamil classics by Tamil scholars. This coalesced with the Non-Brahmin Movement that emerged in the first decades of the twentieth century. The Non-Brahmin Movement had at its core an antagonism to the social base of Indian nationalism which was exploited by the British. What was essentially an upper-caste and elite movement was radically transformed by Periyar in the 1920s. The ideology was radicalised, and its social base was vastly expanded to encompass the large mass of middle and lower castes. With the split in the movement and the formation of the DMK in 1949 the movement joined the mainstream of electoral politics. However, popular misconception notwithstanding, the Dravidian movement was never primarily a secessionist movement. Periyar's articulation of secession – whether for a separate Tamilnadu in 1937–9 or for Dravidastan in the years leading up to 1947, or when he subsequently revised his position to once again ask for a separate Tamilnadu in the 1950s – was always a contingent demand and not an absolute one. Periyar always raised the issue of secession in relation to the lack of power for the backward classes and lower castes. If the Indian Union came in the way of the aspirations of the Shudras he said that he would demand secession. (How else would K. Kamaraj have agreed to rub shoulders with Periyar for over a decade, from 1954 to 1967?) Hardly ever did the DK or DMK actually launch an agitation for a separate state. The DMK saw the Chinese aggression in 1962 as a godsend to have a face-saving way of dropping the secessionist demand.

It is important to note that the intellectual resources for Tamil identity politics were shared by Tamilnadu and Eelam. But a crucial element was missing in Eelam. Sri Lankan Tamils could never identify themselves with the (dominant) non-Brahmin component of the Dravidian movement, nor endorse the radical social reform programme championed by Periyar.

The demand for a sovereign and independent Tamil Eelam emerged only in the 1970s and should not therefore be confused with the Dravidian movement.

Tamil nationalist fringe groups in Tamilnadu have, however, exploited the apparent overlap. Over the last couple of decades these groups have used Sri Lanka to champion a proxy Tamil nationalism which has certainly not helped the Sri Lankan Tamil people and might have positively harmed their interests. It has given a handle to forces inimical to Eelam Tamil interests to depict the entire struggle and the support for it from Tamilnadu as anti-(Indian) national in character.

Is Eelam still a goal or would devolution under the Thirteenth Amendment address the alienation?

The annihilation of the LTTE has left a political vacuum. In the decade preceding the July 1983 pogrom there were many contending political forces in Tamil Sri Lanka – from the moderates to the many groups of armed militants. The systematic elimination of all such forces by the LTTE resulted in the absence of a formation to articulate the grievances of the Sri Lankan Tamils in a language comprehensible to the international community. The sad absence of a spokesman like, say, A. Amirthalingam, a senior leader of the Tamil United Liberation Front (TULF) or a jurist such as Neelan Tiruchelvam is particularly missed. The TULF leaders had a consummate understanding of the global situation, and had a good command over diplomatic language to articulate legitimate Tamil interests within a framework of international affairs and geostrategic interests.

Another aspect is the confusion created by Tamil nationalist fringe groups in Tamilnadu. We are in a strange situation. All the voices that we hear are from those outside Sri Lanka – Tamils in the diaspora and various shades of opinion in Tamilnadu. The Tamils in Sri Lanka themselves seem to have no voice.

The Eelam Tamil diaspora is strongly committed to an independent Eelam. In the present context where democratic rights of the Tamils in Sri Lanka are stifled and dignified existence is a question, their views cannot be ascertained.

Until all the Tamil people are rehabilitated, those in illegal and interminable detention tried, war criminals punished, and the demilitarisation of the traditional Tamil homeland is complete, it would be merely of academic interest to discuss the political future of Eelam Tamils. This might be inconvenient, but this is nevertheless the reality.

Are the people of Tamilnadu really connected to the Sri Lankan Tamils or is it a creation of political parties desperate for issues to rally masses?
The student protests of early 2013, for instance, was only the tip of the iceberg: there is little doubt that the people of Tamilnadu are really connected to the Sri Lankan Tamils. The political parties are only making capital out of this strong undercurrent of empathy and concern.

The chasm that had developed between Tamilnadu and Sri Lanka after Independence began to be bridged after 1983. The steady exchange of people, ideas, cultural artefacts, and others, has been transformed by digital information technology. The role of the Tamil diaspora has to be discussed separately. But suffice to say they have spearheaded the fashioning of a shared culture between Tamils in India and the dispersed Tamil community across the world.

The mental universe of many a thinking Tamil would be seriously impoverished without the poetry of a Cheran or the prose of an A. Muttulingam. This new formation is a virtual community, an imagined community of Tamils, to be seen not as a nation or as a territorial community, but as a cultural community. To mistake it for a political community or even a social community may be to completely miss the point. Perhaps that is why the arena of the last conflict, Mullivaikkal, will be a permanent scar on the Tamil psyche.

Questions posed by V. S. Sambandan

22

DALITS AND
CULTURAL RIGHTS[1]

ON 9 AUGUST 2016 the Madras High Court observed that it was both moral obligation and legal mandate for the state to permit Dalits to worship at the Bhadrakaliamman temple in Kallimedu, a village near Vedaranyam in Nagapattinam district, Tamilnadu, and to perform rituals during the Adi festival. It further hoped that 'some compromise' would be worked out 'so that at least in the next year … the temple festival is performed without any problem or hitch'. With this the curtains have come down on the temple festival even before it could be observed.

In Kallimedu the Bhadrakaliamman temple stands on a site claimed to be some 800 years old. The medieval poet Kalamegam composed a song about it. Now administered by the Government of Tamilnadu through the Hindu Religious and Charitable Endowments Department, its last major *kumbhabhisekham* (re-consecration) was conducted in 1957. The temple's annual festival takes place over five days in the Tamil month of *adi* (mid-July to mid-August). As in many Tamil villages the intermediate castes sponsor and conduct rituals and festivities – called *mandagapadi* – on specific days assigned according to custom. The local Dalits (Adi Dravidars) join the festivities, but do not have the privilege of holding the mandagapadi.

Kallimedu consists of Pillaimars, traditionally a landholding caste, apart from a sprinkling of some service castes. Dalits

[1] Written jointly with J. Balasubramaniam.

live in the adjoining hamlet of Pazhag Kallimedu. The two communities number some 150 families each. The temple is located in between, and the Dalits claim that in the past the temple was situated in their quarters.

The Viduthalai Chiruthaigal Katchi, headed by Thol. Thirumavalavan, has considerable influence and presence among the Dalits. For the last few years Dalits have been claiming mandagapadi rights, a demand stonewalled by the Pillaimars. In August 2015 the headman of the Pazhag Kallimedu, N. Pakkirisamy, filed a writ petition in the high court. Among the prayers was the demand for the deity to be taken in procession through the Dalit quarters. 'Prima facie,' Justice M. M. Sundaresh observed, 'the petitioner cannot be treated differently' and posted the case for a later date to hear respondents' objections.

Matters came to a head in 2016 when the Dalits, unable to make any headway, threatened to embrace Islam. Evidently this was a tactical move. The state and the media promptly paid heed. The Wahhabbist Tamilnadu Thowheed Jamath's associates made an appearance; while extending moral support they stated that conversion should be based on a commitment to Islamic tenets rather than as a form of protest. Can the BJP be far behind? Its state president, Tamilisai Soundararajan, soon made a visit to the village. It is rumoured that a senior Hindutva ideologue too had intervened promising to meet Dalit demands if the conversion threat was dropped. Later a fringe group, the Hindu Makkal Katchi, was involved in negotiating a compromise. As its anti-Dalit image was reinforced by the Una protests in Gujarat and the insult to Mayawati, the BJP was under enormous pressure to shore up its claim to speak for the entire Hindu community.

The district collector hurried to the spot. Soon a minister followed. What followed is described in officialese as 'talks'. In reality it was pressure to maintain status quo. The talks were set in the language of compromise and concessions rather than in the discourse of fairness, rights, and justice – for instance, one of the concessions was the offer of mandagapadi on the sixth day, after the festival is effectively over. When the Dalits did not budge the state administration banned the temple festival. It was against this order that the Pillaimars filed a writ resulting in the observation cited at the beginning of this essay.

TRAGEDY REPEATS ITSELF

Unfortunately those familiar with the history of such disputes may not entertain the same optimism as the learned judge. The Dalits' struggle for an equal share of honours in temple festivals has repeatedly ended in a failure.

Rewind to 1997. In the Swarnamurtheeswarar temple of Kandadevi in Sivaganga district the Devendrakula Vellalars staked a claim to play a full role in the temple festival. The Puthiya Tamilagam party, headed by Dr K. Krishnaswamy, filed a suit in the high court praying for this right. On 6 July 1998 the high court instructed the district collector to ensure the full and complete participation of the Dalits. Apparently to no avail.

In June 2005 the state secretary of the CPI (M), N. Varadarajan, filed a writ petition seeking the enforcement of the above high court direction. A division bench held that the denial of the right to pull the temple car and participate fully in the festival violated Section 21 of the Constitution. Adverting to the token participation of Dalits in the preceding year the bench directed the administration to ensure full participation.

Consequently, the 2005 festival saw the massive deployment of police. Citizens were lulled into believing that the executive was preparing to uphold constitutional rights. As it turned out the reverse was the case. Hundreds of Dalits were rounded up, the pulling of the temple car was advanced by an hour, and the event was truncated to forty-five minutes. Only twenty-six Dalits were permitted to lay their hands on the ropes of the car. The car festivals in subsequent years were suspended.

In 2014 another petition was filed in the Madurai branch of the high court. The judge reiterated that the locally dominant caste of Nattars could not claim first honours, and that full participation of all people irrespective of caste be ensured. Following this the district administration conducted the temple festival without the pulling of the temple car, on the ground that the car needed repairs. The car continues to be under repair ever since!

IN KOVILPATTI

In the Senbakavalliamman temple of Koilpatti an eleven-day annual festival is observed. The Devendrakula Vellalars demanded mandagapadi rights. Coming in the wake of many months of intense and bloody violence involving Devendrakula Vellalars and Thevars starting from the outrage of Kodiyankulam in August 1995 this demand too ended in bloodshed. The car festival remains suspended since then.

More violence followed triggered by the naming of one of the state-owned transport corporations after Sundaralingam, a Devendrakula Vellalar who fought in the anti-colonial army of Kattabomman at the end of the eighteenth century. Buses painted with the Dalit hero's name were stoned, torched, and not permitted entry into Thevar villages. In the event the government decided to drop all names from the transport corporations starting from the venerable Thiruvalluvar.

Again, in mid-2016, in M. Karisalkulam in Sivaganga district, a similar conflict broke out when Dalits demanded the right to take mulaippari in the Muthumariamman temple. After negotiations Dalits agreed to a compromise of performing the ritual in a place earmarked for them.

These are not simple cases of Dalit entry into temples, an issue that animated the Congress during the freedom movement. With the progressive social transformation taking place in Tamilnadu temples have largely been opened up for worship to all communities. The conflict now is in relation to honours. When Dalit communities experience social and economic mobility they become assertive and often stake claim to honours in religious contexts and spaces. In a local rural situation their claims in festivals and rituals become contentious with dominant castes stonewalling their efforts. This leads to a struggle.

It is not difficult to discern a pattern.

In the first instance Dalits assert themselves to a right over social space, a demand often framed in the language of religion. The locally dominant caste refuses to acknowledge it, and depending on the local balance of power and the prevailing political situation (read, the party in power and its predominant support base), the demand is either contained or it flares up. If the local Dalit leadership is sagacious it builds supralocal support and seeks help from a Dalit party. In a bid to attract attention a threat to convert to Islam is issued. The local dominant caste cares little for this demand – and may in fact see it as a resolution to their immediate fears – but this scares the wits out of those with a vested interest in the maintenance of a religious status quo. When legal intervention is sought, courts, thankfully, often uphold the rule of law. And then it is up to the executive to enforce it. But as history bears out, the executive and its political masters (irrespective of the party in power) fail to uphold its spirit if not even the letter. Soon the fear of the collapse of law and order is enough to quieten the courts. A good round of police beating and shooting is enough to serve the twin purpose of teaching the 'upstarts' a lesson as well as educate the court of the cost of upholding constitutional rights. A judicial enquiry is ordered, and little comes out of it. As this process unfolds various political parties maintain a deafening silence fearing the 'stigma' of being branded pro-Dalit.

Sadly such blatant violation of the rule of law scarcely disturbs the conscience of the citizenry, or the larger Hindu community which claims to constitute 84 per cent of India's population.

Kandadevi is neither the first case. Nor will Kallimedu be the last.

23

JALLIKATTU
Catching a Sport by Its Horns

> I suppose, from a moral point of view … the whole bullfight
> is indefensible; there is certainly much cruelty, there is always
> danger, either sought or unlooked for, and there is always death,
> and I should not try to defend it now, only to tell honestly the
> things I have found true about it.
> – Ernest Hemingway, on the Spanish bullfight, in *Death in the
> Afternoon* (1932)

THE TAMIL WORD FOR OX and cattle, *maadu*, also means wealth.
As the unprecedented mass uprising all over Tamilnadu unfolded
in January 2017, jallikattu, the sport of taming the bull, became a
symbol of Tamil pride and identity. The scale and fervour of the
protests caught many by surprise, and left analysts fumbling for
an explanation. How did a sport with origins in a pastoral world
capture the imagination of a vast and differentiated linguistic
community and become its symbol in the modern world?

One reason for the passion jallikattu evoked is its long history
and its embeddedness in the cultural economy of the Tamils.

The earliest evidence of this sport comes from *Kalithogai*,
an anthology of 150 long poems, which forms part of the
classical corpus of Tamil Sangam poetry. Dating to the earlier
centuries of the common era the *Kalithogai* poems from the
section on Mullai – set in the pastoral land – provide the earliest
descriptions of this sport, *eru thazhuvuthal* (literally, embracing
the bull). Attributed to the poet Nalluruthiran, five poems

totalling some 350 breathtaking lines, conjure up jallikattu's thrill, tumult, adventure, and breathless pace.

In the fourteenth century the phenomenally erudite Nachinarkkiniyar, praised as the 'star commentator among scholars', glossed the poems and provided an elucidation. A thousand years after their composition the conventions of jallikattu depicted in *Kalithogai* were evidently familiar to him.

> Cowherds deck themselves with wreaths
> and garlands made from these flowers,
> and gather in the open
> throwing their formidable challenge.
> The killer bulls are let loose into the ring
> whose sharpened horns shine
> like Siva's battle-axe.
> Then come the beating drums
> sounding like thunder.
> Smoke goes up and dust raised.
> Maidens come and stand in a row.
> …
> Look at the silkworm-coloured bull
> piercing his brave adversary
> with his horns and goring him!
> …
> Here is the black-coloured one
> with a bright white spot on his forehead.
> Look at him bearing down on his challenger
> piercing his stomach
> and ripping out his intestines.
> Doesn't he look like the Supreme One,
> digging into the bosom of Death,
> and pulling out his intestines
> to offer them as food for the ghouls?

And now to the white bull with red spots.
His challenger is brave and unafraid
but the bull thrusts his horns
into his chest and disables him. (*Kalithogai* 101)[1]

The sport was deeply imbricated in marriage rituals, and young men could win the hands of the girls they loved only by taming the bulls their family had raised. The girl's friend tells the young man eyeing her friend:

'Young man,
if you can overcome this bull,
angrier than a rutting elephant,
this girl will hold aloft the banner of victory.
We will give our dark-haired girl in marriage
to the young man who will tame
the killer bull that stands beside his master –
the one with a garland,
playing a sad melody on his flute
and holds his staff against his shoulder.' (*Kalithogai* 102)

In another poem, she reiterates:

'She is the one about whom
her parents have made an announcement
by the beating of drums:
she will be given in marriage
only to a young man who fights
their family bull and subdues him.'

'Go, tell her parents
that I accept their challenge!'

---

[2] All translations from *Kalithogai* in this essay are by M. L. Thangappa.

'We will not wait.
Let him come at once,' they said.
'Beat the drums to start the game.'

And after the game is over, the girls sing thus:

'The shepherd maiden shall never hug
anyone afraid of the horns
of the killer bull.
The shepherd maiden will never embrace
anyone not brave enough to face the bull.
Will only accept the hand
of one who confronts
and subdues the bull fearlessly.
The one who is afraid of horns
and clings to his life, not knowing
that it is but a breath of air,
will not win the hand of this maiden.
If the young man lies between the horns of the bull
as if between the breasts of his beloved
our people will not demand
bride price from him.
Let us sing thus,
and dance our *kuravai* dance...' (*Kalithogai* 103)

Sometime after *Kalithogai*, in the great Tamil epic Silappadhikaram, in the chapter on the kuravai dance of the cowherds, there are references to the taming of the bull as a prerequisite for marriage with the cowherd girls. During the seventh to the ninth centuries, as the great wave of the Bhakti movement originated in the south, in the moving devotional poems of the Vaishnava saint-poets, the Alwars, there are a number of references to Kannan (Krishna) taming the seven bulls to take the hand of his favourite *gopika*, the Tamil cowherd girl, Nappinnai. As Friedhelm Hardy, in his authoritative study of Krishna devotion and worship in south India, *Viraha-Bhakti* (1983) points out, this myth is either completely absent in north Indian traditions or appear later, clearly borrowing from Tamil. Further, drawing on the ethnographic study of the Todas by M. B. Emeneau that shows a similar ritual sport involving buffaloes, he argues that bull taming is an ancient folk practice absorbed into early Krishna worship in the Tamil country.

From the evidence of these nearly two-millennium old poems and their medieval commentary it is striking how little the sport has changed over the centuries: the mad rush of the bulls into the ring, the enthusiasm of the young men out to tame them, the spilt blood as man meets bull, the honour at stake, the egging of the spectators…. Perhaps only foreign tourists are missing!

~

Modern Tamil fiction provides even richer descriptions of jallikattu in contemporary times bearing testimony to the continuing tradition. But a few elements have changed. It is no more called eru thazhuvuthal, but goes by the name of jallikattu and *manji virattu*. The participants in this sport are not from the shepherd caste, but belong predominantly to communities with martial occupations such as Kallars, Maravars, and Agamudaiyars.

The pioneer was B. R. Rajam Aiyar, the vedantin and disciple of Swami Vivekananda. His 1893 Tamil novel, *Kamalambal Charithiram* (English translation by Stuart Blackburn, as *The Fatal Rumour*), depicts the celebration accompanying the sport with men and women turning up in huge numbers. Rajam Aiyar also records technical terms associated with this sport. A stubborn bull that stands its ground, unmindful of the intimidating atmosphere, is called *nindru kuthi kalai*.

Ku. Pa. Rajagopalan's 'Veerammalin Kalai' (Veerammal's Bull), a tightly written short story of barely four pages, first published in 1936 in the modernist literary journal Manikodi, lays bare the question of honour – of community and of self – that is deeply imbricated in jallikattu. Veerammal is the local Kallar headman's daughter. She has been betrothed to her cross cousin (the son of her mother's brother; as noted earlier, a preferred form of marriage unique to Dravidian kinship), Kathan, whom she loves deeply. In the communitarian dinner, the day before the event, her father boasts that none dare challenge the bull lovingly raised by Veerammal. Stung by this taunt Kathan takes up the challenge. When Veerammal chuckles instinctively at his bravado Kathan takes insult. Knowing the ferocity of her bull, and fearing for his safety, Veerammal sends word not to persist with the challenge – which only strengthens Kathan's resolve. The next day, in the ring, Kathan bravely takes on the bull, hangs on to its hump, and succeeds in untying the scarf on its horns, the trophy, with his teeth – but not before he is gored. Taken to the hospital he calls for Veerammal and proudly hands over the bloodstained trophy before he collapses. Back at her home a proud Veerammal, flinging a word of abuse, spears her pet bull.

Kothamangalam Subbu (psued. 'Kalaimani') is now largely known for his novel Thillana Mohanambal, later made into the eponymous film starring Sivaji Ganesan and Padmini. Few know that his first foray into fiction, in the 1930s, was with a short story, 'Manji Virattu'. Not satisfied with writing a short story on this theme Subbu serialised a sprawling novel, Rao Bahadur Singaram, again in the popular weekly, Ananda Vikatan. This story, centred on the romance between a young girl who raises a bull and a youth who sets out to tame it, was filmed (Vilaiyattu Pillai, 1970) by the same team that produced Thillana Mohanambal.

But the locus classicus of jallikattu remains C. S. Chellappa's Vadi Vaasal (English translation by N. Kalyan Raman as The

Arena). Conceiving it as a short story Chellappa later expanded it into a novella. Out of print for a quarter of a century after its initial publication in 1959, *Vadi Vaasal* has over the last twenty years been reprinted more than a dozen times – an indication of not only its literary merit, but also the cultural importance accorded to jallikattu.

Many of these works, in their later impressions, were embellished with sketches and paintings by outstanding artistes such as K. M. Adhimoolam and Trotsky Marudhu. An amateur photographer as well, C. S. Chellappa was so fascinated by the sport that he captured some great moments. Meanwhile articles by Panditamani M. Kathiresan Chettiar and other scholars provided an intellectual framework for the celebration of jallikattu as a Tamil sport.

This history of the literary representation of jallikattu is testimony to its enduring allure. A close look at the content of these literary texts provides insights into the changes taking place within the sport and its dynamic interaction with society.

The *Kalithogai* poems depicted the mood of riotous carnival where young men decked in colourful flowers, 'embraced the bull' (*eru thazhuvuthal*), and tamed it. Young women who watched this swore that they would not marry, even in their next life, a man who feared the bulls' sharp horns. The focus of the poems is on the valour and the gore that accompanies this heroic feat. If anyone got hurt it is the youth and not the bull. The term 'bullfight', drawing from the Spanish sport, to describe jallikattu, is therefore unfortunate: for in the Spanish case the bull has to be slowly and artistically killed by the matador, and even when he is gored the bull has to meet its end – it cannot come into the ring again. In jallikattu it is the men and occasionally the spectators who are injured or get killed.

By the time of B. R. Rajam Aiyar the description of the festival becomes naturalistic, written with the eye of an ethnographer.

272 TAMIL CHARACTERS

Unlike the *Kalithogai* poems set in a stylised pastoral zone, the geographical location is now specified as (the erstwhile composite districts of) Madurai, Ramanathapuram, and Tirunelveli. The sport itself is caught in the dynamics of rural power structure. In the tussle between rival zamindars, who fight a proxy war using their bulls, the losing bull pays by being flayed alive.

By the time of Kothamangalam Subbu the fault lines become clearer. '*Manji Virattu*' is set in the year 1927, in Ramanathapuram district. The mood cannot be more festive. As part of the temple festival the sport draws huge crowds from all castes including 'Harijans'. Subbu records the practice of giving endearing and fancy names to the contesting bulls, one of them even being called 'Aeroplane'. By now the sport is caught in the rivalry between Agamudaiyars and Maravars with the latter resenting the economic mobility of the former. This rivalry leads to violence and the festival ends in chaos, harmony being restored only years later – given the Gandhian leanings of the author – with the launch of the Civil Disobedience Movement. By this time jallikattu is described as 'the heroic sport of Tamil peasants'. Soon peasants disappear from such descriptions and it is not too long before the sport becomes a symbol of Tamil pride and valour.

In C. S. Chellappa's hands the sport expands into an exploration of the conflict between man and man, and man and animal; as a vengeful Kaari tames the bull that has gored his father to death years earlier, their interweaving provides subtle insights into the human predicament.

Interestingly all the authors mentioned above were Brahmins, giving the lie to the argument that the sport is the preserve of a few dominant intermediary castes. As a non-corporatised communitarian sport, though undoubtedly reflective of social inequities, especially caste, jallikattu incorporates the entire gamut of the social order and the changes within it. In *Kalithogai*, according to poetic convention the young men and women belonged to the community of shepherds now identified with Idaiyar, Konar, and Yadavar. In the fictional narratives dealt with above the communities that figure are Kallar, Maravar, and Agamudaiyar, castes with martial traditions. By this time, at least in the popular imaginary, jallikattu transcended its regional and caste definition, and became emblematic of Tamil culture.

~

In the wake of the jallikattu protests criticism has arisen that the sport is patriarchal and casteist. As any other sport, jallikattu captures the tensions within society. But it is restrictive to reduce it to only that. It has changed with the times even though retaining its many key elements. If pastoral communities practised the sport, as evidenced from Tamil classical literature, in modern literary representations the political category of Mukkulathor (encompassing Kallar, Maravar, and Agamudaiyar, and other analogous castes) is dominant. However, recent newspaper reports and fieldwork indicates that in many villages Dalit youths and castes such as Nayakkars participate actively. In the Theni region Muslims breed bulls for the contest. In an eye-opening ethnographic piece Ulrike Niklas, the German Indologist, describes how, for over the last half a century, jallikattu is held in the St. Anthony's Church in Kandupatti near Karaikudi. Further, she adds, it has 'exerted a strong influence on orthodox catholic centres in the surrounding area'.

The other change is the slow commercialisation of the sport. In Kothamangalam Subbu's short story, the prize is a scarf; but the scarf is more than a piece of cloth, and stands in for honour. In recent times prizes such as pressure cookers, TVS mopeds, and even the occasional Hero Honda motorbike have become common. With the increasing visibility that the anti-jallikattu activists have willy-nilly garnered for the sport it is set to become even more popular. It is inevitable that bigger sponsors will soon back this sport.

Paralleling the literary depiction of jallikattu is its filmic representation. From the 1960s the taming of the bull by the rural hero became a recurring trope. Embracing the bull not only marks the nativity of the film, but also the manliness of the macho hero. Arguably the first hero to take on the bull was MGR, in *Thaikkupin Tharam* (1956). The film revolves around the taming of the bull and how the hero wins the hand of the heroine by taking on the fierce Senkodan (interestingly bulls always have fearsome names). Gemini Ganesan, as the Maravar lieutenant of the rebellious poligar, repeats the act in the period film *Veerapandiya Kattabomman* (1959). Soon it becomes de rigueur for Tamil heroes to tame the bull and prove their masculinity. This trope continues down to the present generation. The taming of the bull is usually accompanied by a song that equates the bull's prowess to the hero's virility. The convention reached its apogee in Rajinikanth's *Murattu Kaalai* (The Rogue Bull, 1980), AVM's blockbuster which propelled Rajinikanth to superstardom. Not incidentally, Rajini's character is named Kalaiyan (literally, the bull), a quite common name for men in rural Tamilnadu. In Bharathiraja's *Man Vasanai* (1983) the defeat of the heroine's father's bull by trickery lies at the centre of the plot. It continues down to Sarath Kumar's *Cheran Pandiyan* (1991), Prabhu's hundredth film *Rajakumaran* (1994) and Kamal Haasan's *Virumandi* (2004). Younger heroes such as Vijay Sethupathi (*Karuppan*, 2017), and Adhi and Pasupathy (*Aravaan*, 2012) have repeated the act.

In parallel, state recognition of sorts fuelled the patronage of the sport, and Alanganallur, a fixture on the tourist map, became a metaphor for the sport. But surely the credit for unambiguously and unequivocally turning jallikattu into a symbol of all that is Tamil must go to its adversaries, both perceived and real – of animal lovers, of 'north India', of an insensitive central government, of Hindutva, and of the impersonal forces of globalisation.

Over the years animal lovers have launched a legal campaign for the comprehensive ban on jallikattu. Their attitude smacks of elitism, and brings immediately to mind Macaulay's sardonic statement that 'The Puritans hated bear-baiting, not because it gave pain to the bear, but because it gave pleasure to the spectators'. Animal lovers' obsession with the plight of animals can often be misplaced, and comes not without a whiff of anti-humanism. When has one heard of animal lovers talk of, say, the indignity of human scavenging? Ernest Hemingway's observation in *Death in the Afternoon* demands quoting here:

> I believe, after experience and observation ... the almost professional lovers of dogs, and other beasts, are capable of greater cruelty to human beings than those who do not identify themselves readily with animals. It seems as though there were a fundamental cleavage between people on this basis although people who do not identify themselves with animals may, while not loving animals in general, be capable of great affection for an individual animal, a dog, a cat, or a horse for instance. But they will base this affection on some quality, or some association with this individual animal rather than on the fact that it is an animal and hence worthy of love.

But animal lovers, represented by the international NGO People for the Ethical Treatment of Animals (PETA) won the first battle. After winding through the Indian legal system the Supreme Court passed an interim order in early 2017 for its ban. Public protests forced the Government of Tamilnadu to pass an ordinance, and the central government and the Supreme Court to accede, if unwillingly.

The war is far from over. But irrespective of the legislative, judicial, or political outcome of the battle for the bull jallikattu has won the day. But this triumphal moment also calls for introspection. Jallikattu enthusiasts should ensure that the sport is regulated and animals are protected from harm. Increasing media interest is likely to ensure it. In a welcome sign environmental groups, keen on preserving native breeds of bulls, are already in the fray. Hopefully they will take the lead in this matter. More importantly the democratic character manifest in the upsurge should be reflected in jallikattu itself by making it more inclusive with the participation of the high and the low, the dominant and the oppressed.

Jallikattu partisans have much to thank the animal lovers for. Jallikattu now stands enshrined as *the* symbol of Tamil cultural pride.

24

PROHIBITION
'Camphor Ringed by Fire'

EUROPEANS HAVE THEIR FIRST drinks in public and when tipsy they move into the confines of their homes; Tamils, on the other hand, drink under cover and once drunk are out on the streets rolling in the gutter with scarcely a vestment on them, or so C. N. Annadurai once observed with characteristic insight. Drinking is universal. But it is mediated by culture.

Historically societies across the world have consumed alcohol. But, following Anna, we can draw the conclusion that societies handle drink in their own way. Prohibition has always been a much discussed topic in Tamilnadu. But the groundswell of anti-liquor sentiment in 2015 across Tamilnadu provided an occasion to reflect on the history of drinking in Tamil society. Such a reflection is imperative if the battle with the bottle is to succeed.

Sangam literature, our window into ancient Tamil society, is replete with references to drinking. If there is a lively academic controversy in Indological studies about how the Vedic drink of soma was produced, the numerous references to drink in the Sangam poems still leave us in the dark about how much of it was fermented and how much distilled. But there is little doubt that ancient Tamils were tipplers and enjoyed a swig. When the great chieftain Athiyaman died, the original Avvaiyar, the bard (not the grandmotherly author of moral epigrams of popular conception), began her elegy with the words, 'If there was a little toddy he would give it to us. And if there was more he'd share it with us as we sang happily'. Drink was often consumed in social gatherings, especially in the orgy of *undaattu* that followed battle victories. Historically therefore drinking was very much part of sociability. Though Roman wine was imported for the consumption of the elite, much of the liquor was locally produced and consumed. (Purananuru describes it as 'the cool and aromatic liquor in elegant Yavana amphora'.) Not for nothing do two of the primary terms for happiness in the Tamil language, *kali* and *magizhchi*, have their etymology in drinking – these words, now referring to happiness in general, were originally used to describe the specific pleasures of tippling!

However, in the centuries following the Sangam period, a marked shift in attitudes is evident. And it finds its voice in the genius of Thiruvalluvar. Chapter 93 of the Kural, *kallunnamai* (abstinence from drinking), describes in unequivocal terms how drunken stupor brings down a man in the eyes of not only family and society, but oneself as well. And yet the great moralist is not without his ambivalence, when, in the first chapter of the book on love Thiruvalluvar observes with unconcealed delight:

The palm-tree's fragrant wine,
To those who taste yields joys divine;
But love hath rare felicity
For those that only see! (Kural 1090, translated by G. U. Pope)

A nuanced reading of the ten couplets on 'not drinking' could suggest that Valluvar is denouncing excess rather than prohibit outright. It is therefore not merely poetic conceit when Subramania Bharati likens kissing the girl-child Kannamma to 'drink-fed frenzy'. It is this ambivalence about the pleasures of drink and the ills of excessive drinking that lies at the heart of the debates about drink.

Kural is the primary weapon in the prohibitionist arsenal. But though great ideologues do make a definite impact on thinking it does not necessarily translate into action. Kural notwithstanding, little changed in the day-to-day reality of drinking in Tamil society.

From Pallava times down to the advent of the Europeans, though liquor was not directly taxed, a levy called *ezha poochi*, *ezha pattam*, and such like, was imposed on palm-tree climbers. The revenue from this tax could not have been much. Colonialism marks a definite rupture in the culture of drinking.

From brew consumed locally, and mostly seasonally – for the palm tree yields toddy only for some months in a year – the British monopoly on liquor played havoc in peasant and tribal communities. The feared outsider–trader infiltrated traditional society whose sole aim was to maximise income over and above the licence fee shelled out to the rapacious colonial state. Not surprisingly tribal revolts across colonial India targeted the hated middlemen and demanded the right to make one's own brew. In the arresting title of an essay by the subaltern historian David Hardiman, drinking was transformed from being 'custom to crime'.

Abkari came a close second to land revenue in filling colonial coffers. In 1930–1 it yielded 31 per cent (to land revenue's 41 per cent) of the Madras Presidency's revenues. The attempt to increase revenue and follow a Victorian ethic on abstinence resulted in much confused results, with an alarming increase in bootlegging and illicit production and consumption of liquor. Often, licencees themselves sold illicit liquor. This was especially so during the years of the Great Depression.

In urban working-class localities drink proved to be a scourge. So alarming was the impact on productivity that factory owners, borrowing from British working-class experience, advocated temperance, and even encouraged the consumption of tea and coffee. But to little avail.

Not surprisingly liquor became a prime target of nationalist campaign. Under the leadership of Gandhi prohibition was in the forefront of the Non-Cooperation Movement and the Civil Disobedience Movement. Gandhi's views on prohibition found its greatest champion in Rajaji. In the aftermath of the Non-Cooperation Movement he established the Gandhi Ashram in Tiruchengode in 1925 where he tested his ideas on prohibition. He got the then cub journalist, 'Kalki' R. Krishnamurthy, to edit a journal, revealingly titled, *Vimochanam* (Deliverance), exclusively devoted to propagating prohibition. The writings and drawings in the journal represented drinking as an unmitigated evil, and portrayed drinkers in utterly dehumanising terms, denying all agency to the poor villager. By 1930, K. S. Venkataramani's *Desabhaktan Kandan* (translated by the author himself in English as *Kandan, The Patriot*), acclaimed as the first Gandhian/nationalist Tamil novel, had been published. The foreign-returned hero, Kandan, takes part in the picketing of toddy shops and courts arrest. In fact, the novel itself begins in a toddy shop in Akkur. History bears out that such dehumanising portrayals preach only to the converted.

When the Congress assumed power in 1937, Rajaji implemented prohibition first in Salem. A tract on prohibition that Rajaji wrote in 1931 (revised and translated into Tamil as well, in 1943, during World War II, when prohibition was revoked by the governor) makes for interesting reading as it summarised the moral (and medical) arguments against drinking. By 1949, Madras province had implemented a policy of total prohibition.

For a quarter of a century prohibition held, until then Chief Minister M. Karunanidhi, in August 1971, in a desperate bid to raise revenues, withdrew prohibition. A nonagenarian Rajaji, with all the melodrama associated with a Tamil film, drove to the chief minister's home in pouring rain to dissuade him. Karunanidhi's reply, as was his wont, was couched in a metaphor: Tamilnadu was 'a piece of camphor ringed by fire'. When liquor flowed freely in the neighbouring states, especially Pondicherry, how could Tamilnadu afford to be dry? Karunanidhi has been accused of casuistry. But let there be no doubt: the preceding decades were no golden age of teetotalism. If the privileged had access to liquor through the dubious means of the permit system, nearly two million prohibition-related offences were recorded in the 1960s!

As has been demonstrated time and again, prohibition, far from being a panacea turns out to be worse than the malady. Periyar, at the height of the Non-Cooperation Movement, had cut down hundreds of coconut trees on his family farm in response to Gandhi's call. Forty years later, in 1963, he presided over a conference demanding the lifting of prohibition. Prohibition, he argued, discriminated against the poor and corrupted the police.

After a break in the 1970s prohibition was again lifted in 1981 by then Chief Minister MGR, despite his electoral promises targeting his core constituency of the rural poor womenfolk.

But the years following liberalisation were the heyday of drinking. In the wake of the social and political turmoil of the times, many Tamil intellectuals began to celebrate drinking. Backed by postmodernist ideologies they formulated fanciful theories justifying drinking. Scarcely were literary meets held without quite a few participants turning up in an inebriated state. The literary world might have been small, but it was these intellectuals who moved into the media and films at the turn of the millennium, becoming influential opinion makers. The toll that drink took among bright young minds, as a result, is a sad tale.

These intellectuals built a consensus for drinking. In the Tamil cinema of an earlier age only villains drank, or the hero when lovelorn. Immediately after the lifting of prohibition Sivaji Ganesan starred as a drunkard lorry driver in *Needhi* (1972). Rajaji's famous short story, '*Dikkatra Parvati*', was made into an award-winning film soon after. The picture has changed now. It is now mandatory to have one item number set in a Tamilnadu

State Marketing Corporation (TASMAC) shop. Not only the hero, heroines too, to the chagrin of the moral police do not miss an opportunity to drink. One film, fully set in a liquor shop, was even titled *Madupana Kadai* (The Tavern). Film dialogues are peppered with 'cutting' (a measure handed out by pouring half of a 'quarter' – the smallest unit of sales (coming in 180 ml bottles) and 'quarter' (the title of another Tamil film!), and it is supposed to be funny when the hero's sidekick utters such words.

Contorted intellectual justifications apart, the overdetermining factor that legitimated drink was the 2003 decision of the government itself to sell liquor. At one stroke it decimated any moral qualm that the drunkard might have had.

Over the last decade drinking has become a scourge and taken epidemic proportions. All the hypocritical noises made by the dominant political parties do little to disguise the fact that strong vested interests have developed and become well entrenched. The following Q&A occurs in Rajaji's tract on prohibition:

> Q: The drink trade has too much of a hold on municipal and national politics and on the press of the country for any prohibition campaign to be successful.
>
> This does not now apply to India, but may, if we delay.

The prescient fear has materialised. That major distilleries are owned by politicians is an open secret. That this wealth funds further vested interests in education and healthcare is apparently ironical. No quality checks or standards exist or are enforced on liquor manufacture. Steeply priced and heavily taxed, unknown brands of liquor are poured down the throat of the consumer in utterly squalid 'bars'. The biggest price the consumer pays is in terms of dignity.

But the call for total prohibition is misplaced. Its champions little realise that the social and economic costs might actually be higher. Banning liquor in the cultural context of a globalising India is not an option. The moral argument against drinking simply does not work. The killjoy attitude of anti-liquor campaigners can scarcely win converts!

The state, in consultation with civil society, needs to work out a medium- and long-term plan to contain the genie that is out of the bottle. Regulation, overseen by civil society, should be accompanied by a campaign of education. The anti-tobacco campaign and the polio-eradication programme can teach us much. Our hospitals need to be equipped with de-addiction clinics complete with health professionals and peer groups. As demanded by some peasant groups the state may also seriously consider legalising toddy tapping that will provide a cheaper and less harmful substitute for the industrially produced liquor that goes by the name of Indian-Made Foreign Liquor, popularly, IMFL! Most cities in India have little space for socialising, and bars have become locations for youths to get together. Creating newer spaces is a real need.

The cynic might not have much hope. But then hope lies eternal.

25

TAMIL LITERARY SPHERE

LATE IN 2017 THE Tamil writer Perumal Murugan signed a contract with Context/Amazon for the English translation of *Poonachi allathu Oru Vellattin Kathai*. There is a boom in publishing Indian writing in English translation. So this should be no news at all. But it was. Arguably, for the first time in Indian publishing history, the translation rights (for English and eight Indian languages) of an Indian language literary work, a slim novel at that, were auctioned. Major Indian publishing houses put up a bid: Penguin Random House, HarperCollins, and Juggernaut. After some tough negotiations Context/Amazon clinched the deal for a seven figure (rupee) sum.

The story did not end there. Shortly after this Grove Atlantic signed English translations of Perumal Murugan's two novels (*One Part Woman* and *Poonachi*) for North American Rights. The US market had always proven elusive to Indian language writers. So here was a major breakthrough. In another first, rights were sold for German, Korean, and Czech as well. Perumal Murugan has been making waves for the last few years. His *Mathorubhagan* had the dubious distinction of the first Tamil novel to be pirated. For some three years and more, since December 2014, he has been in the news. The *New York Times*, apart from editorialising on him (twice, in fact), profiled him on its centre page.

Over the last twenty years Perumal Murugan has been prolific. He was not a lone swallow. The new millennium has been good for Tamil writing with dramatic changes in literary culture. Perumal Murugan was part of this phenomenon, and his career offers a window into it. But his prominence did not have much to do with these changes. Rather, as we saw earlier, it was the result of unhappy circumstances, the fallout of an unsavoury controversy, an indication of the changed political atmosphere in the country, especially since mid-2014. Right-wing and casteist groups called for the banning of *Mathorubhagan* and threatened violence. Unable to bear the trauma Perumal Murugan left a 'literary suicide' note and withdrew from writing. He was resurrected only after the Madras High Court gave a strong judgement in his favour, with telling obiter on the freedom of expression.

At the time of the controversy Perumal Murugan was in his prime. His literary fiction was being lapped up by a small but burgeoning community of readers. Hailing from a peasant community, a first-generation matriculate/graduate/doctorate, Murugan had developed literary interests at a young age. The western part of Tamilnadu, the Kongu region, where he grew up was dry land, known for its hardy peasants. Dominated by the riverine cultures of Tamilnadu, Kongu did not find a place on the Tamil literary map. Fired by his reading in Tamil literature he made it his life's mission to make his land and his people part of the Tamil literary landscape. The rest, we could say, is literary history.

CHANGING LITERARY LANDSCAPE IN THE NEW MILLENNIUM

This became possible due to changes in the Tamil literary sphere since the 1990s, a period of churning. The downfall of the Congress, the liberalisation of the economy, Mandal–Masjid, the break-up of the Soviet Union, the Ambedkar centenary … all these were not without repercussions in the Tamil world.

The little magazine tradition, which had fostered self-conscious literature over the decades since Independence as the mass-circulated magazines were largely philistine, morphed with these changes. Latin American writing, Dalit writing, postmodernism ... a variety of literary currents made themselves felt. *Nirapirigai*, a self-conscious Dalit periodical, caused a flutter and impacted on the literary landscape, questioning not only the content of the writing, but also foregrounding the caste question. Non-linearity, deconstruction, difference, the fall of grand narratives and the celebration of the fragment, and magic realism were very much the flavour of the season. There was a flurry of obituaries for realism, the credo of the left movement which had a disproportionate influence on Tamil literary standards in relation to its real strength.

At this moment a new literary forum came to be born – the middle magazine. In the late 1980s, Sundara Ramaswamy had launched a literary quarterly, *Kalachuvadu*. It folded up after eight issues and a bumper volume. In later accounts this was often related as the story of the death of the Tamil little magazine. Shortly after *Subhamangala*, a monthly sponsored by a finance company, made a big impact on one troubling aspect of Tamil literary culture. Bringing together Tamil writers across the ideological spectrum was more difficult than herding cats. *Subhamangala* achieved the impossible and opened up possibilities.

In 1994, *Kalachuvadu* was relaunched as a middle magazine. The less than five years separating its two avatars could have well been a quarter of a century. For a beginning the technology of production had changed dramatically. Letterpress had given way to DTP, revolutionising production by splitting the locations of composition and printing. The content, moving away from its focus on literature, became broad covering a range of issues concerning contemporary society and culture. A new collective of young writers was behind the journal, the brainchild of Kannan Sundaram, the son of Sundara Ramaswamy. Within years other middle magazines mushroomed. And contributors and writers groomed in the middle magazines slowly migrated to the popular Tamil press (and the visual media not excluding cinema) in the new millennium. Its pros and cons can be debated, but its impact is palpable. The media now is dominated by a younger generation familiar with the literary world. And a new species, the woman journalist, was also born.

In 2000 an international Tamil conference, Tamil Ini 2000, was organised in Chennai. Despite being marred by a factionalism so characteristic of the Tamil cultural world, the conference was a success. A hallmark of the conference was the significant presence of Sri Lankan writers, both émigré and from the island. Events since the 1983 anti-Tamil July riots and the subsequent rise of armed struggle had resulted in the migration of significant numbers of Sri Lankan Tamils to Europe, Canada, and Australia. Postcolonial national boundaries had cleaved the Tamil-speaking communities in the Indian mainland and in the island, and that was now being bridged. The horror of Sinhala ethnic chauvinism and its resultant processes brought together Tamil writers across the Palk Strait. Over the last two decades or so the Tamil literary market encompasses not only the Tamil mainland and Sri Lanka, but the diaspora as well. Cheran, A. Muttulingam, and Shobasakthi are important writers who command readership across the world. Not to be underestimated are the considerable numbers of young men and women who have migrated to the West, and have rediscovered Tamil. They now form a significant segment of producers and consumers of Tamil writing.

The synergies unleashed by the Tamil Ini 2000 conference were sustained for many years. The back and forth movement of Tamil writers between the subcontinent and the diaspora galvanised Tamil writing. Not incidentally, the conference itself was inaugurated by the literary critic K. Sivathamby of Jaffna. (Sivathamby was deported from India during the 1995 International Tamil Conference; thus it was an expiation of sorts.)

The early decades also saw the emergence of a new crop of Tamil publishers. The culture of Tamil publishing had been set, in the 1940s, by the Nattukkottai Chettiar capital fleeing World War–torn South East Asia. Their stellar role in shaping publishing notwithstanding these firms were conservative and had ossified by the 1980s. In the late 1960s, Vasagar Vattam, and starting in the 1970s, Annam and Cre-A, avant-garde publishing houses, opened new possibilities in both product and content.

By the new millennium newer blood was infused. Kalachuvadu Pathippagam was once again a pioneer. Originating as a publishing house to publish the writings of Sundara Ramaswamy, it soon turned into a game-changing venture. In 2005, a new publishing house, New Horizon Media, entered the field with an investment of five crores – an astronomical amount by Tamil publishing standards – fresh from the sale of a cricketing website, crickinfo.com. Tamil publishing had never known such infusion of capital before. Print media such as *Ananda Vikatan*, *Kumudam*, *Nakkheeran*, and, recently, the *Tamil Hindu* launched publishing imprints. They use 'foreign glaze paper' which has a rather short shelf life – these imprints have nevertheless expanded the market.

In 2004, Tamil was officially declared a classical language. Though this lacked substance the recognition was nevertheless a morale booster for a community forever in search of outside acknowledgement. Without this, for instance, a Tamil chair in Harvard University, now in the offing, with a corpus collected from the Tamil community topped up by the Government of Tamilnadu would have been unthinkable.

EXPLOSION IN THE TAMIL LITERARY FACTORY

Access to publishing has had a profound impact on what could be published. For instance, two major writers – Sundara

Ramaswamy and Ashokamitran – enjoyed in the last phase of their life an access unknown to them for a good half a century. Apart from the quick reprints of many of their earlier books, the reception of their work spurred them to write more. The translation of their works in the Penguin Silver Classics enhanced their national reputation. As noted earlier Ashokamitran was especially fortunate in finding literary advocates in Paul Zacharia and Aravind Adiga.

The collected works of eminent writers of yesteryears were a favourite with many publishers. Every major writer now has more than one edition of his (women writers being few) writings. The list is long: Bharati, Bharatidasan, Pudumaippithan, Ku. Pa. Rajagopalan, G. Alagirisamy, G. Nagarajan…. The Tamilnadu government's policy of nationalising the copyright of Tamil writers and putting their works in the public domain unleashed a volume of copy that has been capitalised by a publishing industry often short of new ideas. That this has also enabled many scholars to work on reliable editions of classics has been a positive spin-off.

There has been an explosion in the number of titles published. As ever there are no figures, reliable or unreliable. About 12,000 annual titles of trade books seem reasonable. The annual Chennai Book Fair is now a cultural phenomenon. Organised by Booksellers and Publishers Association of South India, until twenty years ago it was dominated by English language firms. Back then the fair was like a lovers' park where one could enjoy a leisurely walk. With the boom in Tamil publishing the power has tilted to the vernacular, and it is a surprise, god forbid, there has been no stampede. Without a proper distribution network publishers dependent on book fairs for sales is worrisome, a situation somewhat mitigated by the expansion of online sales.

The changes in the external world and the transformation of the publishing industry have made many things possible. From a time, barely two decades ago, when publishing a book in itself was an achievement with writers unable to find avenues for their literary output, it is safe to say that now no manuscript, worthy or not, remains locked up in the writer's drawer. With the periodical press, both commercial and middle brow, hesitant to carry fiction, the novel is enjoying a bonanza. The average size of the Tamil novel has increased dramatically! Six-hundred-page novels are quite common, and the authors of slim novels now have to be defensive.

Most important has been the advent of writers traditionally at the margins: Dalits, women, and minorities. The wave of Dalit writing that started in the 1990s has now stabilised as part of the mainstream. A Dalit writer is no more new, but very much part of the mainstream. That, according to some, is a sign of appropriation. Women's writing has been the single most important aspect of the last two decades. The puritanical howl castigating the content of women's poetry has ebbed. That few women, with the prominent exceptions of Salma and Bama, have attempted longer forms of writing remains a worry. (Mention also needs to be made of the flowering, in the last two decades, of Tamil Muslim writing in eastern Sri Lanka.)

Salma immediately brings to mind the central place of translations in Tamil literary culture – both into, and from, Tamil. If the first Tamil Muslim's voice flowered with her reading of world literature in Tamil translation, her reputation was made through the translation of her writings into English.

In the days of the freedom struggle translation into Tamil meant Bengali, and, to some extent, Hindi (mostly Premchand) and Marathi (only V. S. Khandekar). Though the Sahitya Akademi and National Book Trust of India published translations from all languages in the Eighth Schedule of the Indian Constitution, the 1960s to 1980s meant mostly Malayalam. (Thakazhi's moment has passed. Vaikom Muhammad Basheer remains evergreen. Occasional dark horses are Balachandran Chullikkad's *Chidambara Smarana*, and the autobiography of a petty criminal, *Thirudan Maniyan Pillai*.) The 1990s saw a wave of Latin American fiction being translated into Tamil. Though, in aping Márquez, many writers often ended up looking like cats fire branding themselves in an attempt to ape tigers, the literary possibilities opened up by Latin American writing cannot be underestimated.

Translations continue to have a good market, and if anything the list is getting longer and expansive. A significant shift is discernible in the process of translation. Earlier translations were often technically illegal, having been published without acquiring rights from the copyright holder. This situation has changed considerably. Acquiring rights is now the norm rather than being an exception. Some publishers have tapped resources from various national literary funds to subsidise works of translation. New languages are now speaking in Tamil. Recently Kalachuvadu published fiction from Chinese, Finnish, Icelandic, Hebrew, Flemish, and Turkish, not to mention a Spanish novel from Paraguay. Despite the limited market for such books new styles of writing and the depiction of life in unknown climes have had their impact on writers.

The other side of translation has been even more empowering. Until the end of the last century translation of Tamil writing into other languages, especially English, was an act of charity on the part of some government agency. Much like getting married to the duchess – more for the honour than for the pleasure – Tamil writers made little, if any, money. Only a few acclaimed writers had their work translated into English. The last decade has seen a dramatic shift.

Translation into English has meant visibility, prestige, and some money which does not hurt. Ambai was one of the earliest to make the breakthrough. In collaboration with the late and greatly lamented Lakshmi Holmström, she also won the

Crossword Book Award. For Salma and Bama their translations into English (and a clutch of other Western languages) has meant a global visibility with frequent participation in international literary festivals. Enjoying the quiet of writers' fellowships to finish work has been a bonus. Starting from East West Press, Macmillan, and Katha in the late 1990s, now all major Indian publishing houses publish Tamil writing in translation: Oxford University Press, Penguin Random House, HarperCollins, Juggernaut, and others. Recently Ratna Sagar has launched a new imprint for Indian writing in translation and the first title was A. Muttulingam's *After Yesterday*. Niyogi has joined the list. The role of Kannan Sundaram of Kalachuvadu Pathippagam in this is worthy of mention. By regularly participating in international book fairs such as Frankfurt he has succeeded in selling the rights of over a dozen Tamil writers: A. Madhavan, Salma, A. Muttulingam, Perumal Murugan, C. S. Chellappa, Devibharati, Sharmila Seyyid, Cho. Dharman, K. A. Gunasekaran, and others. Ambai in French, Salma in German and Catalan enrich this list.

Tamil writers now enjoy a new-found confidence. A Tamil scholar, Tho. Paramasivan, is now a star, and celebrities such as Kamal Haasan make a beeline to visit him at his modest home in far-off Palayamkottai. However, it is still a far cry from Tamil writers taking to full-time writing. Jeyamohan's and S. Ramakrishnan's transition to full-time writing has been cross subsidised by their work in the film world. Perumal Murugan is at the cusp of taking early retirement from his college teaching, but he will be banking on a government pension. A category of writing personalities, called VRS writers, has emerged, sustained by voluntary retirement schemes designed to downsize employee strength. That S. Ramakrishnan has decided to give up on his past publisher to establish his own firm is not a good sign. Though royalties are now being paid few publishers draw up a contract.

All said it is generally a good time to be a Tamil writer. In 1992, just as news of Vikram Seth's advance of 12 million rupees for *A Suitable Boy* was making a splash, cycling in my neighbourhood, I was pleasantly surprised to see Jayakanthan, the celebrated writer. He was waiting at the bus stop for public transport. These days it is unlikely that you will see a Tamil writer at a bus stop.

26

CHENNAI
Changing City

FROM *PETTAI* TO NAGAR

In colonial times Madras had the reputation of being a benighted
province. The city itself, identified with the Brahmin middle
class, was seen as conservative, and a contrast to New Delhi
and Mumbai. A volume of writings on Chennai called itself,
unconsciously perhaps, 'the unhurried city'. In the wake of the
IT boom at the turn of the millennium the city, and perceptions
about it, took a dramatic turn. This is a personal take on the
changes the city is living through.

The distance between Vannarapettai (Washermanpet) and
Kalaignar Karunanidhi Nagar (K. K. Nagar), Google Maps tells
me, is barely ten miles. But the metaphor that comes to mind is
chalk and cheese. In early 1974, when I was about six, my family
moved from the early colonial neighbourhood to the newly
developing suburb – a geographical shift accompanied by a
complete historical, sociological, and cultural reorientation. Our
tenement house in Vannarapettai was on the first floor: a lone
Orient fan suspended from a long rod whirring from the slanted
and tiled roof made little impact on the stifling heat. Three families
shared a single toilet. (My present one-family home boasts of
three.) One stepped on to the narrow Tiruvottiyur High Road,
a busy thoroughfare bustling with traffic and out of bounds for
a boy. Outings meant Sunday visits to Pandian, Maharani, and
Agastya talkies. I have no memory of seeing the sky or even a bird.

The auguries were good the day we moved to K. K. Nagar. Coincidentally it was *thai poosam*, an auspicious day for the Tamil god Murugan. Barely 200 metres from our new home a film shooting was in progress: the veteran actor Sivaji Ganesan, with a healthy paunch and dressed in a lavish coat, was acting the role of a street-side acrobat. The reigning actress Vanisri fitted the stereotype of a snooty actress to a T. Heavy rose powder, the kind some Tamil politicians still daub liberally, passed for make-up. Later I gathered the film shoot was for the blockbuster *Vani Rani*. With the airport a few miles away as the crow flies we gawked at aircrafts as they rumbled overhead.

With well-laid roads and parks and squares, mid-1970s K. K. Nagar was the antithesis of what passes for real-estate development these days. Besides it was the ideal location for shooting films. The land was flat, with nary a tree in sight. Famous film studios, out of which Tamil films would be liberated soon, were just around the corner: AVM, Vijaya, Bharani, Velan. The gardens of M. M. A. Chinnappa Thevar who specialised in making films with animal protagonists (and, it used to be joked, emoted better than human stars) was half a mile away. Once I was woken up to the roar of a lion (or was it a tiger?). Scarcely a day passed without a darshan of a film star.

Each sector – not the town-sized segments in NOIDA and Gurgaon of Delhi, but more a block by American urban definition – enclosed a playground. K. K. Nagar was then dotted with numerous unbuilt plots of land. A variety of weeds – one came with spiked leaves and poisonous-looking berries – overran them. Butterflies flitted past and we took great pleasure in sucking the stalk of the white *thumbai* flowers. Breaking the pods of *erukkam* was a delightful pastime. A mix of (state-defined categories of) HIG (high-income group), MIG (middle-income group), and LIG (lower-income group) apartments, government staff quarters, one ground plots, 800 square feet artisan plots with a slum – Vijayaraghavapuram, now completely gentrified – thrown in, K. K. Nagar was a microcosm of the city with its full complement of social classes.

The playground was a liminal place where everyone joined. By some inexplicable logic, as though by state fiat, games changed overnight. Marbles giving way to tops to seven stones to kite flying. Cricket cut across seasons. Improvisation ruled the day. Puny, with a snotty nose and often the baby of the crowd, I easily made friends across class divides. A gaudily dressed young man who indulged me with goodies and bicycled me around, I later found out, was a petty thief.

Vijayaraghavapuram was the buffer between K. K. Nagar and Vadapalani. Though equidistant the genteel folk of K. K. Nagar preferred K. K. Nagar bus terminus to Vadapalani's.

At the arrack shop, greeting visitors to Vijayaraghavapuram, fried duck eggs and salted fish overwhelmed the reek of alcohol. A local barber doubled as *nagaswaram* player. A small plot of land, now a playground named after Dr Ambedkar, was the venue for feats such as seven days of non-stop cycling. The highlight was the daredevil stunts on the last day after which the athlete was felicitated and given a purse.

An early hero was Arputham – true to his name, he was a real wonder. One day he performed a stunning display of *surul kathi* – actually a bunch of long, rusted tin strips used for packing. One false move and not only would one lose some pounds of flesh, but would make the most potent anti-tetanus serum ineffective. After repeated entreaties Arputham agreed to teach me *silambam* (a traditional Tamil martial art using a staff). Thursdays were auspicious for silambam practice, and it began with a small puja with betel leaves, bananas, and country sugar. The mandated *dakshinai* was a rupee and quarter. On the day when one started practice with a real staff Arputham demanded a vetti. The status of a guru came with gravitas and an otherwise unruly, even rowdy man, Arputham was the very epitome of discipline at class. A knife went through my heart some years later to see my guru, his once muscular body, wasted on drink and women.

Reflecting on those years I value the sociological lessons I learnt as my daughter grows up in a gated community – a bubble that gives little scope for encounters across classes.

The street on which we lived in K. K. Nagar, I later learnt, was named after India's first finance minister. Not only the layout, but the street names of K. K. Nagar also had a method unlike the madness of neighbouring Ashok Nagar with its non-continuous numbers for its streets and avenues, the very antithesis of the American grid system. Jeevanandam, Bobbili Raja, A. Lakshmanaswami (Mudaliar), A. Ramaswami (Mudaliar), 'Sunday Observer' Balasubramaniam (Mudaliar), Muniswamy (Naidu), Alagirisamy, P. T. Rajan, Natesan (Mudaliar), W. P. A. Soundarapandian (Nadar), A. Ponnambalam, A. T. Panneerselvam – streets were named thus, and invariably without caste surnames. To a student studying in a CBSE school these regional names carried no meaning. In the first years of power the DMK's ideological moorings evidently remained strong. It was reflected in the studied choice of street names. The whole pantheon of the Non-Brahmin Movement, from the Justice Party to the Self-Respect Movement to the early communists, was thus memorialised. I suspect the then chief minister of the state who gave the nagar its name was behind it. And not to be left behind, an eager party man gave the name of the chief minister's mother to a nearby neighbourhood – Anjuham Nagar!

Not until I was mentored by a local cultural activist with strong Dravidian movement leanings was I educated about the history behind the names. As I grew into a scholar primarily studying the history of social change in Tamilnadu, these names jumped at me from archival documents and faded newspapers giving it a special resonance. Reading the Dravidian patriarch Periyar's moving tribute to A. T. Panneerselvam on his tragic death in 1940, on his way to join the Secretary of State's India Council in an air crash in the Gulf of Oman, brings to memory the days I cycled on the street named after him.

THE DELUGE

The haphazard nature of development in the wake of the real-estate boom of the new millennium stood exposed during the great rains of 2015.

The great French historian Fernand Braudel explained historical change in terms of structure, conjuncture, and event – the long term and the short term interacting to produce explosive events. It is a fantastic model that could explain the devastation visited upon Chennai in 2015 in two great waves of monsoon fury. Never was the met man more valued. One is not sure if a hundred flowers bloom in this country. But there was enough tolerance for conflicting weather forecasts – with astrologers joining the fray in supremely confident tones. For myself I choose to rely on https://www.facebook.com/tamilnaduweatherman/. *BBC*'s English is good. TamilNadu Weatherman's is not. But he always gets the weather right.

The seductive Braudelian model of change was the last thing on my mind in the midst of Chennai's unfolding disaster. Chennai's terrain is flat, and historically drainage has been a problem. If that is structure, the conjuncture is the state's willing destruction of water bodies, abetment of rapacious real estate barons, and flawed environmental policies. The watery cataclysm is the event.

Caught in a swirl of unceasing rains, eddying waters, call drops, and frenzied tapping of the keyboard to establish communication with marooned friends I was overtaken by end-of-the-world visions: of Siva performing his apocalyptic *oorthuva thandavam*, and my eyes searching the dark firmament for a rider on the white horse.

In the 1970s and 1980s, the neighbourhood I grew up in, piped water supply, sewerage outlets, and storm water drains were taken for granted. Now I live in a 'premium' gated community on Old Mahabalipuram Road (OMR). Sometime earlier a copywriter crafted a clever line to promote one of the many mushrooming apartment complexes on this global software corridor: 'OMR is now OMG!' Prophetic indeed. Never was god invoked by so many mouths with so much fervour than on this highway at the time of the deluge.

To get a road so wrong would be difficult even by design. The OMR runs parallel to the famed East Coast Road (ECR) that hugs the eastern coastline. These two major roadways, despite being barely two kilometres apart, are not connected! Even a brief shower leads to waterlogging – for this great global destination has neither storm water drains nor sewerage lines. When you have ploughed through the water you will have the pleasure of paying toll for the use of the road.

Premium gated communities and Singapore-style buildings of transnational software giants jostle the two sides of the ribbon. But every drop of water that runs through the taps needs to be bought with money somewhat less precious than the aqua nectar. And the used water, processed with STPs (the so-called sewage treatment plants, another expensive bit of equipment), needs to be transported out, at residents' expense, and let out into god-knows-where. No prizes for guessing that the tankers – at least for now separate tankers are used for water and sewerage – are controlled by a water mafia. And when the water and sewerage tax bill arrives at your doorstep every six months it is indeed a cruel joke!

My six-year-old daughter didn't go to school from Deepavali until early January 2016. That's how long this nightmare lasted.

This break outstripped the summer vacation. But there was little joy on my daughter's face or on her friends'. She often wondered how her dear friend Kaku was faring in his marooned home. Parental anxiety is infectious. The constant talk of swirling waters and marooned families cannot but have had its impact.

On 30 November 2015, even as intermittent sharp showers made driving difficult, I braced myself for the coming week carrying enough work home. Previous rainfall records were already on the wayside, and one believed that the worst was over. But the rain gods thought otherwise.

I woke up to a different city. The skies were dark and the downpour, a water curtain. The streets overlooking my home resembled wild streams. People were moving helter-skelter. Calls were dropping, and the few calls that could be made yielded desperate staccato cries. As mobile networks and landlines broke down social media was a blessing. Zuckerberg soon found a place in family altars. Messages for help quickly passed through these media.

On WhatsApp a journalist friend kept a running commentary on water entering his home. It ended abruptly as the level reached his chest. A fellow academic was holed up on the third floor even as water lapped at the threshold of the first. My home guard friend could do little to reach out to him. A poet-friend woke up on his ground floor at daybreak, but by nightfall had steadily moved up to the penthouse on the third floor.

Erratic power supply is the norm on OMR. So the gated communities have diesel generator backup. As diesel supplies ran out power was rationed. During the short intervals of power we were engrossed on our mobile screens.

In between we caught snatches of the unfolding tragedy on the TV screens. *CNN-IBN* did a stellar job, probably the best to cover the Chennai rains with at least six anchors, many of them flown in from outside, wading through the turbulent waters.

A plague on *NDTV* which was covering Delhi pollution and the HT summit as Chennai was reeling under the floods. *Sun TV* did its usual politics telecasting disturbing images of the flooded city to the accompaniment of plaintive strains that accentuated anxiety and triggered panic. *Puthiya Thalaimurai TV* disappointed covering only its studio's vicinity before literally going under water. *Thanthi TV* did not cover itself in glory by interviewing, if you will excuse a tautology, a fake astrologer who claimed to have predicted the disaster weeks earlier; and as if in anger that his words had not been taken seriously, prophesied a more calamitous downpour. If one watched *Jaya TV* one would have thought that the city's problem was the overflow of honey and milk, all the product of Amma's kindness. So when water entered its studios it was a godsend!

Some TV channels played dirty by not focussing on the eighteen deaths at MIOT Hospital's ICU as power failed on the night of 1 December. Instead they gave substantial air time to the self-serving claims of Apollo Hospitals of having provided medical care without a hitch through the rains. A dream marriage between corporate media and corporate medicare! I wonder what would be the rainy-day equivalent of making hay when the sun shines.

The office and press of the venerable Tamil weekly *Kalki* were submerged. In a record for the *Hindu*, the daily suspended its publication for a day – the first time ever in its 137-year-old-history, taking a well-advised decision not to endanger the lives of its distributors and delivery boys.

Many who put up with the privations of the rainy days and bravely organised relief work broke down after hearing tragic tales. On 1 December eighty-eight-year-old writer Vikraman died. Tamil Brahmins cremate their dead in a day. As West Mambalam was a cascade of water there were no graveyards to bury and, with no electricity or logs, no crematoria to burn. Nor were there freezer boxes to keep the body. The veteran writer's corpse lay decaying for four days. U. R. Ananthamurthy's *Samskara* may come to mind.

Stories of the deaths of small children, a loving middle-aged couple in a last embrace, the washing away of bodies as far as the Trincomalee beaches of Sri Lanka ... it'd take a heart of stone not to be moved by such tragedies.

The plight of the living may be no better now. As entire homes submerged, many libraries and bibliophiles lost treasured collections. Tens of thousands lost their television sets, refrigerators, blenders, grinders, and cots.

Home and hearth are comfort zones. The invasion of the watery monster by stealth is a nightmare that can unsettle the most stoic of people. It is as though the ground beneath the feet has slipped.

The remarkable way in which volunteers came together in a moment of unprecedented crisis to provide relief work has been noted. This 379-year-old city is new to disasters. The siege of Chennai by the French during 1758–9 is hardly remembered even by historians. A half-an-hour bombardment of the harbour by the German light cruiser *Emden* was Chennai's only experience of World War I. The city was evacuated in 1942 for Japanese bombers that barely materialised. The tsunami of 2004 was a coastal affair. It is indeed extraordinary that people came together to face what is a crisis of proportions matching Hollywood disaster movies.

The failure is of the political class. The two Dravidian parties – the AIADMK and the DMK – demonstrated their failure by distancing themselves from the grass-roots. In earlier times both parties had strong roots in the local level which stood in good stead in times of crisis. It is no longer so.

My local councillor had a broken down TVS 50 moped at the beginning of his tenure. He now zips around in his Qualis and Scorpio, and it is unfair to expect him to continue to live in the resettlement colony.

The AIADMK failed doubly, both as a political party and as the party in government. Rather than help in relief work and aid the state administration, there were numerous instances of party men hijacking relief material and putting stickers with Amma's images on them.

When the state loses its credibility, rumour-mongers have a field day. A graver natural disaster could not have been imagined. But no command structure was visible. The National Disaster Resource Force was kept waiting for six hours without information and instructions. The politicians and bureaucrats who were on the ground prefaced every one of their statements with the words, 'According to the instructions of Amma/Hon'ble Chief Minister'.

Shockingly enough Jayalalithaa did not address the people. Even Rajiv Gandhi made his infamous statement of a falling banyan tree and the shaking ground three days after Indira Gandhi's assassination. If during the last round of rains she only visited her own R. K. Nagar constituency, it was an aerial survey now. In the face of mounting criticism of the paralysis of the state administration a hurriedly convened press conference was called, but ended swiftly as the chief secretary kept to the script and refused to take questions. The most worshipful mayor of Chennai was invisible for a month. The collector of Salem went viral with the comment that the skies rained according to Amma's orders. The Lal Bahadur Shastri National Academy of Administration, Mussoorie, had better include King Canute's story in its curriculum.

The floods came in a long line of governance failures. But the government remained unmoved. Paradoxically, the AIADMK created history by being returned to power in the 2016 elections (and that without stitching an alliance) though its showing in the city was relatively poor.

The lessons of the 2015 deluge remain, therefore, still to be learnt.

NOTES

Periyar: Published here for the first time.

C. N. Annadurai: First version published as 'C. N. Annadurai: Letter and Spirit', in *India Today*, 21 April 2008. Expanded version published as 'Speaking of Anna', in Anna Centenary Souvenir published by Government of Tamilnadu, 2009.

M. Karunanidhi: Parts of this essay have appeared in Scroll. in, 9 August 2018 (https://scroll.in/article/889723/kalaignar-karunanidhi-a-political-artist-who-left-an-imprint-on-tamil-politics-for-over-50-years)

M. G. Ramachandran: Written specially for this book.

Jayalalithaa: A much shorter profile first published as 'Jayalalithaa: The Iron Woman of Politics', *Mirror*, 6 December 2016. Present version incorporates material published earlier as 'Reading Amma's Mind', *Indian Express*, 17 May 2011; 'Room for a Lotus Bloom', *India Today*, 13 October 2014; 'Amma's Apogee Moment', *Hindu*, 12 May 2015; 'Why the DMK Lost', *Hindu*, 21 May 2016; 'In Sickness and in Health, a Parallel in the Journeys of MGR and Jayalalithaa', https://thewire.in/politics/sickness-health-parallel-journeys-mgr-and-jayalalithaa, 5 October 2016; and 'The AIADMK after Amma', *Hindu*, 7 December 2016.

'Cho' Ramaswamy: Originally published as 'Cho Ramaswamy: The Old Guard', *Economic Times*, 18 December 2016.

C. S. Subramanyam: Longer version published in *Economic and Political Weekly*, 19 January 2013.

Iyotheethoss Pandithar: Combines 'From a Footnote to the Forefront', *Hindu*, 24 December 2014 and 'Nooks of the Past: Close Encounters of the Buddhist Kind', *Telegraph*, 13 August 2018.

Subramania Bharati: Draws from material published as 'Subramania Bharati: In the Pioneer's Penumbra', *Week* (Annual Number), 27 December 2015; 'Why Subramania Bharati, Icon of Modern Tamil Culture, Remains Little Known to the Rest of India', https://www.firstpost.com/living/why-subramania-bharati-icon-of-modern-tamil-culture-remains-little-known-to-the-rest-of-india-4460461.html, 8 May 2018; and 'Subramania Bharati vs Rabindranath Tagore', *Hindustan Times*, 12 May 2018.

Pudumaippithan: First published in Sahapaedia.org.

Sundara Ramaswamy: First published in Sahapaedia.org.

Jayakanthan: Original version published on outlookindia.com, https://www.outlookindia.com/website/story/courting-controversy/227015, 8 April 2005. Expanded and updated here.

Ashokamitran: Originally published as 'Ashokamitran: The Aesthetic of the Ordinary', an afterword to Ashokamitran's novel, *Mole!*, Orient Longman, 2005. Updated, including passages from 'The Tinsel World and Lived Experience', review of Ashokamitran, *Iruttilirundu Velicham* in *Book Review*, December 2000, and an unpublished note on his last novel for nomination to Jnanpith Award, 2017.

M. L. Thangappa: Draws from the obituary published in Scroll.in in, https://scroll.in/article/881097/tamil-poet-ml-thangappa-1934-2018-leaves-behind-a-prolific-and-unparalleled-legacy-of-translations, 3 June 2018; and 'M.L. Thangappa: Shutting Up the Parrot', *Hindu*, 10 June 2018.

Perumal Murugan: First section published as 'In Defence of the Chronicler of Kongu', *Hindu*, 12 January 2015. Longer version published as 'Who Killed Perumal Murugan', in K. Satchidanandan (ed.), *Words Matter: Writings against Silence*, Penguin Viking, 2016. Updated text reproduced here.

Cho. Dharman: Fuller version published as 'Introduction' to Cho. Dharman, *Koogai: The Owl*, © Oxford University Press, 2015.

Non-Brahmin Movement: First published as 'Footprints of the Original "Anti-Nationals"', *Outlook*, 12 December 2016.

Classical Language: First section draws from 'Classical Language', *Economic Times*, 14 November 2008; and 'The "Classical" Language Issue', *Economic and Political Weekly*, January 2009. Expanded text reproduced here with a newly written section.

Against Hindi: First published as 'Tongue-Tied', *India Today*, 31 December 2007. Expanded here with passages from 'Should Hindi Be the Sole Official Language?', *Hindu*, 19 May 2017.

Nationalisation of Copyright: Published here for the first time.

Eelam, Tamils: Published as an interview, 'The "Virtual Community" of Tamils', thehinducentre.com, https://www.thehinducentre.com/the-arena/article4546587.ece, 25 March 2013.

Dalits and Cultural Rights: Written jointly with J. Balasubramaniam as 'From Kandadevi to Kallimedu', *Hindu*, 12 August 2016.

Jallikattu: Published first as 'Catching a Sport by Its Horns', *Hindu*, 21 January 2017. Expanded here along with passages from 'Sharp Like Shiva's Battle Axe' (with M. L. Thangappa), *Hindu*, 13 January 2018.

Prohibition: First published as 'Camphor in a Ring of Fire', *Hindu*, 9 August 2015. Expanded text reproduced here.

Tamil Literary Sphere: First published as 'Tamil Writers No More Wait at Bus Stops', *Biblio*, April–June 2018.

Chennai: First section published as 'Encounters of the Social Kind', *Hindu*, 17 August 2014; and 'From Pettai to Nagar', in *The City and South Asia*, Harvard South Asia Institute, Cambridge, Mass., 2014. Second section published as 'The Deluge and the Deluded', *Open*, 21 December 2015.

INDEX

320 INDEX

ABOUT THE ILLUSTRATOR

Sri Lanka-born poet, illustrator and painter **Mohamed Rashmy Ahamed** studied fine arts at the University of Northampton. He lives in the United Kingdom.